Operational Risk Management

Operational Risk Management

A Case Study Approach to Effective Planning and Response

Mark D. Abkowitz

WILEY

John Wiley & Sons, Inc.

Copyright © 2008 by Mark D. Abkowitz. All rights reserved.

Published by John Wiley & Sons, Inc., Hoboken, New Jersey.

Published simultaneously in Canada.

For general information on our other products and services, or technical support, please contact our Customer Care Department within the United States at 800-762-2974, outside the United States at 317-572-3993 or fax 317-572-4002.

Wiley also publishes its books in a variety of electronic formats. Some content that appears in print may not be available in electronic books.

For more information about Wiley products, visit our Web site at *http://www.wiley.com*.

Library of Congress Cataloging-in-Publication Data:
Abkowitz, Mark David.

   Operational risk management : a case study approach to effective planning and response / Mark D. Abkowitz.

   p. cm.

Includes index.

ISBN 978-0-470-25698-5 (cloth)

1. Risk assessment. 2. Risk management. 3. Emergency management. I. Title.

HD61. A23 2008

658.15′5–dc22

2007045583

10 9 8 7 6 5 4 3 2 1

CONTENTS

PREFACE

The idea for this book actually began several years ago. At the time, I was asked to develop a course on risk management based on case studies of actual historical events. The intent was to examine what went wrong and to extract lessons learned from these events that could improve our quality of life today and in the future. Little did I know where it might lead.

Fast forwarding to the present time, this course has evolved into a steady and popular offering on campus. Each year, cases of historical importance are researched, debated, and reconciled. Some focus on natural disasters, others on man-made accidents, and the remainder on terrorist acts. Could the incident have been prevented? Preventable or not, what could have been done to manage the emergency response more effectively? What actions have we taken since the event occurred to make the world a safer place? Could it happen again?

These are the very same questions that confront and worry families, communities, businesses, and government officials. With media attention devoted to each catastrophe as it occurs around the globe, our anxiety grows, our perception of various risks can become distorted, and a feeling of uncertainty pervades much of how we think and act. Somehow we must be able to sort out the most important risks we face, determine how vulnerable we really are, and decide where our risk management resources can be most wisely used. At the same time, we must come to grips with the notion that some risks are simply beyond our control or are too small to warrant priority attention. In such circumstances, we must learn to become more tolerant of those risks.

Learning from real-world case studies is important and often over-looked. By examining disasters through a retrospective lens, we have a complete history of the event to review and interpret. Hindsight reveals much about the cause, impact, and ripple effect, allowing us to judge how likely it is that history could repeat itself. By going "back to the future," this process enables us to prepare for a better tomorrow.

This book contains many of my favorite case studies. Undoubtedly, you will be familiar with some of them, although perhaps not the important details. They have been carefully selected to cover all three hazard types (man-made accidents, terrorist acts, and natural disasters), in a variety of scenarios across many different industries and environments, both in the United States and abroad.

When you have finished reading, it is my hope that you no longer feel hostage to the anxiety and uncertainty that is limiting our quality of life. My aim is to show that risks can be successfully managed—it is just a matter of dealing with risks in the right way. And you can do your part.

As in any endeavor of this scale, this work would not have been possible without the assistance of many others. I am particularly appreciative of the students at Vanderbilt University who have participated in the risk management class and the encouragement of my colleagues for recognizing the importance of this topic. Special thanks, however, goes to Dr. Derek Bryant, whose dedicated and tireless research formed the basis of the case study narratives. I am also appreciative of his assistance in formalizing the book manuscript. In addition, I would like to acknowledge the support and encouragement of Sheck Cho at John Wiley & Sons, Inc.

Finally, the importance of family in motivating an author to dedicate the time and energy it takes to write a book cannot be understated. For me, the daily interactions with Susan, Alyssa, Kendra, and Jason kept me on an even keel throughout the project. Mom, your confidence in me has been a constant from as far back as I can remember. And Dad, thanks for inspiring me to become a teacher and for instilling in me such important life values. I can only hope that I am living up to them.

CHAPTER I

WHY DO DISASTERS HAPPEN?

It seems like every time we turn on the news, a disaster has occurred. A tornado has touched down creating a swath of destruction, a chemical explosion is spewing toxic fumes into the air, an earthquake has crippled a populated area, wildfires are burning out of control, terrorists have attacked a major public transportation system, a hurricane is ravaging the coastline, buildings are collapsing, ships are sinking. And the list goes on.

Why do these disasters happen? With all of our knowledge, skill, and technology, why can't we do something to prevent them or at least keep them from causing such devastation? The more that we ask this question without a good explanation, the more frustrated and fearful we become of the world we live in. This situation has generated so much uncertainty and anxiety in today's society that our concern for these events seriously affects the way we think and act. It is truly unfortunate . . . and unnecessary.

Disasters come in many different forms, which can be conveniently organized into three groups. *Man-made accidents* are the result of human action or inaction that starts a chain of events leading to a catastrophic outcome. These errors in judgment are not considered intentional or malicious. However, *terrorist acts* are conscious actions made by people with purposeful and destructive intent. These acts are typically well planned, with a specific target in mind, directed at causing heavy casualties and creating mass hysteria. *Natural disasters*, which make up the third category, are considered acts of God, the cause of which is beyond human control. Most natural disasters ultimately can be attributed to weather patterns or movements of the earth's crust. Although humans are not responsible for the occurrence of natural disasters, we can have a profound impact on the severity of the consequences.

While these disaster groups may seem quite different, when one takes a closer look at how these events evolve, there is remarkable similarity. That is to say, there emerges a pattern or "recipe" for disaster. The question that then arises is: What are the ingredients to this recipe, and how do they mix together to form such a lethal outcome?

Each ingredient can be thought of as an underlying *risk factor* that, when present, alone or in combination with other risk factors, erodes into a margin of safety that we normally try to build into our lives. Once that margin of safety is compromised, however, the situation is free to unravel to epic proportions.

I consider there to be 10 basic risk factors:

1. **Design and construction flaws.** Major facilities, such as power plants, skyscrapers, refineries, and ships, are built according to detailed blueprints, otherwise known as design specifications. These specifications are based on engineering analyses that focus on designing the structure to withstand the forces that will be imposed on it, such as load, wind, vibration, puncture, or blast. If there is a flaw in the design process and it is not discovered in time, when those forces are applied to the structure, it will be prone to failure. This failure can lead to a partial or complete collapse of the facility.

   Even when the design specification is valid, problems still can arise if the materials used to fabricate the building components are faulty or the components are not assembled properly. In either case, the integrity of the structure is compromised, making it susceptible to failure, with outcomes similar to those that occur when a design flaw is present. Because of the close relationship between design and construction, it is not uncommon in a structural failure for opposing sides to argue whether the fault rests with a flaw in the design or in the construction.

2. **Deferred maintenance.** In the helter-skelter of trying to keep an operation up and running, discovery of a mechanical problem spurs a debate on whether to shut down the operation and fix the problem immediately, or to keep going and make the repair at a more convenient time. This is a judgment call, where the risk of deferring maintenance is weighed against the benefit of maintaining continuous operations. In these instances, it is human nature to choose to deal with problems at a later time, especially if the system is not actually malfunctioning. Unfortunately, decisions to defer maintenance often lead to the failure of a key system component before the repair can be made, causing a serious accident to occur. Moreover, within a culture where maintenance problems are customarily deferred, the situation is ripe for multiple component failures, allowing the consequences of the ensuing accident to propagate and intensify.

3. **Economic pressures.** As might be expected, one of the more common risk factors involves money. Whether exploring space, building a major facility, moving large quantities of cargo, or protecting a community from natural disasters, one is always dealing with a limited amount of available funding. Therefore, resources must be invested wisely. When a budget is too tight or spending is not controlled adequately, pressure intensifies to implement strict cost-cutting measures. This can translate into shoddy workmanship, purchasing lower-quality materials, eliminating the use of backup operating and safety equipment, or ignoring problems that arise. While economic pressures alone are rarely considered a root cause, they often serve as a catalyst for causing human errors that initiate a disastrous event.

4. **Schedule constraints.** Economic pressures and schedule constraints often go hand in hand as risk factors, as evidenced by the

phrase "Time is money." When a deadline has been imposed, and the project or operation has fallen behind, pressure to make up ground can cause the responsible party to cast a blind eye toward important details. Often this situation leads to the elimination of critical tasks, trying to accomplish tasks in parallel that should be done in sequence, or not pursuing certain considerations in sufficient depth to fully understand their impact on safety. As in the case of economic pressure, schedule constraints are considered a catalyst for committing errors in judgment that can lead to a destructive outcome.

5. **Inadequate training.** Most tasks in today's world have been made more complicated by the complexity of the technology being used and the highly integrated nature of various systems. Consequently, the performance of many important functions requires an individual to be highly trained. At the same time, some organizations view training as a burden because it can be costly to perform and because employees are not being productive while participating in a training program. This short-sighted perspective can place in positions of responsibility individuals whose lack of training causes them to make a mistake that either initiates an accident or allows a crisis situation to intensify.

    Problems with inadequate training go beyond the time when an individual first joins an organization. When there are personnel shortages, individuals may be thrown into an important decision-making role while covering for others, performing a function for which they were not properly trained. Because individuals tend to forget what they were originally taught and because processes change over time and require new learning, lack of retraining can also be a problem.

6. **Not following procedures.** Most organizations have well-defined procedures for how employees should perform a task or function. These procedures are often documented and made available during training and for reference purposes when individuals are on

the job. Moreover, job supervisors have as one of their duties to ensure that each employee is following standard procedures. Surprisingly, procedural errors are a frequent root cause of failure. When engaged in a repetitive activity, complacency can set in, and individuals tend to drift away from following a strict protocol. Consequently, they either neglect to perform certain steps or invent other ways to accomplish the same task, often not considering the ramifications of their actions on safety. Failing to follow procedure can create a hazardous situation, one that is exacerbated by coworkers whose actions are based on assuming that those procedures are being followed.

7. **Lack of planning and preparedness.** Planning and preparedness make up a proactive effort focused on applying resources in advance of an undesirable event to improve understanding and response to the threats with the greatest potential to cause serious harm. Depending on the nature of the threat, attention can be directed at preventing an undesirable event from occurring, mitigating the consequences of an event once it has occurred, or both. Planning and preparedness activities include the gathering of knowledge (intelligence), assessment of the likelihood and consequence of various disaster scenarios, evaluation of alternative risk reduction strategies, and conduct of exercises and drills to determine the effectiveness of ongoing efforts and maintain a state of readiness.

   Unfortunately, lack of planning and preparedness is evident in virtually every catastrophe recorded in history. Because of the luxury of time and the fact that a disastrous event may not have been experienced in recent memory, people tend to place a low priority on making the effort and spending the resources to be adequately prepared for a crisis situation. All too often, little forethought is given to the variety of disaster scenarios that could occur, the magnitude and impact of these events are underestimated if the scenario is considered, or the ability of the response community to handle mass casualty situations is overestimated.

Even in circumstances where significant effort has been devoted to planning and preparedness, the product of this effort can be a written plan that is not practiced or updated, rendering it of little value when a calamity arises.

8. **Communication failure.** This risk factor also is present in nearly every historical disaster, contributing to either the cause or the consequence of the event. Communication failures can occur at various stages, altering an outcome in different ways. One common form of communication failure occurs between members of the same organization. In this instance, critical information is not shared, such as when one group decides to shut down a critical protection system for maintenance while another group is carrying out a dangerous experiment. Poor communication between organizations is also problematic. A typical scenario is two agencies engaged in a response effort, each of which is unaware of what the other is doing. Finally, lack of communication with the public or the provision of inaccurate information can place people at risk either because they do not know the hazards they are facing or because they are not properly advised on how to protect themselves.

9. **Arrogance.** This risk factor is a human trait that can complicate what might otherwise be a safe operation. Arrogance can rear its head in many forms but usually appears as either the person in charge being driven to succeed for individual gain without sufficient regard for the safety of others or an experienced individual who has become overconfident with his or her ability to deal with any problem that might present itself. The former case creates an environment in which concerns expressed fall on deaf ears or, worse yet, a culture of fear of reprisal if an employee complains about personal safety. In the latter circumstance, the individual can underestimate the risk at hand, believing that "I've seen everything before and was able to handle it" or "This is not going to get the better of me." Arrogance displayed in either form can have serious repercussions.

While often associated with a key individual, arrogance can also appear at the institutional level. Such instances occur when the organizational culture has become dominated by an attitude of disregard for the well-being of others, overconfidence in the organization's ability to solve problems, or disdain for individuals whose beliefs threaten the ability to achieve desired goals and objectives.

10. **Stifling political agendas.** Government policies can have a powerful effect on the propensity for disasters. If these political agendas are hard-nosed, with little room for dialogue and compromise, then affected parties can feel that they have little recourse other than to resort to extreme and often hostile measures. Historically, political agendas have been closely associated with the vast majority of terrorist acts, an intentional reaction to what the aggressor perceives to be oppressive governmental policy. This risk factor is not limited to terrorist acts, however. It is also evident in developing countries where governments attempting to become more economically competitive are willing to relax safety standards to attract business, or among nations whose desire for an elevated status in global politics can put its citizens at greater risk.

An interesting observation when reviewing these ten basic risk factors is that we, as humans, are involved in each and every one of them. While this implies that we contribute to the cause or impact of every disaster, it also means that we have an opportunity to control these factors more effectively to achieve a better outcome: a safer tomorrow.

So, where do we begin? A good place to start is to go back in time and carefully review disasters that have occurred in the recent past, selecting a potpourri of those that were accidental in nature, terrorist acts, or due to natural causes. If we can follow the sequence of events that caused each disaster and analyze what went wrong, then we can extract important lessons learned about how to better control these risk factors. Moreover, if we also review actions taken in the aftermath of each disaster so as to reduce the risk of it happening again, we can evaluate our susceptibility to a recurring event in the future. Doing this will allow us to understand how we can become more savvy in making the world a safer place.

The intent of this book is to encourage adoption of such an approach. The parts that follow document and evaluate several case studies of major disasters that have occurred in the past 30 years. Each case study contains a narrative describing what happened, an analysis of what went wrong, a review of what actions have been taken in the aftermath of the event, and a perspective on whether a similar event could happen again. The case studies are separated according to whether they were man-made accidents, terrorist acts, or natural disasters. Also included are cases where disaster was averted because of the exemplary risk management practices of affected individuals and organizations. These success stories become important learning experiences by allowing us to observe what went right. The book closes by summarizing what the case studies have taught us about the ten basic risk factors, followed by a glimpse into what the future could look like if we take these lessons to heart.

PART ONE

MAN-MADE
ACCIDENTS

We live in a society in which technology has provided significant lifestyle improvements that consumers have come to demand as necessities. Our dependence on electric power, advanced telecommunications, household goods, transportation, and other amenities has put considerable pressure on the economy to manufacture large quantities of product in a timely and economical fashion. Beyond this, the human race is not easily satisfied with the status quo, preferring instead to push the technology envelope toward bigger and better things, and doing it sooner rather than later. Whether putting men and women in space, erecting the tallest building, or constructing the largest vessel, we often forgo our common sense in pursuit of these endeavors.

It should therefore come as no surprise that history is filled with disasters of an accidental nature caused by human error. Some of these mistakes were specific in nature, attributed to a single individual who "fell asleep at the wheel." In other cases, the fault rests more with an entire organization, where a sloppy culture fostered a breeding ground

9

for poor decisions. Sometimes the problem began by neglecting to examine a minute detail, which became a catalyst in unleashing a chain of
destructive events. In other circumstances, the opportunity for tragedy
was painstakingly clear and evident to many.

The five cases you will read about in this part involve accidental disasters that have occurred in a variety of disciplines, covering the construction, nuclear, chemical, transportation, and space industries. In
one instance, separate tragedies occurred several years apart, due to
similar causes. All of these events were considered preventable, and
some were met with such public scrutiny that the perception of safety
in certain industries continues to suffer to this day, even though the
events took place decades ago.

CHAPTER 2

HYATT REGENCY WALKWAY COLLAPSE

A tea dance hosted in the atrium of the Hyatt Regency Hotel in Kansas City on July 17, 1981, ended in tragedy when the second- and fourth-floor skywalks collapsed onto a crowded dance floor, leaving 114 people dead and another 216 injured. Flaws in a simple design change made to a support mechanism went unnoticed, allowing the skywalk to buckle at the worst possible moment.

The Hyatt Regency hotel opened its doors in Kansas City in July of 1980. A facility over four years and $50 million in the making, the building stood 45 stories and 500 feet tall, occupying a prominent position on the city skyline. The most notable of its eye-catching design elements was a 60-foot, four-story glass atrium lobby, crossed by three skywalks, one each on the second, third, and fourth floors. On a summer night in 1981, the beauty of these features would be all but forgotten, as two of the skywalks crashed to the floor in one of the worst structural failures in U.S. history.

Construction of the Kansas City Hyatt dated back to early 1976, when Crown Center Redevelopment Corporation (CCRC) began the initiative, retaining PBNDML Architects, Planners, Inc. as the project architect. In April 1978, the firm of Gillum Colaco was hired to provide structural engineering services. One of the subsidiaries of this firm, Jack D. Gillum & Associates, was subcontracted to perform all of the engineering work for the hotel construction. Gillum, engineer of record for the project, was an experienced professional who held more than 20 professional engineering licenses throughout the United States. He had won several awards for his work on other high-profile projects, including facilities for the Olympic Games and other buildings for the CCRC. At the time he took on this assignment, Gillum was in charge of up to 100 engineers and specialists, working on as many as 70 projects. Daniel Duncan, one of the engineers under Gillum's supervision, was designated as project engineer for the Kansas City Hyatt.

The Hyatt project was scheduled according to the "fast-track" construction method. This building technique, which became popular in the late 1970s, involved commencing construction before the final designs were complete, thereby reducing the amount of time taken to build a facility. Eldridge Construction Company (ECC) was selected as the construction contractor. ECC subsequently sub-contracted with Havens Steel Company (HSC) to fabricate and erect the atrium steel.

In mid-1978, the first plans for the hotel's trademark skywalks were drawn by Gillum & Associates, with construction on the hotel tower already under way. The design called for the fourth-floor walkway to hang directly above the second-floor walkway, with the third-floor skywalk offset, suspended parallel to the others. The engineering sketch called for the second- and fourth-floor walkways to hang from a single set of rods, anchored to the atrium ceiling (see Exhibit 2.1). According to these drawings, each rod had to be threaded continuously from one level to the next to accommodate the nuts that would support the walkways. The details of the design for connecting the walkways to the hanger rods were left up to the fabricator (HSC), a practice not uncommon in Kansas City in the late 1970s.

On the construction site, it became apparent that using a single set of rods to hang both walkways would not be feasible. It is unclear whether this was due to the inability of HSC to obtain rods of sufficient length or from a realization that threading the rods continuously would be impractical and potentially unsafe. In early January 1979, HSC's engineering manager called Gillum & Associates to request that the design be changed to incorporate two rods, offset at the fourth floor (see

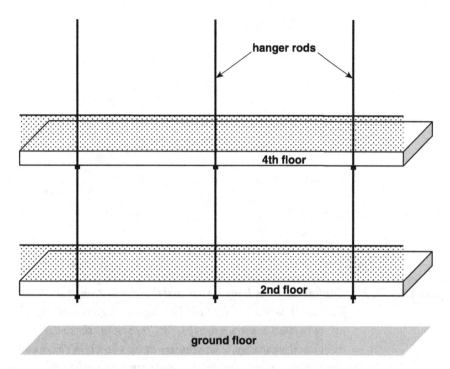

EXHIBIT 2.1   *Configuration of the second- and fourth-floor walkways (not to scale)*

Exhibit 2.2). The structural engineer agreed to the change over the phone but requested that the change be submitted formally. HSC's engineer later testified that he viewed the change as minor and never submitted it through official channels, though Duncan and Gillum both admitted to being aware of the change and approving it. On January 12, 1979, HSC halted work on the project and subcontracted it to an experienced outside engineering firm for detailing to free up resources for a larger, newly awarded project.

HSC had not flagged the change in the design of the rod/walkway connection in the shop drawings before handing the plans over to the detailer. As a result, the detailer assumed that the design process for the connection was complete and did not redesign it to account for the doubling of the weight placed on the nuts supporting the fourth-floor

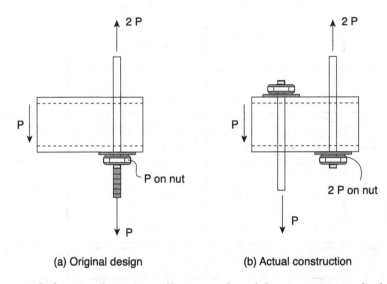

(a) Original design   (b) Actual construction

EXHIBIT 2.2   *Configuration of hanger rods and the connection at the fourth-floor walkway according to the original engineering sketches (a) and actual construction (b). "P" represents the weight of an individual walkway. The configuration shown in (b) doubles the weight supported by the nuts on the underside of the fourth-floor walkway.*

Source: *Marshall, R.D., et al.* Investigation of the Kansas City Hyatt Regency Walkways Collapse. *Washington, DC: National Bureau of Standards, 1982.*

walkway. When the subcontractors completed the drawings, they reviewed them for consistency, but the change to the hangers went unnoticed.

On February 16, 1979, the drawings were delivered to Gillum & Associates for review. ECC, under increasing pressure to erect the walkways, requested an expedited approval of the plans. Due to personnel changes within Gillum & Associates and a heavy workload, review of the drawings was assigned to an unlicensed, but highly experienced, senior technician rather than one of the project leaders. Despite questions raised about the hanger/walkway system by the technician and at least six inquiries to Duncan about the implications of the design change, the plans were approved, sealed by Gillum, and handed over to the contractor on February 26.

The atrium was erected during the summer of 1979. The following October, construction work on the atrium was revealed to be deficient when a section of the roof collapsed. Gillum called the quality of construction an "abomination" and promised CCRC that his firm would check the design of all of the connections in the atrium roof. CCRC, in turn, hired an independent firm (Seiden-Page) to inspect the construction of the atrium while Gillum & Associates carried out its review of the atrium design. While these reviews did uncover other potentially serious design flaws with the roof, the structural integrity of the skywalks went unnoticed. In fact, the design of the connections in the walkways was never even checked, despite Duncan's written assurance to the contrary.

Hotel construction continued without any major setbacks after the roof collapse. Seven weeks prior to scheduled completion, a worker noticed deformation of the walkway and reported it to the architect's on-site representative. Unfortunately, this report was never followed up. The Hyatt subsequently held its grand opening in July 1980. The following February, two more observations were made of deformation in the walkways, but both were discounted.

On the night of July 17, 1981, a year after the Hyatt's opening, a party was being held in the atrium. Diners in the restaurant overlooking the lobby watched as nearly 2,000 local residents gathered for a weekly tea dance, featuring big band music and a dance contest. Suddenly, at 7:05 PM, there was a loud snap and a deafening roar as the fourth-floor skywalk began to break free. The walkway fell 30 feet to the floor below, but not before landing on the second-floor sky bridge, causing it to collapse as well. Over 70 tons of debris fell, crushing or trapping hundreds of partygoers, some of whom could not be reached for more than seven hours.

Emergency crews arrived on the scene within minutes. Despite being hampered by gas leaks and broken water pipes that flooded the lobby, a well-organized response ensued, due in large part to a preformulated citywide disaster plan and the resources afforded by an urban environment. Despite this organized and dedicated effort, the number of casualties was staggering. Faced with over 100 fatalities, hotel rooms had to be transformed into makeshift morgues. Taxis, buses, helicopters, and more than 40 emergency vehicles were used to evacuate over 200 people injured in the collapse.

In the hours after collapse of the second- and fourth-floor walkways, responders noticed that the third-floor walkway had separated from the atrium walls and was itself in danger of collapsing. Six days later, despite the possibility of obstructing investigations into the cause of the accident, the third walkway was removed, circumventing further disaster.

The cause of the walkway collapse was attributed directly to the change in connection design and the resulting increased weight on the hanger bolts supporting the fourth floor. This configuration allowed the supporting beam to fail at the point of the nuts and slide downward over them (see Exhibit 2.3). In hindsight, this problem could have been solved with very minor design changes, such as the addition of a stiffening plate to the fourth-floor support beam, thereby providing sufficient strength to the connection.

While poor design of the hanger connections was the mechanical reason for failure, the catalyst was poor communication and inability to follow procedures among the many parties involved in project design and construction. HSC's request to Gillum & Associates for a change from a single-rod to a double-rod system was conducted over the phone with no written follow-up by either party. This lapse in communication undermined the formal review process for such a critical change and helped it to remain unnoticed throughout the rest of the design and construction process. Because of a drafting error made at Gillum & Associates, the weight of the walkways was left off the sketch of the connection. Without this information, HSC began redesigning the

EXHIBIT **2.3** *Fourth-floor box beam showing a hole where it pulled free from the ceiling suspension rod. The hanger rod to the second floor is still in place.*

Source: http://ethics.tamu.edu/ethics/hyatt/hyatt2.htm.

connection to the two-rod configuration and was unable to account for the resulting change in weight that the connection would need to support. Before the redesign was finalized, HSC sent the drawings out for completion without indicating which elements remained incomplete. The outside detailer hired by HSC assumed that all of the drawings it received were essentially complete and never addressed the strength of the fourth-floor connection. Clearly, the delegation of duties created a high-risk environment in which individuals carried out work with a lack of accountability.

Ironically, had the hanger design not been changed, the original connection still would have violated local safety standards. According to Kansas City building code, in order to safely support the walkway and any load it might bear, the connections should have been designed to hold approximately 17 tons. Yet the connections as indicated by the engineering drawings for the single-hanger system would have supported only 10.25 tons, barely more than the 10.15-ton weight of the walk-ways and nearly 40% below its required capacity. This oversight might also explain why the third-floor walkway was in the process of experiencing structural failure.

The fact that the walkways did not meet the local building code highlights deficiencies in the building inspection process. This is a common problem when local building departments are involved with monitoring regulatory compliance of large construction projects. That Kansas City suffered from this problem finally surfaced in 1983, when 19 building code officials were fired, suspended, or forced to retire early after an investigation revealed that construction sites were not being inspected properly.

Schedule constraints also played a key role in the walkway collapse, creating an environment that reduced the likelihood of discovering design and construction errors. The project's "fast-track" approach encouraged personnel to cut corners in order to finish the project quickly. With construction under way prior to completion of the drawings, the design team, including the engineers, likely felt added pressure to keep ahead of the construction crew. One example of this situation was ECC's request to the engineers for an expedited review of the technical drawings. A longer, more thorough review would have allowed greater opportunity to discover mistakes such as the faulty fourth-floor connection.

Economic pressure may have also been a factor. On three separate occasions, Gillum requested that CCRC authorize the placement of an engineer on site to monitor construction activity. CCRC, however, rejected the request each time due to the added expense involved.

Despite the presence of these risk factors, project engineers missed several opportunities to discover the walkway connection problem. During design review, following collapse of the atrium roof in 1979, Gillum & Associates never checked the walkway connections. Duncan was also asked several times about the strength of the hanger rods and the change to a two-rod configuration. Rather than checking the design and making the necessary calculations, Duncan reassured the questioning parties with answers from memory, thus forfeiting at least six separate opportunities to discover the fatal flaw. Such repeated disregard for good engineering practice suggests that Duncan and Gillum were cavalier about the way in which Gillum & Associates conducted business.

The years following the tragedy witnessed the filing of numerous lawsuits against CCRC, which were eventually settled for more than $100 million. In 1983, an investigation was launched by local and federal officials to determine if any criminal wrongdoing had led to the collapse of the walkways. In December of that year, the county prosecutor and the U.S. attorney in Kansas City announced that there was insufficient evidence to convict anyone for criminal negligence.

Meanwhile, the Missouri Board of Architects, Professional Engineers and Land Surveyors, recognizing that the Hyatt disaster had shaken public confidence in the engineering profession, decided to take action. On February 4, 1984, the Missouri Attorney General, John Ashcroft, filed a complaint on behalf of the board, charging Gillum and Duncan with gross negligence and other inappropriate conduct in the practice of engineering. This case marked the first time that a state licensing board had filed a formal complaint against any of its professionals. The complaint alleged that the two engineers (1) did not make the necessary calculations or run checks that would have ensured the safety of the system and compliance with building codes, and (2) failed to review their design following the collapse of the atrium roof in October 1979.

During the trial, a number of engineers testified on both sides of the case, describing what they considered to be standards of responsible practice in structural engineering. The variations in testimony served to indicate a lack of consensus regarding such standards. Some witnesses testified that they personally work through calculations on each structural connection in projects that they oversee, while others testified that they rely on the fabricator for such details. Duncan and Gillum also testified that it is common practice for engineers to put their seal on plans that they have not personally reviewed, despite Missouri licensing law that makes a professional engineer responsible for every piece of information on documents he or she seals.

On November 15, 1985, Gillum and Duncan were both found guilty of gross negligence and misconduct. Gillum was also cited for unprofessional conduct. The state then gave the board permission to revoke the engineers' licenses, which it did in January 1986. Days after this action, both Gillum and Duncan offered their letters of resignation to Ketcham, Konkel, Barrett, Nichol & Austin, the firm where they were employed at that time. One month later, both men were "relieved of engineering duties" at the firm. Daniel Duncan has not worked as an engineer since that day.

Further scrutiny of Gillum's performance was subsequently carried out by the American Society of Civil Engineers (ASCE). In the summer of 1986, ASCE's Committee for Professional Conduct recommended that Gillum be permanently expelled from the professional organization (Duncan was not an ASCE member). ASCE's board of directors subsequently revoked Gillum's membership for three years, based on a finding that he was "vicariously responsible . . . but not guilty of gross negligence or of unprofessional conduct." Although eligible to do so, Gillum has chosen not to reapply for membership.

As a result of the State of Missouri decision, 27 of the 28 states in which Gillum was recognized as a professional engineer either revoked or chose not to renew his license. Nevertheless, he continued a structural engineering practice. In 1992, Gillum became president of a firm in California, where he was later reinstated as a professional engineer. He has since held a number of positions, including that of an adjunct faculty member in the Department of Civil Engineering at Washington University in St. Louis.

Today, the Kansas City Hyatt atrium no longer features the three hanging skywalks. In their place stands a single walkway, which is supported from below by thick concrete columns, intended to impart a feeling of safety to hotel guests.

While the collapse of the Hyatt Regency atrium remains a vivid memory to many and the disaster caused the engineering community to take a closer look at its ethical responsibilities, there are no assurances that building collapses of this kind will not happen again. Although our technology has improved in identifying design and construction flaws prior to the onset of a major structural failure, it still boils down to whether individuals involved in the project are diligent in carrying out their responsibilities. Unfortunately, building collapses due to structural failure happen routinely and with increased likelihood during "construction booms" due to diminished oversight. Rarely have the consequences been as dramatic as what was experienced in Kansas City that night, however, since most collapses have not occurred under such crowded conditions.

REFERENCES

Crewdson, John M. "Third Hyatt Walk Removed Despite Protest from Mayor," *New York Times*, July 24, 1981.

DeArmond, Mike, et al. "46 Killed in Hyatt Collapse as Tea Dance Turns to Terror," *Kansas City Times*, July 18, 1981.

"Disaster Began with a 'Big Snap, Like Lightning in Your Backyard,'" *New York Times*, July 19, 1981.

"Engineers' Negligence Charged in Kansas City Hotel Disaster," *New York Times*, February 4, 1984.

"45 Killed at Hotel in Kansas City, Mo., as Walkways Fall," *New York Times*, July 18, 1981.

Gillum, Jack D. "The Engineer of Record and Design Responsibility," *Journal of Performance of Constructed Facilities* 14 (2000): 67–70.

Haskins, Paul J. "Collapse of Hotel's 'Skywalks' in 1981 Is Still Reverberating in Kansas City," *New York Times*, March 29, 1983. www.skyscraperpage.com.

"Jack Gillum—Department of Civil Engineering—Washington University," undated. http://cive.seas.wustl.edu/About/People.asp?PersonID=26&Org=CivE.

"The Kansas City Hyatt Regency Walkways Collapse," undated. http:// ethics.tamu.edu/ethics/hyatt/hyatt1.htm.

Luth, Gregory P. "Chronology and Context of the Hyatt Regency Collapse," *Journal of Performance of Constructed Facilities* 14 (2000): 51–61.

Marshall, R. D., et al. *Investigation of the Kansas City Hyatt Regency Walkways Collapse*. Washington, DC: National Bureau of Standards, 1982.

Moncarz, Piotr D., and Robert K. Taylor. "Engineering Process Failure— Hyatt Walkway Collapse," *Journal of Performance of Constructed Facilities* 14 (2000): 46–50.

Orr, Steven M., and William A. Robinson. "The Hyatt Regency Skywalk Collapse: An EMS-based Disaster Response," *Annals of Emergency Medicine* 12 (1983): 601–605.

Pfatteicher, Sarah K. A. "'The Hyatt Horror': Failure and Responsibility in American Engineering," *Journal of Performance of Constructed Facilities* 14 (2000): 62–66.

"2 Engineers Replaced for Role in Hyatt Case," *New York Times*, December 26, 1985.

"2 Hyatt Hotel Engineers Offer Their Resignations," *New York Times*, November 20, 1985.

CHAPTER 3

NIGHTMARE IN BHOPAL

On the night of December 2, 1984, 40 tons of methyl isocyanate (MIC) was accidentally released from a chemical plant located in Bhopal, India, owned and operated by a subsidiary of Union Carbide Corporation. The MIC formed a toxic cloud that drifted over residents of Bhopal while they were asleep, leading to catastrophic consequences: 3,800 fatalities and 11,000 injuries, with many residents still suffering from the long-term effects of chemical exposure. Plant workers allowed water to seep into the MIC tanks, causing a reaction that led to the release, following which poorly maintained safety systems failed to contain its movement.

In 1934, the Union Carbide Corporation (UCC) became one of the earliest U.S. companies to establish a subsidiary in India. The country was seeking to attract foreign investors in order to strengthen its economy and often did so, like many other developing countries, by relaxing safety standards or ignoring violations. Over the next 50 years, this safety culture, low labor costs, and untapped markets in India would help UCC to gain a competitive advantage. Unfortunately, it also led to the worst disaster in the history of the chemical manufacturing industry.

In the 1960s and 1970s, developing countries around the globe were becoming participants in the "Green Revolution," an agricultural movement utilizing improved practices and technology. These countries were able to increase domestic food harvests drastically and thus reduce reliance on imported crops. In India, as in other Green Revolution

23

countries, rising crop production led to a growing demand for pesticides. In keeping with India's economic goals, the country decided to manufacture the necessary pesticides domestically rather than obtain them through foreign import. Consequently, in 1969, UCC and its Indian subsidiary, Union Carbide India Limited (UCIL), established a pesticide factory in Bhopal, India.

By the late 1960s, UCIL had expanded to encompass 14 factories with over 9,000 employees. Its stock was publicly traded on the Calcutta Stock Exchange with UCC retaining majority (51%) ownership. The remaining UCIL shares were held by Indian financial institutions and private investors.

Bhopal, located in the Indian state of Madhya Pradesh (see Exhibit 3.1), was a growing city of several hundred thousand people in 1969. Building a pesticide factory in Bhopal was a logical choice for UCC and UCIL based on the city's central location in India, access to electricity, existing rail infrastructure, a large potential labor force, and the availability of a reliable water supply.

The plant was situated near a residential area just north of the city. Soon after the facility was constructed, more densely populated settlements began to grow around it. These settlements became so large that, in 1975, Bhopal's administrator of municipal planning requested that the plant be relocated to protect these inhabitants. This idea was rejected by both the company and local government officials.

MIC was one of many chemicals used in the production of pesticides at the Bhopal plant. MIC is a highly reactive, extremely hazardous substance and is known to cause severe damage to the lungs, digestive tract, skin, reproductive organs, and eyes, even under very short-term exposure. Furthermore, MIC vapor is heavier than air, which causes the chemical, when released, to stay close to the ground where it can come into contact with humans, animals, and plants.

On the night of December 2, 1984, 132 gallons of water seeped into MIC storage tank 610 at the Bhopal facility. The water reacted with MIC, causing approximately 40 tons of deadly vapors to leak out of the tank. Around 11:30 PM, MIC unit workers, noticing their eyes

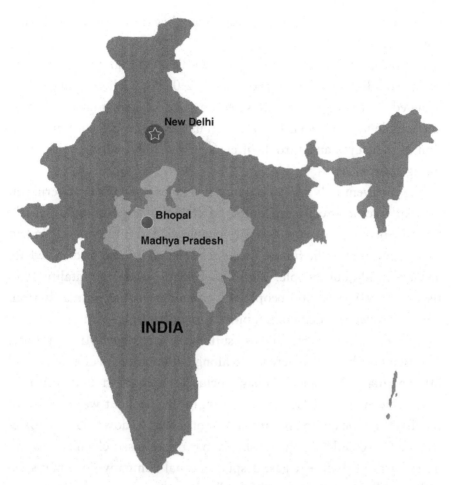

EXHIBIT 3.1   *Map of India depicting the location of Madhya Pradesh and the city of Bhopal*

beginning to water and burn, notified the shift supervisor of a suspected leak. The supervisor did not take any action until 12:20 AM (December 3), when he contacted the plant superintendent. By 12:25 AM, MIC had completely filled the air in the unit, yet operations were allowed to continue for another 20 minutes. Shortly after 12:50 AM, the first toxic gas alarm was activated to notify workers and the local rescue squad. Responders initially tried to stop the spread of gas by spraying it with water. When this approach proved futile, both plant workers and responders began to flee upwind from the plant.

The public was finally notified of the leak more than two hours after it was first discovered, at approximately 2:00 AM, when plant officials sounded the toxic gas siren. Residents awoke, coughing uncontrollably and unable to catch their breath. Victims experienced a burning sensation in their eyes and throat, often followed by vomiting, with some losing consciousness.

The gas eventually spread as far as five miles downwind, covering an area of over eight square miles, affecting a population of nearly 900,000 people. As many as 4,000 people died that night while in bed or trying to escape the fumes. Estimates of those injured or disabled are as high as 400,000 people. Within three days, estimated fatalities had risen to 7,000 to 10,000 people, the casualties coming primarily from the poor, overcrowded communities surrounding the plant.

Animal life and vegetation also suffered as a result of MIC exposure. Thousands of livestock were killed along with numerous dogs, cats, and other animals. Ecological damage included extensive tree defoliation.

On December 4, UCC headquarters in Connecticut was notified of the disaster. The company's initial response was to downplay the toxicity of MIC. One UCC official stated that the released chemical was no more harmful than tear gas, despite internal company documents describing MIC to be potentially deadly.

Chairman and chief executive officer Warren Anderson and a small technical team traveled to Bhopal on December 4. Upon arrival, Anderson was placed under arrest and charged, along with UCC, as having committed culpable homicide. Anderson promptly posted $2,000 bail and returned to the United States. In the meantime, the UCC technical team helped dispose of the remaining MIC on site and began an inquiry into the cause of the leak.

The disaster sparked an enormous legal battle between UCC and the Indian government, which had assigned itself the authority to act on behalf of the victims. The Indian government filed an initial suit in U.S. court, seeking $3.3 billion in damages. However, the court refused to hear any suits related to Bhopal because of the location of the incident, the nationality of the victims, and the fact that UCC did not appear to closely manage operations at UCIL. The two parties eventually settled out of court in February 1989. The settlement called for UCC to pay $470 million to victims of the disaster, with the stipulation that the money was not an indication of any civil or criminal wrongdoing.

Unfortunately, victims soon discovered that obtaining a share of this settlement would be a difficult task. Those who filed claims had to register, prove their identity with photos and medical records, receive notification of a hearing, be categorized according to the severity of their injuries, receive a judgment, and, for some, undergo the appeals process. As a result, over the ensuing three years, the Indian government had distributed only a small portion of the financial settlement to victims. This process continued until July 2004, when the Indian Supreme Court ordered the government of India to distribute the remaining settlement funds to victims of the gas leak. An initial deadline for compliance was set for November 2004, but it was later extended to April 2006, more than 21 years after the disaster.

In 1994, the Indian Supreme Court allowed UCC to sell its assets in India for the purpose of funding a hospital in Bhopal. The sale of UCC's stock in UCIL provided $90 million for the hospital, which eventually began operating in 2001. With no holdings left in India and UCC officials ignoring court summonses (for which Anderson was declared a fugitive from justice in 1992), criminal cases against the corporation became increasingly difficult to pursue.

In 1999, UCC merged with and was subsumed by the Dow Chemical Company. Dow subsequently disavowed responsibility for any UCC liabilities in India despite accepting responsibility for UCC liabilities within the United States.

Three years after the merger, the Indian government reaffirmed its charges of culpable homicide against Warren Anderson and, in 2003, formally sought his extradition from the United States. A year later, this request was rejected in the U.S. court.

The environment in and around Bhopal continues to show the effects of the disaster. As many as 15,000 more people have since reportedly died from residual MIC exposure. Hundreds of thousands of other victims continue to deal with effects of the disaster, suffering from blindness, chronic eye disease, lung and gastrointestinal ailments, neurological disorders, reproductive issues, muscular and skeletal problems, weakened immune systems, miscarriages, infant mortality, and cancer. Moreover, many victims were forced to change occupations, work fewer hours, or stop working altogether as a result of their illnesses or due to business disruption.

Today, groundwater containing high concentrations of toxic chemicals is still used for drinking and other purposes. Soils in the area are similarly polluted. The UCIL factory remains, although it has not been in operation since the night of the gas leak. Stocks of hazardous chemicals lie scattered and abandoned throughout the facility, serving as a constant threat and reminder to the people of Bhopal of that fateful night.

The Bhopal disaster can be attributed to such a large number of risk factors, that the occurrence of a catastrophe was not so much a matter of "whether" but more a case of "when."

The event that initiated the leak on the night of December 2, 1984, was the introduction of water into a MIC holding tank. UCC contends that this was the result of sabotage by a disgruntled employee, citing the results of an independent investigation by a third-party consulting firm. However, the name of the saboteur has never been released and no charges have ever been filed. Workers at the plant generally believe that the water seeped into the tank while being used as part of a routine cleaning procedure. It is unclear whether this seepage stemmed from an inability to follow proper procedures or if it was due to inadequate training.

Once the leak occurred, the toxic gas was able to escape due to a series of failures attributed to poor design and deferred maintenance (see Exhibit 3.2). Initially, water was unable to drain because of clogged bleeder lines. Eventually the water worked its way through a series of leaky valves into the MIC tank. Because temperature and pressure gauges in the MIC unit were known to be unreliable, workers initially ignored the gauge readings that indicated a problem was occurring in the storage tank. The refrigeration system for keeping the MIC cool, and therefore less likely to overheat, was also not functioning. An alarm that should have indicated the temperature rise in the storage tank did not work. The gas scrubber, used for neutralizing any escaping MIC, was designed to handle only one-fourth of the gas that was actually released; moreover, it had been shut down for maintenance at the time of the incident. A flare tower for burning off any escaping MIC also had a

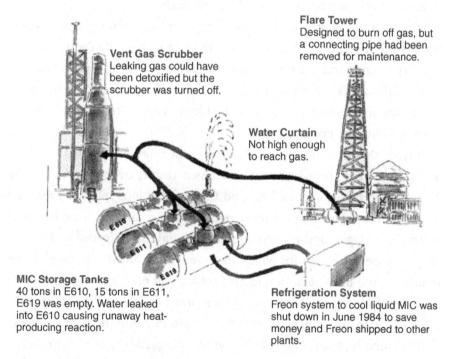

EXHIBIT 3.2   *Some of the major safety and containment failures during the Bhopal gas leak*

Source: SEMCOSH, "Bhopal Diagram," 2004. www.semcosh .org/bhopal_diagram.htm.

design capacity of less than the volume of the release; it, too, had been turned off for maintenance. The water curtain (for containing any gas that may have escaped the scrubber and flare tower) was operational, but proved to be too short to reach the source of the escaping MIC. Finally, the storage tank that ruptured was filled beyond its recommended capacity and an overflow tank designed to capture excess MIC was already full of the chemical.

That MIC was allowed to be stored at the factory was, in itself, a recognized hazard. The Bhopal plant kept a 30-day supply of MIC on hand, which the Council for Scientific and Industrial Research determined to be both unnecessary and hazardous. This situation prompted a local attorney, in March 1983, to write a letter to the Bhopal plant manager threatening legal action for storing hazardous substances and releasing toxic waste to the local environment.

What is remarkable about these design and operational flaws is that these system components were implemented to provide redundant capability in containing a potential release. It was only through their collective failure that an event of such disastrous proportions could occur.

Economic pressure faced by UCIL likely contributed to such dilapidated conditions. From the time MIC production began until the release occurred, the Bhopal plant had not been profitable. This led UCIL to search for ways to reduce expenses. As a result, over one-half of the MIC workers had been laid off and the maintenance staff was reduced to only two people. Those who remained behind suffered from job insecurity, low wages, and no promotion potential, often forced to fill in as needed to perform jobs for which they were not trained. The work force reduction and limited resources also took a toll on equipment performance, resulting in decisions to use temporary or inferior low-cost solutions, defer maintenance, or shut down system components altogether.

Additionally, the Bhopal operation was plagued by poor communication, attributable perhaps to UCC's hands-off approach to managing UCIL. It has been alleged that UCC did not effectively transmit information to its subsidiary about the hazards present at the Bhopal facility. Such communication breakdowns are not unusual in multinational corporations, as they involve parties separated by distance, working under different cultural norms, and speaking different languages. For example, operating manuals at the Bhopal plant were written in English rather than in Hindi, the predominant native language of the region. Communication problems were not limited to international dialogue, however, for interactions within the plant, and between the plant and the community, were also suspect.

Lack of planning and preparedness is also present as a risk factor in this case. There is no indication that any formal emergency response plan existed in the event of a chemical spill, as evidenced by the inability of the responders to perform effective mitigation and the inexcusable length of time before the public was notified of the release. When residents finally were made aware of the threat, most did not know what to do and many fled into low-lying areas where conditions were even worse than what they had left behind. Furthermore, when hospitals in Bhopal became overwhelmed by the enormous flood of patients, staff could do little to help since UCC did not make known what type of gas had escaped from the factory nor how to treat the victims.

Looming larger than all of these other risk factors, perhaps, was the culture in which the Bhopal facility was designed, constructed, and operated. Many of the plant's safety hazards were well known to UCIL and UCC management but were never addressed. In fact, chemical-related accidents began occurring at the site shortly after the plant began manufacturing MIC. In the early 1980s, there were at least three incidents involving the release of MIC and one of its constituents (phosgene) that exposed numerous workers, killing one and injuring dozens of others. Two separate safety investigations followed these incidents, one conducted by UCC and another by the Madhya Pradesh government, the findings of which were provided to company executives. UCC's audit report cited over 60 safety hazards at the plant, 30 of which were considered major, with 11 of these associated with the phosgene/MIC units. The report specifically discussed the significant likelihood of a major release of hazardous chemicals due to mechanical and operating problems. An August 1984 letter from the secretary general of the facility's workers' union to company officials voiced a similar concern about deteriorating safety conditions at the plant. A number of articles also appeared in the local press, including one published in June 1984 entitled "Bhopal: On the Brink of a Disaster."

While no remedial measures were taken by UCC or UCIL at the Bhopal plant in response to any of the audits, letters, or articles, ironically, action was taken to address similar problems at a UCC plant in West Virginia. The improved safety at the West Virginia plant, in comparison to its Indian counterpart, can be explained only by a different standard of health and environmental safety regulations imposed by the two countries. Disadvantages faced by Bhopal workers not experienced by their West Virginia counterparts included high storage time for MIC, no emergency scrubber to neutralize MIC, no computerized monitoring of equipment, use of a storage tank coolant that is highly reactive with MIC, poor worker training, and inadequate personal safety gear.

The blame for allowing such a culture to exist rests squarely on the political agendas of both the Indian government and UCC. From the outset, it was apparent that economic development was India's highest priority, motivating a desire to create a highly favorable business climate for foreign investment. Among the incentives offered was a set of lax safety laws and an "understanding" that enforcement of safety practices would not be taken seriously. This strategy likely influenced UCC to create UCIL and build substantial operations in India. Culpability does not belong to the Indian government alone, however, because it was UCC's decision to apply a different safety standard to its U.S. plants than to those operating in India. In doing so, UCC abdicated corporate responsibility to treat employees equally on a worldwide basis, in deference to maximizing the bottom line.

To a large extent, such arrogance on the part of both UCC and the Indian government did not change in the aftermath of the MIC release. UCC distanced itself from responsibility for the incident and engaged in a relatively passive relief effort that reflected poorly on the company's image. By designating itself as the legal representative for all disaster victims, the Indian government removed any rights individuals had for restitution based on their particular circumstances. Moreover, by allowing UCC to rescind its holdings in UCIL, the Indian Supreme Court effectively closed the door on any further recourse that victims may have had. Some contend that the process established by the Indian government for obtaining a share of the settlement was made purposely difficult to discourage timely and widespread distribution of funds, serving notice to other foreign investors that India was still a welcoming place for business development.

Bhopal served as a bellwether event for the chemical industry and a catalyst for safety reform. In the year following the disaster, the Chemical Manufacturer's Association (now known as the American Chemistry Council [ACC]) began implementing a number of voluntary initiatives designed to reduce the possibility and effects of chemical accidents. It began with the launch of the Community Awareness and Emergency Response (CAER) program. This program was designed to encourage ACC member plants to inform local communities about chemicals located on site and to coordinate response efforts in the event of a release. A year later, the ACC adopted the Canadian Responsible Care Program, which established industry practices to reduce risks to workers, the community, and the environment. Subsequently the CAER program was incorporated into the Responsible Care program. In order to avoid another tragedy like Bhopal, all ACC members, which account for over 90% of U.S. chemical production, are required to follow Responsible Care guidelines. Other industry trade groups, such as the Synthetic Organic Chemical Manufacturers Association (SOCMA), have followed this lead.

In August 2003, the United Nations created a set of guidelines to protect human rights in the face of increasing economic globalization. The UN Norms on the Responsibilities of Transnational Corporations and Other Business Enterprises with Regard to Human Rights define standards to ensure that multinational corporations, their overseas plants, and surrounding communities are connected by a common set of values. Many of these guidelines would have applied directly to the Bhopal plant, including principles calling for multinational corporations to be responsible for the impact of their activities on human and environmental health, to report actual or anticipated releases of hazardous or toxic substances, and to use best management practices to reduce the risk of accidents or damage to the environment.

Despite these changes in the aftermath of Bhopal, not everyone is convinced that chemical safety has reached an acceptable level. Critics of the Responsible Care program charge that it is a purely voluntary measure on the part of the chemical industry, primarily a public relations campaign with no major effect on plant safety. They argue that government regulations and stringent enforcement are required to effect real change in industry practices.

The jury is still out on the UN reforms, as well. For this initiative to be successful, it will require a meaningful partnership between an industry willing to make reforms and governments willing to adopt and enforce stricter safety standards. Many people doubt that the pendulum has swung far enough in this direction, acknowledging that all too often the fervor over promoting economic development trumps safety concerns.

Meanwhile, chemical accidents continue to occur, in the United States and abroad, resulting in casualties and community evacuations. Yet nothing of Bhopalian proportions has been experienced since that December night. Whether something so dreadful could happen again, and how likely that would be, is a much-debated subject.

REFERENCES

ABC News. "Timeline: Disaster in Bhopal." www.abc.net.au/news/ newsitems/200412/s1256762.htm.

Amnesty International, *Clouds of Injustice—Bhopal 20 Years On*. London: Amnesty International Publications, 2004.

Amnesty International. "Dow Chemical Company, Union Carbide Corporation and the Bhopal Communities in India," www.amnestyusa .org/business/sharepower/bhopal.html.

Amnesty International. "UN Human Rights Standards for Businesses." http://web.amnesty.org/pages/ec-unnorms_2-eng.

Dawson, Bill. "Chemical Industry Catching Up on Safety," *Houston Chronicle*, February 18, 1986.

Greenpeace. "Bhopal Timeline." www.greenpeace.org/international/ campaigns/toxics/toxic-hotspots/bhopal-timeline.

Patel, Trupti. "Bhopal Disaster in India and Trade Aspects." *TED Case Studies: Environmental Accidents as Crimes*. www.american.edu/ted/ bhopal.htm.

Population Estimates for Bhopal, India, 1950–2015. http://books .mon gabay.com/population_estimates/full/Bhopal-India.html.

Reisch, Marc S. "Twenty Years after Bhopal," *Chemical & Engineering News* 82 June 2004,(): 19–23.

Union Carbide Corporation. "Bhopal Information Center." www.bhopal .com.

CHAPTER 4

MELTDOWN AT CHERNOBYL

A planned experiment gone badly at the Chernobyl nuclear power plant in the Soviet Union on April 25–26, 1986, created a reactor core explosion that sent a huge radioactive cloud into the atmosphere (see Exhibit 4.1). Thirty-one people died from immediate radiation poisoning, 130,000 residents were evacuated, and radiation effects were felt across most of Europe and beyond. The long-term human health effects of radiation exposure are now being realized, and a large area around the plant site remains off limits to human habitation. Many believe that this event was the catalyst to ending the Cold War.

In the mid-1980s, the Soviet Union (USSR) was locked in a decades-old power struggle with Western Europe and the United States known as the Cold War. As participants on both sides of this conflict attempted to gain political, economic, and military advantage, new technologies were developed to strengthen their cause. One of these was the nuclear reactor for creating electricity.

In 1978, the USSR unveiled the first nuclear reactor at its new power plant near the town of Chernobyl. The plant was situated in what is now Ukraine, approximately four miles south of the current Ukraine–Belarus border (see Exhibit 4.2). The facility sat on the banks of the Pripyat River, two miles from a town of the same name that had been constructed to house workers at the plant. In the years that followed the opening of the Chernobyl plant, several more reactors were added,

EXHIBIT **4.1**   *Remains of Chernobyl reactor No. 4 after the April 26, 1986, accident*

Source: *"Chernobyl Tour." www.allvirtualware.com/ ukrainianweb/images/chernobyl/chernobyl_reactor.jpg.*

culminating in 1983, when reactor No. 4 came online. All four of the Chernobyl reactors were of a Soviet design known by its Russian acronym, RBMK.

Nuclear power generation involves breaking atoms of uranium fuel apart, a process known as fission, to produce heat. When a uranium atom fissions, it sets off a chain reaction in which ejected pieces of the split atom, called neutrons, cause other atoms to fission. For this reason, control rods must be inserted into the uranium fuel to

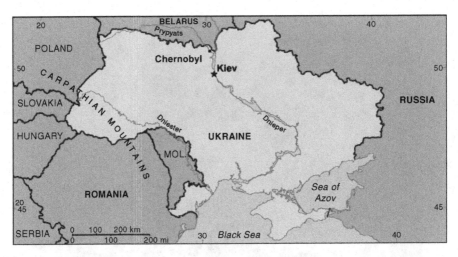

EXHIBIT **4.2**   *Map of Ukraine showing the location of Chernobyl*

Source: US Central Intelligence Agency. "Ukraine," World Factbook, 2006. www.cia.gov/cia/publications/factbook/geos/ up.html.

absorb neutrons and control the reaction. Heat from the fuel is absorbed and carried away by a loop of water gas coolant, which ultimately drives a turbine to create electricity. Most reactors also use coolant to moderate, or sustain, the fission process. Thus, if coolant is lost, the reactor will experience a decrease in energy production. By contrast, RBMK reactors use a graphite moderator. Because of this design change, if coolant is lost, a RBMK reactor will increase power output.

On the night of April 25, 1986, the No. 4 reactor at the Chernobyl plant was scheduled to reduce production to approximately half-power to allow for routine maintenance to be performed. During this period, an experiment was also programmed to test the ability of emergency equipment and cooling pumps to operate until backup generators came online. This procedure has since been likened to airline pilots experimenting with a plane's engines in midflight.

The initial step of reducing reactor production to half-power, 1,600 megawatts (MW), was accomplished successfully. In accordance with the test, the emergency cooling system would then be disabled and the reactor power further reduced to 700 to 1,000 MW. This process went awry at approximately 11:00 PM, when operators mistakenly allowed power production to fall all the way to 30 MW, or 1% of full power. Such low-power conditions in the RBMK design can cause the reactor to become extremely unstable. Recognizing this problem, workers attempted to raise the operating power by manually extracting some of the control rods from the uranium fuel. At 1:00 AM on April 26, the reactor stabilized for a short period of time at 200 MW. Soon thereafter, however, energy production began to wane, prompting the workers to extract most of the remaining control rods.

Meanwhile, as the power production had decreased, coolant pumps powered by the decelerating turbine had begun providing less coolant to the reactor. This decrease in coolant resulted in an increase in steam pressure, causing a power surge of more than 100 times the normal operating power. Operators attempted to reinsert the control rods to lower the power output but could not act quickly enough. The fuel rods ruptured and reacted with the steam from the coolant system. When the uranium came in contact with the coolant, an explosion with the force of 2,000 pounds of TNT occurred, blowing a 1,000-ton steel-and-cement shield off the top of the reactor.

At 1:23 AM, workers in Chernobyl's No. 1 reactor felt the ground shake and saw the lights flicker. They were ordered to report to reactor No. 4 immediately. Upon their arrival, however, reactor No. 4 co-workers told them to run and save themselves. "We are already dead," they said, "Go away."

A second explosion followed shortly afterward, contributing to the release of tons of radioactive material into the atmosphere and touching off fires in the reactor, some burning as hot as 2,800°F. Of the approximately 600 workers present at the Chernobyl plant during the explosion, 2 were killed and 134 received high doses of radiation, 28 of whom would die within the following four months.

As dawn broke on April 26, a typical day was beginning in Pripyat, a town of roughly 45,000 residents. People went about their business that day and into the next with no reason for alarm. It was not until 36 hours after the explosion that the population of Pripyat was officially informed of the incident and ordered to evacuate. By the following week, over 130,000 people had been evacuated from a 19-mile area around the plant.

For 12 days following the accident, an immense plume of radioactive material more than 400 times the magnitude of that released at Hiroshima spewed from the explosion site into the upper atmosphere, where weather patterns carried it north over Russia, then northeast over Poland and Scandinavia. Danish and Swedish nuclear monitors began detecting elevated levels of radiation within days of the incident. However, the first media coverage did not occur until April 29, when a German newscast reported that there had been a major nuclear incident at Chernobyl. Though the Soviet government initially denied the allegations, increasing international pressure finally caused Soviet leaders to acknowledge what had taken place.

Meanwhile, at the Chernobyl plant, 3,400 responders were attempting to put out fires started by the explosion. From April 27 to May 4, 1,800 helicopter flights dropped 5,000 tons of sand, lead, and boron on the reactor to extinguish the flames. On May 15 and 16, new blazes ignited, releasing even more radiation before firefighters could bring the flames under control. Over the next year, 200,000 workers were exposed to high radiation levels as they attempted to decontaminate the site and construct a concrete "sarcophagus" around the reactor to contain the radiation. Eventually, over 600,000 people would be involved in the cleanup and containment activities.

In the weeks following the explosions, the radioactive plume migrated beyond Scandinavia to the United Kingdom and Ireland. Changing weather patterns then carried it southward over most of Europe. Radiation from Chernobyl eventually was detected throughout the entire northern hemisphere, including countries as far away as Japan and the United States. Because no one had anticipated the vast extent of such a disaster, most nations had no contingency plan for the situation and limited their response to the radiation threat to banning food suspect of being contaminated.

Radioactive exposure from Chernobyl has caused a number of long-term medical problems. In Belarus, which received approximately 70% of the fallout, cases of childhood leukemia have reportedly increased by 50%. In parts of Belarus, children have become 30 times more likely to develop thyroid cancer. Adult cancer cases have increased by 40% in some areas of Belarus, including a doubling of the incidence of breast cancer. Additional carcinogenic impacts are expected, as experts acknowledge that some radiation-caused cancers may not appear until 30 years after initial exposure. Beyond cancer, exposed populations have experienced increased incidences of weakened immune systems, reproductive diseases, stillbirths, premature births, birth defects, infant mortality, and psychological trauma.

The accident also caused staggering economic losses for the USSR and the former Soviet nations. Damage estimates are in excess of $200 billion each for the Ukraine and Belarus, attributable to crop loss, power shortages, decontamination efforts, relocation of affected populations, payments to victims, and impacts on labor and industry. Upon dissolution of the USSR, Belarus and Ukraine were forced to levy emergency "Chernobyl taxes" on businesses to help offset expenses from the disaster, initially accounting for 22% and 15% of each country's national budget, respectively. These taxes continue to be collected, although they have been decreased to 6% of each country's budget, corresponding with the decline in disaster-related impacts over time.

The financial impacts of Chernobyl outside of the USSR, although not as extensive, were still significant. Sweden and Austria lost an estimated $144 million and $80 million, respectively, in agricultural products, and the United Kingdom lost millions in livestock. The economies of Eastern European countries, such as Poland, were hurt by bans imposed by the Western European community on the import of potentially contaminated foods.

Radioactive fallout from the accident also rendered large areas of land unusable. To this day, the region within a 19-mile radius around the plant remains off limits to human habitation. Even larger swaths of land have been deemed unsafe for crop production for a minimum of 30 years after the accident. Bioaccumulation of radioactivity has also left fish, grazing animals, and especially predators, such as wolves and foxes, highly contaminated.

A number of risk factors contributed to the Chernobyl accident and intensified its effects on human and environmental health. The decision to test the emergency system of reactor No. 4 while operating at half-power was a risky endeavor, one that significantly increased the likelihood of a reactor failure. When power was reduced much farther than intended, due to an operator error, reactor instability was too much to overcome. That such an experiment was designed to take place without complete interruption to power production suggests that schedule constraints may have been a factor. Knowledge that if the test could not be completed at the time, it would have to be deferred for another year caused stressful conditions that created more opportunity for operator error.

Aspects of poor design of the Chernobyl reactors also elevated the risk of a major nuclear accident. Arguably the most significant of these was the use of a graphite moderator. This design allowed the fission process to spiral out of control once steam started forming in the cooling loop, reducing the flow of coolant into the core. As the design of the reactor core also made quick insertion of control rods virtually impossible, there was no way to deal with a major power surge. Additionally, the reactors at Chernobyl had no containment structure to confine the explosion or the radiation it released. In contrast, reactors built in the United States and other western countries include containment structures built to withstand the force of an airline crash. If there had been a shield present around reactor No. 4, it may have contained the blast and reduced the severity of the accident.

Chernobyl was also plagued by an inability to follow standard operating practices. Plant workers appeared to employ ad hoc procedures in a desperate attempt to regain control of the reactor. For example, when power output fell to dangerously low levels, workers manually extracted nearly all of the control rods, despite requirements that at least 30 remain in place. This action, while intended to be helpful, ultimately served to accelerate and intensify the explosion.

When the disaster occurred, the Soviet government's eagerness to preserve national honor in the midst of the Cold War took precedence over protecting human health. This political agenda kept the USSR from reporting the incident immediately and further denying accusations that a nuclear event had occurred. This also led to an intentional strategy of poor communication with the victims. Official news of the incident was kept from the local population for 36 hours, during which time many people were unknowingly exposed to high levels of radiation. Iodine tablets that would have protected the population against thyroid cancer were not distributed until nearly a month after the accident, far too late to be of any therapeutic value. Moreover, propaganda focusing on heroism was used to motivate cleanup crews and downplay the hazardous conditions in which they were forced to work.

Even after publicly acknowledging the incident, the Soviet government continued to limit the flow of information that may have helped protect its people. For example, initially Soviet citizens were forbidden to use dosimeters to measure their radiation exposure, and maps showing the extent of contamination were not published until 1989. Such behavior reflects an attitude of arrogance on the part of Soviet leaders, willing to sacrifice Chernobyl's victims in order to save face on the world chessboard.

Following the explosions that destroyed reactor No. 4, the Chernobyl plant continued to produce electricity with its remaining reactors. Three years after the accident, in 1989, a decision was made to scrap plans to construct two new reactors, No. 5 and No. 6. The following year, emergency measures had to be taken to thwart an impending chain reaction of the remaining nuclear fuel contained in the wreckage of reactor

No. 4. Then, in October 1991, a fire broke out in the No. 2 reactor, which subsequently had to be shut down. By December 14, 2000, No. 3, the last operating reactor at the Chernobyl site, faced technical problems so severe that it could no longer function. The following day marked the ceremonial closing of the Chernobyl facility; Ukraine's president, Leonid Kuchma, ordered the reactor to cease operations, declaring that the world would be a safer place without its power.

Despite closing of the facility, the radiation threat at Chernobyl lingers. The site still contains hundreds of tons of radioactive fuel, a problem compounded by the fact that the concrete sarcophagus built in 1986 to contain radiation was designed for a maximum lifetime of only 20 to 30 years. With that containment now crumbling, a new $800 million structure is planned to encase the reactor until a permanent solution can be found. Because of the danger posed by radiation on site, the new covering will be erected several hundred yards from its ultimate destination and slid into place, making it the largest movable structure ever built (see Exhibit 4.3).

Since the accident, there have been several advances in the safety culture involving the production of nuclear energy, both inside and beyond former Soviet borders. Within Russia, the number of safety inspectors at nuclear plants has increased fivefold. In former Eastern Bloc countries, more stringent requirements now govern plant procedures, maintenance, and employee training. In some instances, new technologies also have been employed. For example, catalytic recombiners have been introduced in German reactors, which bond hydrogen released from a reactor accident to oxygen, creating water and preventing an explosion. Throughout the nuclear industry, accident management has been enhanced to better train and equip response teams, address response duties that may cross national borders (such as the timely distribution of iodine tablets), and improve the international early-warning system.

With the end of the Cold War, increased cooperation between former Soviet states and the West has helped to mitigate the long-term consequences of the Chernobyl disaster. The member countries of the Group of Seven and European Commission have supported Ukraine in shutting

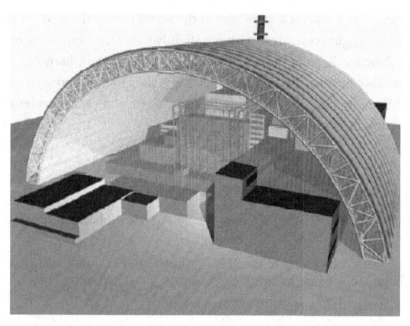

EXHIBIT **4.3**   *Artist rendering of the new containment structure for reactor No. 4*

Source: Eric Schmieman et al., "Conceptual Design of the Chernobyl New Safe Confinement—An Overview," 14th Pacific Basin Nuclear Conference. Honolulu, Hawaii, March 21–25, 2004.

down the Chernobyl reactors and decommissioning the plant, building a new structure to enclose reactor No.4, addressing the social issues faced by its citizens as a result of the disaster, and finding new ways to meet demand for electricity. In 1996, ten years after the accident, the Chernobyl Center for Nuclear Safety, Radioactive Waste and Radioecology was opened near the disaster site. Funded by the United States and Ukraine, the center now works with dozens of international agencies to improve the safety of nuclear power within and beyond Ukraine.

Despite improvements in the safety culture and international cooperation since the accident, certain forms of nuclear power production are still considered a high-risk endeavor. A recent study by the German Association for Reactor Safety placed the chances of a total meltdown occurring at a reactor somewhere in the world during the next 40 years at 40%, a figure consistent with but slightly lower than estimates by the U.S. Nuclear Regulatory Commission just prior to the Chernobyl accident. This surprisingly high figure is due in part to the continued use of RBMK reactors, 17 of which remain in operation or are under construction throughout Russia and Latvia.

REFERENCES

BBC. "The Chernobyl Disaster," 2004. www.bbc.co.uk/dna/h2g2/A2922103

BBC News. "Lost City in Pictures." http://news.bbc.co.uk/1/shared/spl/hi/pop_ups/06/in_pictures_chernobyl0s_lost_city/html/1.stm.

"Chernobyl Information." www.chernobyl.info.

Chornobyl Center for Nuclear Safety, Radioactive Waste, and Radio-ecology. "Chornobyl Center." www.chornobyl.net/en.

CNN. "Chernobyl Horror Remembered," 2006. www.cnn.com/2006/WORLD/europe/04/26/chernobyl.anniversary/index.html.

CNN. "Chernobyl Limps toward Shutdown," 2000. http://archives.cnno.com/2000/WORLD/europe/12/13/ukraine.chernobyl/index.html.

Gougar, Hans, et al. "Chernobyl: An Update." http://users.owt.com/smsrpm/Chernobyl/.

Guess, Marc. "Chernobyl Accident, Environment and Trade Impacts." *TED Case Studies* 4 (1995). www.american.edu/TED/chernob.htm.

Nave, Rod. "Chernobyl." http://hyperphysics.phyastr.gsu.edu/hbase/nucene/cherno.html.

"The Next Nuclear Meltdown," *New York Times*, May 8, 1985.

Nuclear Energy Institute. "Security Effectiveness." www.nei.org/index.asp?catnum=2&catid=279.

Organisation for Economic Co-operation and Development, Nuclear Energy Agency. *Chernobyl—Assessment of Radiological and Health Impacts*. Paris: OECD, 2002.

Stone, Richard. "The Long Shadow of Chernobyl," *National Geographic* (April 2006): 32–53.

U.S. Environmental Protection Agency. "Nuclear Incidents: Three Mile Island Nuclear Plant," 2006. www.epa.gov/radiation/rert/tmi.html.

U.S. Nuclear Regulatory Commission. "Backgrounder: Chernobyl Nuclear Power Plant Accident," 2006. www.nrc.gov/reading-rm/doc-collections/fact-sheets/chernobyl-bg.html.

CHAPTER 5

EXXON VALDEZ

A few minutes after midnight on March 24, 1989, the crew of the *Exxon Valdez* grounded the vessel on a reef located in Alaska's Prince William Sound, puncturing the cargo hold in eight places. In the ensuing hours, over 11 million gallons of crude oil escaped from the tanker, contaminating one of the world's most pristine areas. The severity of the spill, coupled with an ineffective response effort, resulted in an environmental and economic disaster. Members of the *Valdez* crew, the parent company, and other organizations all contributed to this outcome.

In the late 1980s, the *Exxon Valdez* was the newest and largest vessel in Exxon's oil tanker fleet. Its primary purpose was to transport crude oil from a pipeline terminal located in the town of Valdez on the southern coast of Alaska to cities in California, notably San Francisco and Long Beach. By March 1989, the tanker had made 27 such trips without a major mishap.

The captain of the *Valdez* was Joseph Hazelwood, an experienced seaman who had been employed by Exxon for more than 20 years. Hazelwood had been hired by Exxon following graduation from college in 1968. He quickly worked his way up through the ranks to become the youngest captain in Exxon's fleet at 32 years of age. The *Valdez* was placed under Hazelwood's command in 1987, subsequently receiving an Exxon award for "safety and performance" in each of the next two years.

On March 22, 1989, the *Valdez* docked at the Alyeska Marine Terminal in Valdez, Alaska, to take on its cargo of crude oil from the Alyeska Pipeline Company, a consortium of oil companies that included Exxon, operating in Alaska. Loading of the ship began the following morning, just after 5:00 AM. Six hours later, Hazelwood and two fellow crew members left the terminal and ventured into town. While there, Hazelwood conducted some official business, ordered Easter flowers for his wife and daughter, and drank beer and vodka in local bars. The three men hailed a taxi to return to the ship, cleared security, and boarded the vessel around 8:30 PM. Upon arrival, the trio was informed that the scheduled departure time had been moved up from 10:00 PM to 9:00.

After a rushed preparation for departure, the Valdez embarked at 9:12 PM, just a few minutes behind schedule. At 9:21, shortly after clearing the dock, Captain Hazelwood left the bridge while the harbor pilot guided the vessel toward the open waters of Prince William Sound (see Exhibit 5.1). Hazelwood was absent from the bridge for the next two hours, in violation of a company policy that requires at least two officers to be on the bridge while passing through the Valdez Narrows.

At approximately 11:15 PM, Hazelwood returned to the bridge, and the harbor pilot, having performed his duty, disembarked shortly thereafter. Hazelwood notified the Vessel Traffic Center at 11:25 that he was accelerating to sea speed. He further informed the center that if there were no incoming vessels, he would divert the *Valdez* from the outbound shipping lane to the inbound lane to avoid floating ice. This was a common procedure used to maneuver around small icebergs that often broke free from the nearby Columbia Glacier.

At 11:30 PM, Hazelwood notified the Vessel Traffic Center that he was turning the ship eastward toward the inbound lane. The captain also noted that he was slowing the ship's speed to navigate through the ice, although engine logs would later reveal that the ship's speed continued to increase. The Valdez began working its way eastward out of the outbound lane, across the half-mile-wide traffic separation zone, and

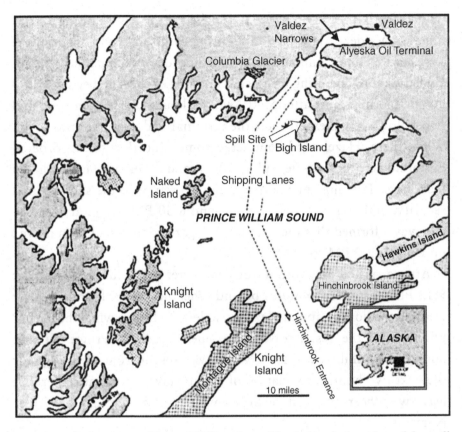

EXHIBIT 5.1   *Map of Prince William Sound depicting the location of the spill*

> Source: National Response Team, The Exxon Valdez Oil
> Spill: A Report to the President *(Washington, DC: Govern-*
> *ment Printing Office, 1989).*

into the inbound lane. Then, without further communication with the center, the *Valdez* turned southward on a course that would take it beyond the inbound shipping lane. At 11:39 PM, Hazelwood ordered that the ship be placed on autopilot and a few minutes later ordered initialization of computer software that would ramp up the ship's engines to full speed over the course of the next 40 to 50 minutes. Hazelwood then discussed the procedures for returning the *Valdez* to its assigned traffic lane with Third Mate Gregory Cousins and returned to his cabin to complete some paperwork. Although his cabin was only 15 feet and one stairway away, Hazelwood's departure again violated company policy by leaving Cousins as the only officer on the bridge.

Around this time, Second Mate Lloyd LeCain was scheduled to relieve Cousins, who was nearing the end of his six-hour shift. Cousins, however, knowing that LeCain was tired from a long day of working on the ship's loading operations, told the second mate to take his time getting to the bridge.

Around midnight, Cousins determined that it was time to turn the boat back toward the shipping lanes. He ordered the helmsman to begin turning the ship, turned off the autopilot, and called Hazelwood to notify him that the turn was under way. At approximately the same time, the lookout reported seeing a buoy light near Bligh Reef. However, instead of the light appearing on the port (left) side of the ship, where it was expected, she had spotted it off of the starboard (right) side. The position of the light relative to the Valdez meant that the tanker was accelerating straight toward the reef. Cousins urgently ordered that the ship be turned harder and phoned Hazelwood again. "We are in trouble," he told the captain as they both felt the first jolts of the tanker grinding over the reef. The time was 12:04 AM, on March 24.

Hazelwood rushed to the bridge, arriving as the Valdez came to rest on top of Bligh Reef. He began giving orders, trying to free the ship. Chief Mate James Kunkel reported that eight cargo and two ballast tanks had been punctured and oil was spilling into Prince William Sound. After unsuccessful attempts to free the ship, Hazelwood notified the Vessel Traffic Center of his situation at 12:26 AM.

Upon notification of the spill, the center closed the port of Valdez to all vessel traffic and notified the National Response Center in Washington, D.C. Representatives from the coast guard and the Alaska Department of Environmental Conservation began arriving on scene approximately three and one-half hours after the incident to assess the situation.

In the first five hours following the grounding, more than 11 million gallons of crude oil spilled into Prince William Sound and began spreading rapidly. By 7:30 AM, the oil slick had grown to 1,000 feet wide and four miles long. The spill was quickly becoming the largest in U.S. history and no one, not Exxon, Alyeska, the state of Alaska, nor the federal government, was adequately prepared to handle it.

Alyeska immediately responsibility for the cleanup and began activating its two emergency operations centers. The coast guard On-Scene Coordinator (OSC) and Exxon started coordinating efforts to ensure that the *Valdez* would not capsize and thereby dump the remaining 80% of its cargo. Alyeska and the National Oceanic and Atmospheric Administration (NOAA) had identified environmentally sensitive areas prior to the spill and began taking measures to protect them. Four fish hatcheries were assigned highest priority, but when containment equipment became scarce, the OSC was forced to choose between protecting other ecological resources or containing the spill.

This equipment shortage was just one of many instances in which the necessary resources were not available for timely and effective spill response. While Alyeska had been quick to mobilize once notified of the incident, it soon realized that an effective response would be impossible. Though the company's spill contingency plan called for an initial response time of five hours, the barge designated for such operations was missing vital equipment that had been removed for repairs. Reloading the barge was made especially difficult because cranes used for the task had been positioned for use by other Alyeska vessels. As a result, the barge did not arrive on scene until 12 hours after the spill began. Even then, the available equipment amounted to only two skimmers for collecting oil, two 1,000-gallon collection bladders, and 8,000 feet of containment boom. These were no match for a spill of such magnitude.

Other response supplies were similarly inadequate. Alyeska had only four miles of additional boom on hand, which was already insufficient by the time response vessels began arriving at the scene. Similarly, Alyeska had less than 4,000 gallons of chemical dispersant available at the time of the spill. While another 16,800 gallons of dispersant were available in other towns in the Valdez region, hundreds of thousands of gallons would have been required to break up a spill of this size.

The available dispersant was eventually applied to the oil slick by helicopter at 6:00 PM on the March 24, 18 hours after the spill began. Calm waters and winds kept the dispersant and oil from mixing and effectively breaking up the oil for the first three days after the accident. Burning off the oil was also attempted, but this was abandoned when residents downwind reported eye and throat irritation from the smoke. Mechanical methods of oil recovery proved to be the most effective, but complications also plagued this technique. Fragile containment booms had to be towed very slowly to avoid breaking, and, because Prince William Sound is so large, it took considerable time to place booms in the desired locations. Furthermore, skimmers were generally ineffective as time passed because the increasingly weathered oil thickened and clogged skimmer hoses. With no effective means for collecting or containing the oil, the slick continued to grow (see Exhibit 5.2).

While containment and recovery activities progressed, Exxon pumped oil out of the *Valdez* to another vessel to reduce the likelihood of additional spillage. By April 4, the remaining 43 million gallons of crude oil had been transferred from the *Valdez* to the *Exxon Baton Rouge*. While the oil was being pumped out of the *Valdez*, Exxon was also busy establishing a communication network for response crews, creating a refueling station for helicopters, bringing in additional response supplies and equipment, and contracting for the services of numerous ships and aircraft.

At the peak of the response effort, approximately 100 aircraft, 1,000 ships, and 10,000 workers were involved, representing Alyeska, Exxon, various state and federal agencies, and at least five foreign countries. Utilization of this workforce and equipment enabled the collection of up to 200,000 gallons of oil per day, although only 14% of the spilled oil would ever be recovered. By the time all of the response resources had arrived, however, the spill had grown to encompass an enormous area, eventually covering more than 11,000 square miles. It spread from Bligh Reef to parts of the Alaska peninsula, located 470 miles southwest, contaminating 1,300 miles of shoreline along the way.

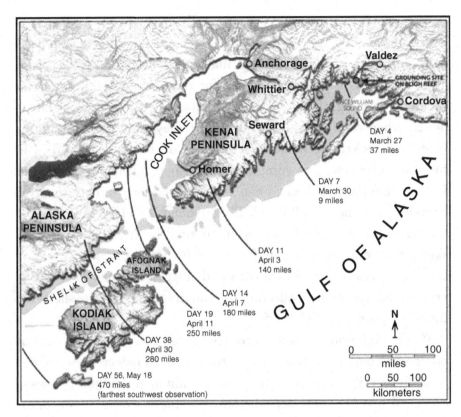

EXHIBIT 5.2 *Extent of the* Valdez *oil slick*

Source: Exxon Valdez *Oil Spill Trustee Council. www.evostc .state.ak.us.*

Despite early efforts by Alyeska and various federal agencies to protect sensitive species and ecosystems, many indigenous animals and shoreline habitats fell victim to the spill. Wildlife casualties included approximately 300,000 birds, 2,500 sea otters, and 300 harbor seals. The oil also severely damaged the region's fisheries, the economic foundation for the area's many small fishing communities. Other spill casualties included subsistence resources (fish, shellfish, mammals) for local Alaskan native populations, dozens of archeological sites, and a number of recreation and tourism destinations.

Oil removal from beaches, using pressure washing, excavation, and bioremediation, continued for more than three years after the

accident. In June 1992, the coast guard recommended that cleanup activities cease based on a cost/benefit analysis that indicated diminishing returns on investment. Pools of oil remained on many beaches,
however, and decades later, smaller-scale environmental restoration
projects remain ongoing. Cleanup efforts cost Exxon an estimated
$2.1 billion, not including funds in settlements and damages from
lawsuits, some of which have also been applied to environmental
cleanup and restoration.

Despite not even ranking among the world's 50 largest oil spills,
the *Exxon Valdez* accident is widely regarded as the most destructive to the environment. Like 80% of all maritime accidents, the
cause of the spill itself was attributed to human error, although
organizational behavior was certainly a contributing risk factor.
The consequential damage, however, resulted from a combination
of poor planning, economic pressures, political agendas, and suspect vessel design.

The fact that Captain Hazelwood had been consuming alcohol in
the hours prior to the accident received much attention after the event.
Hazelwood had been a serious drinker since his college days in the
mid-1960s. As his career progressed, he began drinking heavily and
openly on ships, a violation of Exxon company policy. In 1982, he was
sued by another seaman who claimed that Hazelwood had hit him in a
drunken rage. Hazelwood later lost his driver's license on three separate occasions due to drunk driving, one such incident occurring just
months prior to the *Valdez* accident.

Exxon became aware of Hazelwood's drinking problem and, in accordance with company policy, encouraged him to seek treatment
rather than punish him. In 1985, Hazelwood entered a rehabilitation
center. After a 28-day stay, Exxon monitored the captain closely, with
supervisors checking in on him at least twice a month for the next two
years. Despite this scrutiny, however, the company missed signs that

Hazelwood had begun drinking heavily again. Meanwhile, Exxon started supplying low-alcohol beer to crewmen aboard its tankers, a situation that could only have served to make sobriety more difficult for Hazelwood.

Hazelwood has since admitted that he consumed alcohol in the afternoon and early evening of March 23. His cab driver and a port security guard later testified that Hazelwood did not appear drunk when he returned to the vessel, although a ship's agent and the harbor pilot both suspected he had been drinking. A test administered 10 hours after the grounding measured Hazelwood's blood-alcohol level at approximately 0.06%, in excess of the 0.04 limit set by the coast guard for seamen operating a moving vessel. Exxon fired Hazelwood upon learning of this violation. It remains uncertain, however, if his elevated test results were caused by alcohol consumption before or after the accident had occurred.

Crew fatigue was also a likely factor in the grounding of the Valdez. In the late 1960s, when Hazelwood began his career with Exxon, as many as 40 sailors were assigned to tankers smaller than the *Valdez*. By the time of the accident in Prince William Sound, crew size had been slashed significantly, presumably for economic reasons. The crew on board the *Valdez* that day consisted of only 20 people and was set to be trimmed to 15 on future voyages to further reduce costs. As a result, crew members were often overworked, regularly putting in 12- to 14-hour days. It has been estimated that at the time of the grounding, Third Mate Cousins had been working for 18 consecutive hours. In terms of human error rates, being awake for such a long period of time, without taking into account exhaustion from labor, is equivalent to having a blood-alcohol level of 0.05%. Thus, Cousins may have been as unfit to command the ship as Hazelwood.

It is uncertain as to whether Cousins was even qualified to command the *Valdez* at the time of the accident. In June 1989, the commandant of the coast guard reported that Cousins had been "fully qualified" to pilot the ship. Later that year, he changed his view, saying that Cousins "was competent, but not technically qualified." The rules governing

Cousins's qualifications to command the ship at the location and time of the incident are unclear. When the Alaska Pipeline opened in 1977, the coast guard required a pilotage endorsement to steer a vessel anywhere between the sound entrance and the port of Valdez. Such a restriction would have made Cousins unqualified. However, in 1986, this rule was relaxed to allow unendorsed pilots beyond a certain point in the sound, given good visibility. Following the accident, the coast guard maintained that the point in question lay at Bligh Reef, where the *Valdez* struck ground. Others argued that the coast guard had waived the endorsement requirement farther north, to the point where harbor pilots disembarked from outgoing vessels. If the latter scenario was the case, Cousins would have been qualified to steer the *Valdez* at the time of the accident, although the presence of only one officer on the bridge still would have violated company procedure.

As Hazelwood and Cousins guided the *Valdez* south and out of the traffic lanes, they were operating with incomplete information. The Vessel Traffic Center could not monitor the ship's movement due to range limits on the station's radar. This kept the center from providing the *Valdez* with information on its whereabouts or warnings that may have helped it steer clear of the reef.

Once the *Valdez* ran aground, vessel design became an important risk factor. It is widely known that single-hull designs, like that of the *Valdez*, are susceptible to puncture accidents; based on historical records, this type of accident is associated with 70% of all oil spills. If additional containment was included in the vessel, such as the presence of an internal (second) hull, perhaps no oil would have spilled when the external hull was punctured or, alternatively, less oil would have spilled because the puncture opening might have been smaller.

Once it was known that the *Valdez* was spilling oil, poor response exacerbated the problem. There were at least six spill contingency plans in place for such an event, yet none of them proved to be effective. These plans, established by Alyeska, Exxon, and various governmental entities, were not coordinated nor did they establish a clear hierarchy of command. Moreover, some of these plans were too general to be of any value in the event of an actual spill. Exxon's plan, for example, contained no location-specific information for the port of Valdez terminal or Prince William Sound, and was missing a list of available equipment and description of its use.

The federal government's initial reluctance to get more heavily involved in the spill response effort could be seen as politically motivated. Critics point to the delicate balance between the economic importance of domestic oil production and the outcry from environmentalists over the magnitude and consequences of the spill. They argue that the federal government stalled in its decision making with the hope that the spill would be controlled rather quickly and media attention would wane. This would allow for the incident to pass quietly from the public conscience, leaving intact a future agenda for opening up Alaska's other oil reserves.

In terms of resources, the response agencies were totally unprepared for a spill of such magnitude. Because the likelihood of a spill event of this scale had been estimated to be extremely low, Alyeska concluded that storing all of the necessary response equipment was not cost effective. Thus, when the *Valdez* struck Bligh Reef, Alyeska's only barge had been stripped of its equipment, and other available booms, skimmers, and dispersants were in limited supply. Responders were also short of personnel, many of whom were at home for the Easter holiday. As the spill spread, when even more response workers were required, few possessed the skill to perform containment or cleanup.

The response environment was also afflicted by the mountainous terrain surrounding Prince William Sound, which hindered radio communication among involved parties. This situation was further complicated by the large number of vessels using the airwaves, resulting in simultaneous transmissions. Similarly, telecommunications infrastructure in a town the size of Valdez was unable to handle the sudden increase in calls from response teams and media representatives. Several thousand phone calls were not connected during the first week after the spill, further delaying requests for supplies and information. Valdez also had only a small airstrip, prompting the Federal Aviation Administration to build and staff a temporary air traffic control tower to handle the increase in flights. Nevertheless, larger planes were forced to fly into Anchorage, where supplies had to be unloaded and driven nine hours by truck in order to reach Valdez. Upon arrival at the port, the supplies had to be offloaded and reloaded onto a vessel for a two-hour boat ride to the spill site. Such long transit times necessitated the use of helicopters; however, they were largely ineffective because of limited access to refueling stations.

In 1990, Hazelwood was acquitted of criminal mischief, reckless endangerment, and operating a boat under the influence of alcohol. He was, however, convicted of negligently discharging oil, and sentenced to serve community service and pay a $50,000 fine. Unable to find employment as a captain, Hazelwood was hired to teach classes at his alma mater, the Maritime College of the State University of New York, in 1992. He has since worked as a claims adjustor for the New York–based law firm that represented him during the trial.

Exxon completed delivery of its $900 million civil settlement in 2001. In addition to restoration efforts, the money was used to protect 650,000 acres of land, support scientific studies in Prince William Sound, and establish a new aquarium in Seward, Alaska. In June 2006, in accordance with the settlement, the U.S. Justice Department and the State of Alaska asked for an additional $92 million from Exxon when it became apparent that further cleanup efforts were needed.

In the decades following the spill, wildlife and the environment remain damaged. While many of the affected animal populations have shown signs of recovery, some, like the harbor seal, Pacific herring, and harlequin duck, have not.

To guard against the occurrence of such disasters in the future, a number of changes in legislation, port procedures, and industry practices have occurred. In 1990, Congress passed the Oil Pollution Act (OPA), which included a provision requiring all oil tankers using U.S.

ports to have a double-hull design by the year 2015 (see Exhibit 5.3). This design provides a buffer between the cargo hold and a ship's outer hull, in theory making puncture spills less likely. OPA also increased the cost of spill response for the responsible party. In the port of Valdez, tugboats now escort tankers, radar systems have been improved, and emergency drills are held on a monthly basis. The oil industry has invested $1 billion to create the Marine Spill Response Corporation, which continuously staffs a 210-foot cleanup vessel for quick response to catastrophic spills.

After the spill, the *Valdez* was floated and towed to San Diego, where it received $30 million worth of repairs. The ship was subsequently renamed the *SeaRiver Mediterranean*. The vessel was not allowed to operate in Prince William Sound, as a provision in the 1990 OPA prohibits any ship that has spilled more than 1 million gallons anywhere in the world from entering the environmentally sensitive area. This meant that the *Mediterranean* would have to be assigned to international shipping, a task for which it was not designed. By 2002, continued operation of the *Mediterranean* proved to be too costly. It was stripped of its cargo, fuel, and supplies, and anchored at an undisclosed port in Asia to await its fate. Its sister ship, the *SeaRiver Long Beach*, continues to operate in the port of Valdez, despite having once been forced into emergency dry dock for leaking oil through fractures in its hull.

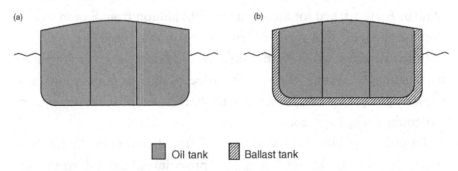

EXHIBIT 5.3   *Cross section of an oil tanker with (a) a single hull and (b) a double hull*

Oil spills have continued to plague the petroleum industry since the grounding of the *Valdez*, with many occurring in similarly environmentally sensitive locations. For example, in a seven-month period beginning in July 2000, oil spills endangered wildlife in the Galapagos Islands; internationally renowned waterfalls along the Iguacu River in Brazil; penguin colonies on Dassen Island, South Africa; and shellfish beds and waterfowl hatcheries along the lower Mississippi River. In the coming decades, however, the industry's regulation-induced adoption of double-hulled vessels will likely help to alleviate environmental damage stemming from grounding accidents. Comparisons of groundings involving single- versus double-hulled ships at identical locations have shown double hulls to be an effective prevention against spills. With the total transition to these safer vessels in the U.S. fleet nearly complete and the imminent ban of single-hulled ships in the European Union stemming from a 2001 spill off the coast of Spain, the majority of the world's tankers will soon be double-hulled.

REFERENCES

Alaska Oil Spill Commission. Spill, the Wreck of the *Exxon Valdez*: Implications for Safe Transportation of Oil. 1990.

Allen, Scott. "Worst Oil Spill in US Has Lingering Effects for Alaska, Industries," *Boston Globe*, March 7, 1999.

Australian Maritime Safety Authority. "Comparison of Single and Double Hull Tankers," 2002. www.amsa.gov.au/Publications/Comparison_of_single_and_double_hull_tankers.pdf.

Barrenger, Felicity. "$92 Million More Is Sought for Exxon Valdez Cleanup," *New York Times*, June 2, 2006.

BBC. "EU to Ban Single-Hull Tankers," December 6, 2002. http://news.bbc.co.uk/1/hi/world/europe/2551721.stm.

Behar, Richard. "Joe's Bad Trip," *Time Magazine*, July 24, 1989.

"Captain Joe Goes to College," *Time Magazine*, May 18, 1992.

CNN. "African Penguins Airlifted from Oil Spill Zone," July 4, 2000. http://archives.cnn.com/2000/NATURE/07/04/safrica.penguins/index.html.

CNN. "Brazil Stops River Oil Spill Far from Key City," July 19, 2000. http://archives.cnn.com/2000/NATURE/07/19/brazil.spill.wildlife/ index.html.

CNN. "Crews on Mississippi Tackle Largest Oil Spill Since Exxon Valdez," November 30, 2000. http://archives.cnn.com/2000/US/11/ 30/oil.spill.ap/index.html.

CNN. "Exxon Valdez Banned from Spill Site," November 1, 2002. http://archives.cnn.com/2002/WORLD/europe/11/01/valdez.ban.glb/ index.html.

CNN *Moneyline* transcript, November 19, 2002. http://transcripts.cnn .com/TRANSCRIPTS/0211/19/mlld.00.html.

CNN. "New Hurdles Hamper Galapagos Oil Spill Cleanup," January 26, 2001. http://archives.cnn.com/2001/NATURE/01/26/galapagos .spill/index.html.

CNNMoney.com. "Its 100 Tugs and Barges Ply Coastal Waters, Delivering Petroleum," July 11, 2007. http://money.cnn.com/news/newsfeeds/ articles/newstex/IBD-0001-18071068.htm.

Crowley, Lauren E. "*Exxon Valdez* Crash," *TED Case Studies* 2 (1992). www.american.edu/TED/exxon.htm.

Exxon Valdez Oil Spill Trustee Council. www.evostc.state.ak.us.

Exxon Valdez Oil Spill Trustee Council. "*Exxon Valdez* Oil Spill Restoration Plan: Update on Injured Resources and Services." Anchorage, AK, 2002.

Exxon Valdez Oil Spill Trustee Council. 2004 Annual Report. www .evostc.state.ak.us/History/Downloadables/AnRpt04.pdf.

Hunter, Don. "Alcohol Stains Record of Skilled Sea Captain," *Anchorage Daily News*, March 24, 1989.

Little, Robert, "Even Renamed, Exxon Valdez Can't Outlive Stain on Its Past," *Baltimore Sun*, October 15, 2002.

National Research Council. "Double-Hull Vessels Could Significantly Reduce Oil Spills, But New Design Standards Are Needed," Publication Announcement. 1997. www8.nationalacademies.org/onpinews/ newsitem.aspx?RecordID=5798.

National Response Team. *The* Exxon Valdez *Oil Spill: A Report to the President*. Washington, DC: Government Printing Office, 1989.

Newton, L. H., and C. K. Dillingham. *Watersheds 2: Ten Cases in Environmental Ethics*. Albany, NY: Wadsworth Publishing Company, 1997, chap. 6: "Oil and Waters—*Exxon Valdez* and the Cleanup."

"Notebook," *Time Magazine,* May 26, 1997.

O'Connor, Anahad. "Wakefulness Finds a Powerful Ally," *New York Times*, June 29, 2004.

Toomey, Sheila. "$50,000 Check Settles Hazelwood's Alaska Debt," *Anchorage Daily News*, May 16, 2002.

U.S. Environmental Protection Agency. *Understanding Oil Spills and Oil Response*. Cincinnati: National Service Center for Environmental Publications, 1999.

"Where Are They Now: The Captain: Joe Hazelwood," *Anchorage Daily News*, May 13, 1999.

CHAPTER 6

CHALLENGER AND COLUMBIA: DÉJÀ VU

T he U.S. space shuttle program suffered a serious setback on January 28, 1986, when the shuttle *Challenger* disintegrated shortly after takeoff, killing the entire crew. The official cause of the disaster was a mechanical design problem, but it was discovered that NASA and its contractor knew of the existence of this design flaw yet allowed the flight to proceed. NASA subsequently took corrective actions to ensure that such institutional failures would not allow the repetition of another shuttle disaster. Yet history repeated itself some 17 years later, on February 1, 2003, when the shuttle *Columbia* tore apart during reentry into Earth's atmosphere. Once again, compelling evidence of NASA's institutional failures figured prominently in the postaccident investigation.

Since its inception in 1958, the U.S. National Aeronautics and Space Administration (NASA) has made tremendous scientific and technological strides in our understanding of the universe. One such accomplishment has been the development of the Human Space Flight Program, which produced the first manned U.S. space flight in 1961. This program has put scores of astronauts into space, carried out countless scientific experiments, accomplished six lunar landings, and placed numerous satellites and space stations into orbit.

In the late 1960s, as lunar expeditions were under way, NASA began forming plans for the next generation of space exploration. The agency

EXHIBIT **6.1**　*Mission patches for the final* Challenger *(at left) and* Columbia *flights*

Source: (a) http://science.ksc.nasa.gov/shuttle/missions/51-l/51-l-patch.jpg and (b) http://spaceflight.nasa.gov/gallery/images/shuttle/sts-107/html/sts107-s-001.html.

decided to develop a reusable space vehicle to enable the transportation of humans and resources between future space stations as well as to facilitate exploration of other planets within our solar system. In 1972, President Nixon officially announced plans for such a program, proclaiming that the new vehicle would revolutionize space transportation by "routinizing it."

It took approximately $6 billion and another nine years to produce the vehicle, which had come to be known as the space shuttle. This massive effort resulted in one of the most complicated and impressive machines ever created, comprised of over 2 million parts and able to travel 25 times the speed of sound.

The shuttle consists of four main elements (see Exhibit 6.2): the orbiter, main engines, external tank, and solid rocket boosters (SRBs). The orbiter is a glider similar in size to a commercial airliner, and carries the mission crew and payload. Attached to the orbiter are the three main engines, fueled by a large external tank containing liquid oxygen

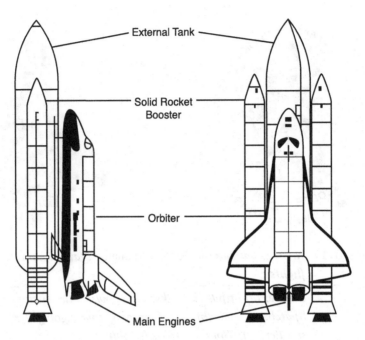

External Tank

Solid Rocket Booster

Orbiter

Main Engines

EXHIBIT 6.2   *Four major elements of the space shuttle*

and hydrogen fuel. Attached to this tank are the two SRBs. These rockets provide the majority of the thrust needed to propel the shuttle into orbit.

April 12, 1981, ushered in a new era of space travel when the shuttle *Columbia* began its first flight. It was piloted safely back to Earth two days later and would complete three more missions over the next 15 months. As *Columbia* touched down to end its fourth flight on July 4, 1982, President Reagan announced to the world that with its next mission, the shuttle would be fully operational, beginning an age of regular, low-cost access to space.

Over the next three years, the shuttle program grew to include four orbiters, the *Columbia, Challenger, Discovery,* and *Atlantis.* By the end of 1985, the shuttles were flying nine missions a year. It seemed that spaceflight was indeed becoming routine, so much so that two U.S. legislators flew on one mission and a high school teacher was scheduled to fly on another.

In late January 1986, the *Challenger* was set to fly the twenty-fifth mission of NASA's shuttle program. The flight would be the tenth for the *Challenger,* three more than any other shuttle. The mission plan called for placing two satellites into orbit, conducting experiments related to a fly-by of Haley's Comet, and initiating the "Teacher In Space" project to raise interest among youth in the space program and in education.

Preparations for this *Challenger* flight had begun as far back as 1984. The shuttle crew started training 37 weeks prior to lift-off, and periodic reviews of the mission began 7 months in advance. While there were some obstacles to overcome in mission planning, such as the addition of a crew member and payloads, flight preparations generally went smoothly. Despite delays in astronaut training resulting from the previous shuttle flight being behind schedule, all seven crew members and mission flight controllers were able to complete their training and were certified for flight. On January 15, 1986, the Flight Readiness Review was conducted for the *Challenger* mission. This review is the last in a series of evaluations to ensure the readiness of a shuttle mission and to address any questions that may have arisen during flight preparation.

The *Challenger* mission had originally been scheduled to launch on January 22, but several delays were experienced due to earlier shuttle flights being off schedule, poor weather conditions, and a mechanical problem with a hatch handle, among others. The mission was finally set for the morning of January 28.

The weather forecast for the night of January 27 and the next morning was unusually cold, with temperatures expected to drop several degrees below freezing. NASA management ordered its engineers to determine the effects of such low temperatures on the launch. No concerns were presented to NASA officials, and the countdown continued.

By the morning of January 28, water running from the launch structure had caused a buildup of ice on the launch pad and structures surrounding the shuttle, including emergency escape paths for the crew.

There was some concern that the ice might break loose during liftoff and damage the orbiter. An ice inspection team was sent to monitor and report on the situation as launch time drew closer. Based on reports from the inspection team, the shuttle program manager decided to delay the launch to allow more ice to melt. Finally, at 11:15 AM, with temperatures 15 degrees colder than any previous launch, the countdown was resumed.

Just before 11:38 AM, *Challenger*'s engines roared to life. Seconds later, the SRBs ignited and the shuttle lifted off from the launch pad. Unnoticed by anyone at the time, puffs of black smoke began emanating from one of the joints on the right SRB. In seconds, the shuttle was hurtling through the air, performing maneuvers necessary for escaping Earth's gravitational field. To the ground control crew and the astronauts onboard the orbiter, everything about the flight seemed to be proceeding according to plan.

Suddenly, 73 seconds into the mission, all signals from the *Challenger* were lost. Video coverage showed a cloud of smoke where the shuttle had been, and NASA's radar system began displaying multiple objects rather than the single vehicle. The *Challenger*'s external fuel tank had exploded, exposing the orbiter itself to aerodynamic loads so intense that it was immediately torn apart (see Exhibit 6.3). The two SRBs continued flying independently after the explosion and were detonated remotely by NASA officials to ensure the safety of people on the ground.

The cabin of the *Challenger* fell toward Earth for nearly three minutes before impacting the Atlantic Ocean. It would later be determined that at least some of the crew survived the initial explosion and had even activated their emergency air supplies, though it is unlikely that they were conscious at the time of impact.

Less than six hours after the disaster, President Reagan addressed a stunned nation. In his speech, the president praised NASA and the *Challenger* crew for their devotion and effort, and promised a continued commitment to space exploration. President Reagan also reminded the nation that, despite public perception that space travel had become

EXHIBIT **6.3**   *Explosion of the* Challenger's *external fuel tank and breakup of the orbiter. Diverging trails of smoke are from the independently operating SRBs.*

Source: NASA. Image # 86-HC-220, 1986. http://dayton.hq
.nasa.gov/ABSTRACTS/GPN-2004-00012.html.

so common as to be unremarkable, such exploration was still in its infancy.

One week later, President Reagan established the Rogers Commission to investigate the cause of the accident and to determine how another such occurrence could be prevented. The commission concluded the primary technical reason for the *Challenger* disaster was the failure of a joint between two sections of the right SRB. Specifically, rubber seals, referred to as O-rings, did not keep hot gases from escaping through the joint. These gases burned into the external tank, causing it to explode.

A possible explanation for O-ring failure centered on low-temperature conditions. Testing on O-rings showed them to be less resilient at low temperatures, meaning that when pressure is relieved from the joint, the ring material is slow to expand and maintain a seal. If the seal is not maintained, hot gases can escape around the O-rings. Evidence of this flaw was found on all four prior shuttle flights that had been launched when the air temperature was 61°F or lower. In contrast, only 4 of the 21 flights launched above that temperature had experienced similar O-ring deterioration.

The performance of the putty used to insulate the O-rings from direct contact with the gases was similarly susceptible to degradation at low temperatures. Under such conditions, the putty can keep the O-rings from sealing for several seconds after ignition of the SRBs, sufficient time to allow hot gases to escape around the rings.

Ice buildup in the joint also may have contributed to O-ring failure. Water had been present in the SRB joints on at least one previous shuttle flight. A similar occurrence in the *Challenger* would have resulted in a buildup of ice that could have prevented the O-rings from sealing upon ignition of the SRBs.

Beyond these technical considerations, however, that an O-ring failure was allowed to occur was attributed to institutional problems that plagued NASA. The Rogers Commission discovered that engineers' concerns regarding O-ring performance were not communicated to NASA officials who made the decision to proceed with the launch. The problem of gases escaping around the O-rings had been recognized since mid-1985, at which point the O-rings were designated as "launch constraints." This label meant that Flight Readiness Reviews would have to consider the problem before going forward with a launch, which would then only be possible by issuing a waiver for the launch constraint. These waivers were issued for each of the seven shuttle missions flown after the launch constraint designation, including the *Challenger*. After the disaster, however, NASA officials in charge of signing the waivers claimed that they had not been aware of the seriousness of the problem. Although engineers at Morton

Thiokol, the contractor that produced the SRBs, voiced serious concerns about the possible effects of the O-ring problem, neither Morton Thiokol nor NASA project managers felt that the situation warranted notifying NASA officials in charge of issuing waivers.

Another case of questionable decision making arose when project engineers expressed concern regarding the proposed launch time temperatures and the possibility of ice damaging the shuttle. Ironically, NASA managers decided that this concern would not be communicated to higher-ranking officials unless the contractor could prove that conditions were *unsafe* rather than the standard procedure of having to prove that it was *safe* to launch.

Another disturbing trend involved the safety program workforce, which was reduced as the number of flights increased. At the time of the *Challenger* disaster, only 20 safety workers were assigned to the program, and none of them was included in the decision to launch on January 28, 1986. Further complicating matters was the lack of standard requirements and incentives for identifying and reporting critical issues for the consideration of NASA managers.

After reviewing these events and decisions, it becomes clear that the NASA culture was governed to a large degree by political agendas more so than a concern for safety. This culture became more pronounced and showed signs of arrogance as shuttle launches became routine and NASA grew complacent. The effects of NASA's internal deficiencies were magnified when coupled with economic pressure and schedule constraints that confronted the agency. The shuttle faced market competition before it had even flown its first mission. In the early 1970s, the European Space Agency developed an expendable commercial vehicle for carrying satellites into orbit. This vehicle, known as *Ariane*, began operating in 1979, nearly two years before the first shuttle flight. The competition for commercial contracts pushed NASA not only to pronounce the shuttle operational prematurely, but also to offer launch services to customers for only one-third of the actual flight cost.

This situation created the pressure to fly more often in order to reduce the cost per flight. An early NASA objective was to fly one mission

a week, but before the time of the *Challenger* accident, it became apparent that even a schedule of two flights a month was too aggressive.
Turnaround times on flights had ballooned from a projected 10 days in
1975 to an average of 67 days by the time of the disaster. The expense
of the shuttle program had risen in a similar fashion, with a single flight
costing $140 million, more than seven times higher than originally
projected.

This environment clearly led to increased risk for the shuttle and its
crew. The demanding schedule for the program meant less time for flight
crew training, analysis of previous flights, and changes to account for
safety concerns. Economic constraints led to the reuse of SRBs and sharing of critical elements among the four operating shuttles, which increased
the possibility of component failure due to greater handling and wear.

In the years following the loss of the *Challenger*, a number of changes
were instituted within NASA and to the shuttle itself. Many of these
modifications were based on the findings and recommendations of the
Rogers Commission, including a redesign of the SRB joints, moving
shuttle program management to NASA headquarters in Washington,
DC, to facilitate better communication, revising the shuttle manifest to
follow a more realistic schedule, and establishing an independent Office
of Safety, Reliability and Quality Assurance that reported directly to the
NASA administrator. Changes beyond the commission's recommendations included the end of NASA's launching of private satellites, a focus
on improving expendable launch vehicles, and the abandonment of a
future launch site in California. Also during this period, construction
began on a new shuttle, *Endeavor,* to replace *Challenger.*

On September 28, 1988, the shuttle returned to space with the flight of
the orbiter Discovery. This flight was followed by an Atlantis mission two
months later. After the shuttle's return to space until early 2003, 87 missions were flown, with as many as 8 per year. During this period, these
missions launched and repaired the Hubble Space Telescope; carried out

numerous scientific research projects; rendezvoused with the Russian space station Mir; launched probes to the Sun, Jupiter, and Venus; and delivered the first U.S. components of the International Space Station.

Following the *Challenger* disaster and into the start of the new millennium, the political climate surrounding NASA experienced a major shift. NASA had originally been created in response to the Soviet space program and its success with *Sputnik*, the world's first artificial satellite. With the fall of the Soviet government and the end of the Cold War in the late 1980s, the political impetus behind high-profile achievements in U.S. space exploration had diminished. Consequently, NASA's funding was dramatically reduced and the shuttle program budget was correspondingly decreased by 40%. By the year 2000, NASA's budget was only one-third of what an independent commission deemed necessary for the agency to fulfill its mission.

Complicating this situation were demands placed on the shuttle program by the International Space Station. This project required NASA to maintain a regular and predictable flight schedule to transport station crews and to serve as the sole means for delivering components for the station's continuing construction. NASA responded to the intense schedule demands and reduced funding by focusing on improving efficiency rather than cutting programs. Such improvements in efficiency meant downsizing (25% of the workforce in the 1990s), deferment of shuttle upgrades, and reducing operating costs.

These pressures served to increase the risk inherent in human spaceflight. By 1990, shuttle reliability was estimated to be approximately 98%. This prompted an independent committee to predict that NASA would lose another shuttle within the next few years. This prediction became reality on February 1, 2003, in the final moments of the twenty-eighth flight of the *Columbia*.

The *Columbia* and its seven-person crew lifted off on the morning of January 16, 2003, for a 16-day scientific mission. Much like the flight of the *Challenger*, a problem occurred during launch that initially went unnoticed. Eighty-two seconds into flight, as the shuttle was traveling at more than twice the speed of sound, a piece of insulating foam that covers the external tank broke free, striking the heat-resistant reinforced carbon-carbon (RCC) panels on the leading edge of the orbiter's left wing. It was not until the following day that NASA became aware of the incident during routine reviews of launch video and photography.

NASA's image team made three separate requests to acquire high-resolution images of the shuttle wing in orbit in order to determine the extent of any damage, all of which were denied by senior management. With no imagery to confirm the presence or absence of damage to the orbiter from the foam strike, NASA's debris assessment team was forced to rely on mathematical modeling of the incident. Analysis over the next six days indicated that there would likely be some localized heat damage to the wing during reentry to Earth's atmosphere, but not necessarily structural damage to the orbiter.

On January 23, the foam debris incident was communicated to the *Columbia* crew, who was told that there was "no concern for RCC or tile damage." The crew was further reassured that since this situation had been encountered on previous missions, there was "absolutely no concern for [re-]entry."

After the conclusion of around-the-clock experiments, the crew prepared to return to Earth on the morning of February 1. Shortly after 8:00 AM, the mission commander and pilot began maneuvering the shuttle for its descent from a 175-mile-high orbit. By 8:53, *Columbia* had crossed over the California coastline and was heading eastward. At this point, friction from the atmosphere normally causes the leading edge of an orbiter's wings to heat up to approximately 2,800°F. It was then that observers in California and Nevada began to notice a bright streak following the vehicle. This trail was the first indication that debris was being shed from the *Columbia*.

Meanwhile, at NASA Mission Control, the landing appeared to be proceeding as planned until 8:54 AM, when four of the shuttle's sensors began indicating hydraulic levels too low to measure. Four minutes later, as NASA controllers discussed the problem, a tile fell off of the orbiter's left wing as it passed over western Texas. At 8:59, ground crews were unable to get a reading on the pressure sensors in the shuttle's left landing gear tires. Mission Control notified the shuttle crew that it was aware of the unusual sensor readings and was evaluating the situation. When the commander of the *Columbia* attempted to respond, his message was cut off in midsentence. This partial transmission marked the last information received from the orbiter. Videos filmed by observers on the ground later showed the *Columbia* disintegrating seconds after 9:00 AM, killing all seven crew members onboard.

With the passing of Columbia's scheduled landing time of 9:16, NASA set in motion its contingency action plan that had been established after the loss of the *Challenger*. As part of this plan, the Columbia Accident Investigation Board was activated and all material (e.g., data, hardware, facilities) relating to the mission was impounded for review. The NASA Mishap Investigation Team was also called into service to oversee debris recovery efforts.

Shortly after the accident, President George W. Bush declared east Texas a national disaster area, authorizing other federal agencies, including the Federal Emergency Management Agency and the Environmental Protection Agency, to assist in response and recovery. Eventually, more than 700,000 acres were searched, leading to the recovery of 84,000 pieces of the orbiter, primarily in a band stretching from western Texas to western Louisiana. Much of the vehicle was not recovered; what was found represented only 38% of the shuttle craft by weight.

The *Columbia* postaccident investigation would reveal risk factors eerily similar to those of its *Challenger* predecessor. More specifically, design flaws, deferred maintenance, economic pressure, schedule constraints, poor communication, arrogance, and political agendas all appear to have contributed to the *Columbia*'s demise.

Based on an analysis of the recovered articles and their positions, combined with a review of flight data, the Columbia Accident Investigation Board determined the cause of the accident to be the foam strike incident that occurred during launch. The foam had damaged the RCC panels on the left wing's leading edge, allowing superheated air to penetrate the wing during reentry. This air melted the wing's aluminum frame until the intense aerodynamic forces experienced at high speeds in Earth's atmosphere caused the wing to fail and the shuttle to disintegrate.

As with the loss of the *Challenger,* however, structural failure was but one of numerous risk factors that included many institutional problems and external pressures. NASA was aware of the flaw that led to *Columbia*'s demise years prior to the disaster. In fact, foam debris had been considered a serious threat since the beginning of the shuttle program, when over 300 damaged tiles had to be replaced on the first flight in 1981. The orbiter thermal protection system, which included heat-resistant tiles and RCC panels, was designed to withstand only minor impacts. It was considered so vulnerable that parts of it could be damaged by "lightly pressing a thumbnail into it."

Because of this susceptibility to damage, NASA design specifications required that no debris emanate from the external tank during launch. Damage from debris, however, had occurred on every shuttle flight prior to the *Columbia* disaster, and most had involved the loss of external tank foam. At least seven of the flights had even lost foam from bipods attached to the external tank, the exact location of foam loss in *Columbia*'s final flight. The first such incident occurred during the second launch of the *Challenger* in June 1983. After the mission, the problem was recognized and coded as an "in-flight anomaly," meaning that before the next launch, the problem would have to be resolved or proven not to be a threat. During preparations for the following flight, a review of the problem was completed, though documentation reveals only that repairs were made, not that the cause of the foam shedding was resolved.

Foam loss from the same location was also experienced on the flight of the shuttle *Atlantis* less than three months before the loss of the *Columbia*. In the *Atlantis* incident, which was the most severe encountered up to that point, the tank's bipod foam broke free during liftoff and struck the left SRB, causing a four-inch-long, three-inch-deep dent. Following that mission, foam loss was classified as an action item rather than an in-flight anomaly, meaning that the issue would have to be addressed but would not preclude the launching of other flights. The resolution of the action item was not due until after two more shuttle missions had been completed, the next flight of *Endeavor* and *Columbia*'s last flight.

During the flight readiness review for the *Endeavor* mission, the foam problem was declared to be an "acceptable risk." After 111 flights without the loss of a shuttle due to foam debris, despite foam regularly impacting the vehicle, NASA management no longer viewed the problem as a significant threat. *Endeavor* was cleared for flight, paving the way for the flight of the *Columbia* two months later. By the time of the *Columbia* mission, many NASA engineers and managers felt that the foam was no longer an issue for concern. Consequently, it was not even mentioned during the flight readiness review.

The labeling of the foam problem as an "acceptable risk" despite the damage it caused during the launch of the *Atlantis* may be attributable to scheduling pressures related to the International Space Station. Construction of the space station had begun two years behind schedule in 1998, and by the beginning of the twenty-first century, NASA was under increasing pressure to complete the station core. Had the *Endeavor* mission been delayed, astronauts onboard the station would have been forced to overstay their 180-day limit, and the core section of the station would not have been completed by the February 19, 2004, deadline.

Once the *Columbia* was in orbit and NASA's image team had identified the possibility of damage to the orbiter, mistakes similar to those made prior to the *Challenger* disaster resurfaced. While NASA engineers and those of its contractors quickly identified the foam shedding and used models to determine that it presented a risk to the shuttle on reentry, they were unable to get the attention of upper management. Soon after the possible problem was identified, mission managers consulted a tile expert, who assured them that strike damage was only a maintenance concern and that imaging of the orbiter to search for damage was not necessary. Thus, when NASA engineers made multiple requests for visual evidence to confirm or deny the results of their modeling, they were repeatedly rejected. Once again NASA management was requiring that engineers prove a situation to be *unsafe* in order to take action. Management's position that the foam impact did not present a problem stifled further communication from engineers who were concerned with being ridiculed for presenting a dissenting opinion. In this way, further information regarding the situation did not progress up the chain of command.

Since the *Challenger* accident, NASA had made efforts to incorporate safety personnel in discussions regarding technical problems. According to the Rogers Commission, this change should have been a significant step toward increasing the safety of the shuttle program. During review of the *Columbia*'s foam strike, however, safety personnel, while included in discussions, were not involved in the decision-making process.

In 2004, crew members of the two destroyed shuttles were awarded the Congressional Space Medal of Honor by President Bush, who had reaffirmed America's commitment to space exploration following the loss of the *Columbia*. Consistent with that commitment, NASA has continued to deliver payloads to space, carry out scientific research, and conduct work connected with the International Space Station. In August 2007, the agency was even able to resume the Teacher In Space program, once thought to be one of the many casualties of the *Challenger* disaster.

NASA has made numerous changes to the shuttle and launch area in an attempt to avoid another disaster. A total of 107 cameras have been installed around the launch pad and on the orbiter, external tank, and SRBs to provide ground crews with adequate imaging for identifying debris damage. Sensors have been incorporated into the RCC panels on the leading edges of the wings to help improve damage detection capability. Several shuttle elements have been redesigned to reduce the likelihood of debris shedding. New methods for examining and repairing damage in orbit have also been developed, including the use of a boom for imaging the underside of the orbiter and the availability of tile filler and patches for in-orbit repairs.

With these improvements in place, NASA returned to space on July 26, 2005, with the thirty-first flight of the shuttle *Discovery*. Once again, pieces of the external tank's insulating foam came loose during the launch. Upon inspection of the orbiter's thermal protection system, no major damage from the debris was found. Two astronauts did use the newly installed boom to perform a spacewalk for an unrelated repair to the tile system, however. After delivering much-needed supplies to the International Space Station, the *Discovery* returned to Earth without incident on the morning of August 9, 2005.

After the *Discovery* flight, NASA announced that all future shuttle flights would be put on hold until the foam issue was resolved. Consequently, the next flight, which had been scheduled for September 2005, was eventually pushed back to July 2006. This flight also experienced foam shedding from the tank during liftoff, but the particles broke loose after the time determined to be critical to shuttle safety. A similar incident occurred on the next shuttle mission two months later. During the August 2007 flight of the *Endeavor* in which the Teacher In Space program was resumed, a piece of foam from the external fuel tank struck the underside of the orbiter, creating a deep gouge in one of the thermal tiles. After nearly a week of deliberation, NASA officials decided against repairing the damage in orbit and the shuttle returned to Earth without incident.

In August 2006, NASA announced that a new vehicle would soon be replacing the aging space shuttle fleet. The new ship, known as *Orion*, will incorporate numerous technological improvements in a design considered 10 times safer than its predecessor.

While these developments give the appearance of an organization that may have finally learned its lesson, the Columbia Accident Investigation Board, as part of its final report, issued this sobering message:

> The organizational causes of this accident are rooted in the space shuttle program's history and culture, including the original compromises that were required to gain approval for the shuttle, subsequent years of resource constraints, fluctuating priorities, schedule pressures, mischaracterization of the shuttle as operational rather than developmental, and lack of agreed national vision for human space flight.[1]

The report goes on to say:

> Based on NASA's history of ignoring external recommendations, or making improvements that atrophy with time, the Board has no confidence that the Space Shuttle can be safely operated for more than a few years based solely on renewed post-accident vigilance.

REFERENCES

Associated Press. "Shuttle Enters Space after 'Majestic Launch.'" www.cnn.com/2006/TECH/space/09/09/space.shuttle.ap/index.html.

Associated Press. "Teacher-Astronaut Heads for Space Station," August 8, 2007. www.cnn.com/2007/TECH/space/08/08/space.shuttle.ap/index.html.

BBC News. "Discovery Returns Safely to Earth." August 9, 2005. http://news.bbc.co.uk/1/hi/sci/tech/4134986.stm.

BBC News. "Space Shuttle: Return to Flight." http://news.bbc.co.uk/1/shared/spl/hi/sci_nat/05/shuttle_guide/html/default.stm.

CNN. "NASA: No Concern on Fallen Foam." July 6, 2006. www.cnn.com/2006/TECH/space/07/05/shuttle.launch/index.html.

CNN. "NASA Remembers 'Columbia Seven.'" February 5, 2003, www.cnn.com/2003/TECH/space/02/04/sprj.colu.shuttle.memorial/index.html.

CNN. "Shuttle Lands Safely in Florida," August 21, 2007. www.cnn.com/2007/TECH/space/08/21/space.shuttle/index.html.

Columbia Accident Investigation Board. *Report,* vol. 1. Washington, DC: Author, 2003.

Kerwin, Joseph P. Letter to NASA Associate Administrator Richard H. Truly. 1986. http://history.nasa.gov/kerwin.html.

NASA. "NASA's Orbiter Fleet." www.nasa.gov/centers/kennedy/shuttleoperations/orbiters/orbiters_toc.html.

NASA. "Orion Crew Vehicle." www.nasa.gov/mission_pages/constellation/orion/index.html.

NASA. "Return to Flight." www.nasa.gov/returntoflight/main/index.html.

NASA. "Shuttle Missions." www.nasa.gov/mission_pages/shuttle/shuttlemissions/list_main.html.

NASA History Division. "Congressional Space Medal of Honor." http://history.nasa.gov/spacemedal.htm.

NASA History Division. "Human Space Flight." http://history.nasa.gov/tindex.html#5.

NASA History Division. "STS-1 History." http://history.nasa.gov/sts25th/history.html.

Presidential Commission on the Space Shuttle *Challenger* Accident. *Report to the President.* Washington, DC: Author, 1986.

Reagan, Ronald. "Address to the Nation on the Explosion of the Space Shuttle Challenger." 1986. www.reagan.utexas.edu/archives/speeches/1986/12886b.htm.

Reagan, Ronald. "Remarks Announcing the Establishment of the Presidential Commission on the Space Shuttle *Challenger* Accident." 1986. www.reagan.utexas.edu/archives/speeches/1986/20386b.htm.

NOTE

1. *Columbia* Accident Investigation Board, *Report,* vol. 1 (Washington, DC: Author, 2003).

PART TWO

TERRORIST ACTS

It is an unfortunate sign of the times that we live in an age in which deliberate acts of terrorism have become so prevalent. While our world has never been free from sabotage and other violent acts, in the past typically these events have been directed at an offending party and not society as a whole. The type of terrorism we are experiencing today has a different motivation: to inflict mass casualties for the purpose of creating political and social unrest. Over the past decade in particular, numerous high-profile acts of terrorism have occurred, attacks carried out by various parties in different locales.

The cases included here have occurred on three different continents. Two of these incidents have taken place on U.S. soil, one carried out by a domestic group and the other by an international organization. All either utilized transportation as a weapon or were directed at a transportation target. In each case, the impact was significant, resulting in mass casualties and considerable damage. Moreover, the shock of these events reverberated throughout the international community, creating an intense feeling of fear and anxiety.

Against this backdrop, however, emerges a better understanding of how these incidents evolved, what intervention could have occurred, and what opportunities we have to deter similar attacks in the future. The cases also remind us of our need to be vigilant and resilient, determined not to let the ambitions of a few dictate the way in which we live.

CHAPTER 7

OKLAHOMA CITY BOMBING

Timothy McVeigh, an ex-military, right-wing extremist, and his accomplices carried out a devastating domestic terrorist act by detonating a truck bomb outside of the Alfred P. Murrah Building in Oklahoma City on April 19, 1995. The truck, loaded with 4,800 pounds of explosives in 55-gallon drums, collapsed much of the building into rubble, killing 168 people, including children attending a day care center (see Exhibit 7.1). Lack of domestic terrorism intelligence, inadequate building protection, and ease of obtaining supplies and instructions on how to build and deploy such a bomb were widely blamed for allowing the incident to happen.

On the morning of February 28, 1993, agents of the U.S. Bureau of Alcohol, Tobacco, and Firearms (ATF) attempted to arrest the leader of a religious cult in Waco, Texas, for possessing illegal weapons. Cult members, known as the Branch Davidians, opened fire, touching off an intense shootout that left several federal agents and cult members dead. In the hours and days that followed, other federal agencies dispatched officials to the site, including the Department of Treasury and the Federal Bureau of Investigation (FBI). With scores of women and children inside the Davidian compound, the federal government chose to negotiate with cult leaders rather than attempt another raid. The negotiations turned into a even week standoff between the two groups. After determining that a negotiated solution was no longer possible, in the

EXHIBIT 7.1   *168 empty chairs serve as a memorial to those killed in the April 19, 1995, Oklahoma City bombing.*

Source: *Hugh Scott,* The Oklahoman. *www.newsok.com/ bombing/photos/.*

early-morning hours of April 19, federal agents began pumping tear gas into the complex, hoping to force cult members to flee the compound with minimal casualties. Within minutes, the Davidians began firing back, prompting agents to increase the tear gas intensity. At approximately noon, cult members began setting fires throughout the compound, and gunshots could be heard coming from within the buildings. Rather than surrender, the Davidians chose to commit mass suicide. Hours later, when the fire was finally extinguished, 75 cult members were found dead, including 25 children.

One man, Timothy McVeigh, had been paying close attention to events that unfolded at the Davidian complex. McVeigh was a decorated veteran who had served during the Gulf War but had grown increasingly disillusioned with the federal government. In rants to local newspapers, he complained about taxes, crime, and corruption, even suggesting that bloodshed might be required to change the political landscape. A fanatic gun collector, he became obsessed with the Second Amendment of the U.S. Constitution, which guarantees the right to bear arms. McVeigh eventually became convinced that the federal government was conspiring to disarm the American people and enslave them.

McVeigh's views were also influenced by a siege that took place in 1992 at Ruby Ridge, Idaho, in which a woman and child were killed by federal agents attempting to arrest Randy Weaver, a white separatist, on weapons-related charges. The passage of the Brady Handgun Violence Prevention Act in 1993, which required background checks for the purchase of a handgun, further bolstered McVeigh's hatred and distrust of the federal government. To McVeigh, the Waco event was just another example of government tyranny. He believed that the U.S. government had executed the Davidians in Waco, drawing "first blood" in a war against the people. He decided to fight back in such a dramatic way that it would motivate other Americans to join his revolution.

McVeigh's plan for revenge eventually coalesced into a plot to bomb the Alfred P. Murrah Federal Building in Oklahoma City. McVeigh believed that bombing this structure would not only serve as excellent propaganda in the recruitment of other Americans to his revolution, but would also avenge the massacre at Waco by destroying the ATF offices he mistakenly believed to be housed within the building. He also considered the Murrah Building to be a particularly vulnerable target, with easy access, little security, and many glass windows for maximum effect.

In the summer of 1994, McVeigh began formulating his plan with the help of Terry Nichols, whom McVeigh had befriended during his time in military service. Nichols held similar views of the federal government, going so far as to officially renounce his U.S. citizenship earlier that year. The two men began buying the necessary supplies to create a massive truck bomb, finding much of what they needed simply by searching the telephone book. They purchased 4,000 pounds of ammonium nitrate fertilizer from a farm supply store in Kingman, Arizona, and 165 gallons of nitromethane fuel from a raceway in Dallas, Texas. Next, McVeigh and Nichols burglarized a rock quarry in Marion, Kansas, stealing detonation cord, an explosive known as Tovex, and hundreds of blasting caps. The pair then robbed a gun trader in Arkansas to help cover the expenses of renting storage facilities for the bomb components. They subsequently enlisted a former army friend, Michael Fortier, to help them transport and sell the stolen guns.

Around the time of the robbery, in early November, McVeigh visited his sister in New York. He created a document on her computer entitled "ATF read," anticipating that federal agents would search the belongings of family members in the days following his attack. In the letter, he declared that all agents of the federal government would "swing in the wind one day for your treasonous actions against the Constitution and the United States." He concluded with the words "Die, you spineless cowardice [sic] bastards."

McVeigh chose April 19, 1995, as the date for the bombing. The date was significant not only because of its connection to the burning of the Davidian compound, but also because it is "Liberty Day," the day the American Revolution began in 1775. McVeigh even listed April 19 as his birthday on the fake identification he used to rent the truck that would carry his bomb.

By December 1994, McVeigh became increasingly bold, disclosing to others that he was involved in a major plot against the government. He warned his sister that "something big is about to happen" and that it would occur in March/April of the following year. He even took Fortier to the Murrah Building and detailed his plan for the day of the bombing.

On April 16, 1995, McVeigh activated his plan. He drove to Oklahoma City, met Nichols, and parked his car on a street near the Murrah Building, to be used in fleeing the scene after the bombing. The next day, he rented the truck that would carry the bomb from a body shop in Junction City, Kansas. On April 18, McVeigh and Nichols loaded the explosive materials into the truck and constructed the bomb. It consisted of 16 drum barrels filled with explosives, surrounding a detonation device. The barrels were arranged in a semicircular pattern, favoring one side of the truck, to focus the blast toward the Murrah Building.

At 7:00 AM on April 19, McVeigh awoke and drove the bomb-laden vehicle into Oklahoma City. Shortly before 9:00 AM, a security camera filmed a large rental truck being parked outside of the Murrah Building. The workday was just beginning. Children were filing into the day care center, and people were forming lines inside the building at the Social Security Administration, Federal Credit Union, and snack bar. At 9:00, a meeting was convened next door in the Water Resources Board Building. Two minutes later, a tape recorder set up to record the events of that meeting captured the sound of a sudden, massive explosion.

The bomb had detonated with such force that it ripped away the face of the Murrah Building, causing one-third of the nine-story structure to collapse (see Exhibit 7.2). The explosion damaged more than 300 buildings, overturned automobiles, and shattered windows over a 50-block area. The blast created a nearly seven-foot crater in the ground and registered 6.0 on the Richter scale.

One hundred sixty-eight people lost their lives as a result of the bombing, including 19 children in the building's day care center and 1

EXHIBIT 7.2   *Aerial view of the damaged Murrah Building*

Source: *U.S. Army Corps of Engineers. www.hq.usace.army .mil/cepa/pubs/aug01/murrah.jpg.*

rescue worker. Eight hundred fifty-three people were injured, more than 400 were left homeless, and approximately 7,000 employees lost their workplace.

Response to the explosion was quick, with authorities initially alerted by the thousands of security alarms triggered by the blast. Within minutes, the Oklahoma City fire department established a command center near the scene of the disaster to direct search-and-rescue efforts. By 9:25 AM, a state emergency operations center had been established. An hour later, President Clinton declared Oklahoma City a federal disaster area, thereby authorizing the Red Cross to oversee relief efforts and mobilizing the Federal Emergency Management Agency.

Meanwhile, McVeigh had casually left the scene and driven out of the city after listening to the explosion from a nearby alley. At 10:17 AM, 78 miles north of Oklahoma City, a state trooper stopped McVeigh because of a missing license plate. The trooper, unaware of any connection to the bombing, found a concealed, loaded handgun inside McVeigh's jacket and promptly arrested him. At the time of his arrest, McVeigh was wearing a T-shirt emblazoned with two phrases: "sic semper tyrannis" (a Latin phrase translated as "thus always to tyrants") and "the tree of liberty must be refreshed from time to time with the blood of patriots and tyrants."

While McVeigh was being detained, federal agents found, among the rubble, the rear axle of the rental truck that had contained the bomb. They used the vehicle identification number on the axle to track the truck to the rental agency and eventually to McVeigh. A search of McVeigh's car later revealed documents describing his hatred of the federal government, including a letter in which he alluded to the bombing as his "contribution to defense of freedom" and a "call to arms."

Two days later, Terry Nichols turned himself in to police. Michael Fortier was later taken into custody and, in August 1995, agreed to plead guilty to weapons charges and testify against McVeigh and Nichols in exchange for leniency.

On June 2, 1997, McVeigh was convicted in federal court on charges of conspiracy to use a weapon of mass destruction, use of such a weapon, destruction of a federal property by explosives, and first-degree murder of eight federal agents. He was executed by lethal injection on June 11, 2001, becoming the first person executed by the federal government in 38 years. Nichols was found guilty in both federal and state courts for his role in the bombing and is currently serving a life sentence without the possibility of parole. Fortier was sentenced to 12 years in prison and a $200,000 fine. He was released early in January 2006 for good behavior.

Although an explosion was directly responsible for the catastrophic consequences of this event, the cause of the Oklahoma City disaster ultimately lies in the political motives of Timothy McVeigh. His ability to carry out what was, at the time, the worst terrorist attack on American soil was facilitated by insufficient security combined with access to low-cost materials and sensitive information. The impact of his actions was exacerbated by communication failures during the response effort.

Terrorist acts against the United States and its citizens had occurred numerous times prior to the Oklahoma City disaster, including the 1983 bombings of the U.S. embassy and marine barracks in Beirut; an explosion aboard Pan American Flight 103 over Lockerbie, Scotland, in 1988; and the 1993 bombing of the World Trade Center in New York City. None of these attacks, however, was carried out by U.S. citizens. Because such attacks were planned and performed by foreign terrorists, U.S. counterterrorism efforts in the mid-1990s had become increasingly focused on international extremist groups. Since domestic terrorism was not viewed as a security priority, there were no federal laws in place to allow for the investigation or prosecution of many potential sources of domestic terrorism, particularly if these sources operated within a single state. Thus, McVeigh, and other domestic militants of the time were able to conspire without alerting, or interference from, federal officials.

The lack of security around the Murrah Building indicated that Oklahoma City and the federal agencies within the building did not regard the site as a potential target for terrorism. A local paper expressed this view the day after the bombing: "This is the place, after all, where terrorists don't venture—the Heartland." This false sense of security led to vulnerabilities that McVeigh was able to exploit. For example, the Murrah Building had been designed and constructed in the mid-1970s according to all applicable building codes of that time, but did not include any measures for resisting a vehicle bomb blast. As a result, the building partially collapsed during the explosion, adding to the number of casualties and complicating response efforts. Not only was McVeigh able to construct a truck bomb that could penetrate the structure, but he was also able to detonate the explosives within 14 feet of the building, increasing the damage caused by the blast.

The bomb components McVeigh and Nichols used were relatively inexpensive and easy to acquire. Using a simple telephone book, they were able to find suppliers and purchase most of the necessary materials for a few thousand dollars. McVeigh and Nichols relied on literature readily available to the public to learn how to mix the bomb ingredients and construct the device, including such details as how to run a fuse cord from the cargo area of the truck to the cab to enable lighting of the fuse from the driver's seat. With such easy access to information and materials, they were able to plan and execute an attack with little to no outside help, reducing the chances of being discovered.

While the response to the disaster benefited from a strong state and federal government presence in Oklahoma City, it was also complicated by the partial collapse of the Murrah Building. Rescuers on the scene encountered numerous obstacles as they attempted to locate and extract victims, including live electric lines, pools of water from broken plumbing, falling debris, and wailing fire alarms. In the first 90 minutes following the blast, workers were evacuated from the building and the incident command center was relocated after at least two false reports of additional bombs. The structural integrity of the building was also a concern, forcing the entire search-and-rescue operation to be conducted without the use of heavy machinery.

In the early stages of the response, communication among rescue workers was especially problematic. The local ambulance service switchboard became clogged with incoming calls immediately. Shortly thereafter, all communication by telephone became impossible due to system overload, forcing agencies to interact exclusively via handheld radios.

Five years after the disaster, a memorial was dedicated on the grounds once occupied by the Murrah Building. A major feature of the memorial is 168 empty chairs, symbolizing those whose lives were lost in the tragedy. In May 2004, a new federal building was opened near the blast site. This structure is set back from the street, includes strict vehicle access control, and features shatterproof windows to resist the type of attack that destroyed the Murrah Building.

In response to the Oklahoma City bombing and similar terrorist attacks, federal buildings throughout the United States implemented enhanced security measures, including the use of concrete barriers, improved surveillance, and parking restrictions. One such example is the federal courthouse in Albuquerque, New Mexico, which features controlled underground parking, a large setback from the street, planter-barriers to prevent parking near the building, small windows on the lower floors, and a variety of access-control technologies to prevent bombs from being carried inside. New design standards have also been developed for future construction of critical federal facilities. Nonfederal government agencies and private businesses have pursued similar bomb deterrence initiatives.

In 2005, nearly 10 years after the triggering event, the State of Oklahoma took a step aimed more specifically at eliminating the threat posed by homemade bombs, when it became the third U.S. state to regulate the sale of ammonium nitrate fertilizer. Purchasers of this fertilizer, which was a critical component in McVeigh's bomb, now must provide identification and sales are tracked.

Despite the increased focus on domestic terrorism motivated by the bombing of the Murrah Building, terrorists continue to operate within the United States. Between 1996 and 1998, a right-wing militant named Eric Rudolph carried out a series of four bombings in the southeastern states, killing 2 people and injuring more than 100 others. With heightened awareness among law enforcement officials since the September 11, 2001, attacks, authorities recently have been more successful in thwarting terrorist attacks before they occur. In 2004, for example, authorities arrested two people in Texas for stockpiling vast amounts of chemical weapons, explosives and ammunition, though their specific target was uncertain. Months later, authorities foiled a plot by a Tennessee man to attack federal buildings using explosives and chemical weapons.

Complacency and a redirected focus may, however, be a harbinger that such violence will reappear soon. The sale of ammonium nitrate fertilizer remains unregulated in 47 states. Also, notably absent in a recent Department of Homeland Security planning document is a budgetary provision for combating sources of right-wing domestic terrorism, the very kind that McVeigh and Nichols proved to be so deadly.

REFERENCES

Aita, Judy. "Nairobi Embassy Bomber Given Life Sentence" U.S. Department of State. June 12, 2001, http://usinfo.state.gov/is/Archive_Index/Nairobi_Embassy_Bomber_Given_Life_Sentence.html.

"Alfred P. Murrah Federal Building Bombing April 19, 1995": City of Oklahoma City, July 1996.

Associated Press. "McVeigh Co-Conspirator to Be Freed." January 18, 2006, www.cnn.com/2006/LAW/01/17/okla.fortier.ap/index.html.

Barnes, Steve. "Oklahoma: New Federal Building," New York Times, May 4, 2004.

CNN. "Fortier's Sentence Thrown Out in Oklahoma Bombing." June 30, 1999, www.cnn.com/US/9906/30/fortier/index.html?eref=sitesearch.

CNN. "New WTC Tower Design Made Public." June 29, 2005, www.cnn.com/2005/US/06/29/wtc.tower.redesign/index.html.

CNN. "Oklahoma Bombing Victims, Fortier Emotional at Sentencing Hearing." May 27, 1998, www.cnn.com/US/9805/27/fortier/index .html?eref=sitesearch.

CNN. "The Trial of Eric Rudolph." www.cnn.com/SPECIALS/2005/ rudolph.

Copeland, Larry. "Domestic Terrorism: New Trouble at Home," *USA Today*, November 14, 2004.

Dougherty, Jon. "McVeigh Diagrams ANFO Bomb," World Net Daily. May 25, 2001, www.wnd.com/news/article.asp?ARTICLE_ID=22963.

Freeh, Louis J. Opening Statement before the U.S. House of Representative Committee on the Judiciary Subcommittee on Crime, May 3, 1995.

German, John. "Bracing Ourselves against Terrorism, Natural Disasters, and Deterioration," *Sandia Lab News*, August 28, 1998.

Horton, Scott, and NewsOK.com. "9:02 April 19th," www.newsok .com/bombing/intro.

McFadden, Robert D. "Terror in Oklahoma: John Doe No. 1—A Special Report; A Life of Solitude and Obsessions,"*New York Times*, May 4, 1995.

McLaughlin, Amber, and Bob Wyatt. "Factual Chronology." January 22, 1996, www.pbs.org/wgbh/pages/frontline/documents/mcveigh.

"McVeigh: A Time Line," *Las Vegas Review-Journal*, June 10, 2001.

Mlakar, Paul F. Sr., W. Gene Corley, Mete A. Sozen, and Charles H. Thornton. "Blast Loading and Response of Murrah Building." In *Forensic Engineering*, ed. Kevin L. Rens. Reston, VA: American Society of Civil Engineers, 1997.

Oklahoma Department of Civil Emergency Management. *After Action Report* (Oklahoma City: Author, 1995).

"Oklahoma Rules to Regulate Selling of Fertilizer," *New York Times*, February 18, 2005.

President's Critical Infrastructure Protection Board. "The National Strategy for the Physical Protection of Critical Infrastructures and Key Assets." 2003. www.whitehouse.gov/pcipb/physical.html.

Scott, Hugh. The Oklahoma City Bombing. *The Oklahoman*. www.newsok.com/bombing/photos.

Thompson, Bennie G., et al. "10 Years after the Oklahoma City Bombing, the Department of Homeland Security Must Do More to Fight Right-Wing Domestic Terrorists," April 19, 2005. www.globalsecurity.org/security/library/report/2005/050419-RightWingTerrorists.pdf.

U.S. Department of Justice. *Responding to Terrorism Victims: Oklahoma City and Beyond*. Washington, DC: Author, 2000.

U.S. Department of Justice. "Report to the Deputy Attorney General on the Events at Waco, Texas, February 28 to April 19, 1993," Redacted version. Washington, DC: U.S. Government Printing Office, 1993.

U.S. Department of State. "Bush, Cheney Observe 10th Anniversary of Oklahoma City Bombing." April 19, 2005, http://usinfo.state.gov/xarchives/display.html?p=washfile-english&y=2005&m=April&x=20050419145407xkelyp0.8344385&t=xarchives/xarchitem.html.

U.S. District Court, District of Colorado. Criminal Action No. 96-CR-68. Opening Statement by the Defense, April 24, 1997.

U.S. District Court, District of Colorado. Criminal Action No. 96-CR-68. Opening Statement by the U.S. Government, April 24, 1997.

CHAPTER 8

AUM SHINRIKYO: TERROR IN JAPAN

A terrorist group in Japan, hiding behind the shroud of a religious organization, carried out a well-coordinated sarin gas attack on the Tokyo subway system on March 20, 1995. Sarin was released from packages on five trains, all converging at the center of the city. The attack killed 12 people, injured over 5,000 others, and created widespread fear and panic. Japanese authorities had good reason ahead of time to believe that this group had the capability and motivation to carry out such an attack. Yet nothing was done to apprehend the group's masterminds before their plan could be implemented.

In 1984, a partially blind masseur named Chizuo Matsumoto founded a publishing company and yoga school near the Japanese capital of Tokyo (see Exhibit 8.1). Matsumoto subsequently changed his name to Shoko Asahara, or "Bright Light," and began shaping his new operation into a religious cult. The cult, which in 1987 Asahara named "Aum Shinrikyo," or "Supreme Truth," was centered on Buddhism but incorporated a number of other religions, including Hindu (the cult's central deity was Shiva, the Hindu god of destruction and rebirth), Zen, and Christian philosophies.

Asahara recruited converts to Aum with claims of his supernatural powers, including the ability to levitate. New members took vows of chastity, turned all of their possessions over to the cult, and cut off all ties to their previous lives. In their subsequent quest for enlightenment,

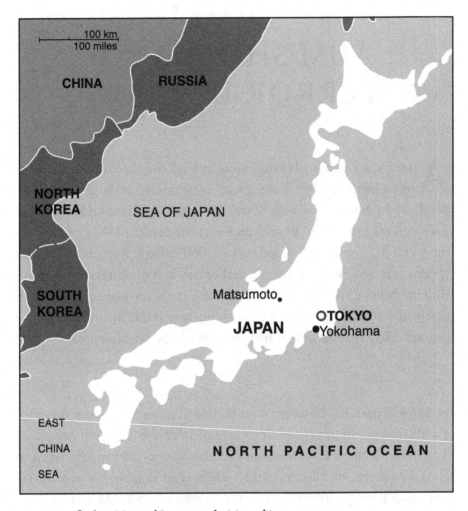

EXHIBIT 8.1   *Map of Japan and cities of interest*

Source: Adapted from World Travels, 2007. www.worldtravels
.com/Travelguide/Countries/Japan/Map.

cult members engaged in unusual rituals and endured a wide variety
of physical and financial hardships. Asahara's followers were often
forced to go without food or water to the point of malnourishment.
Aum members wore battery-powered helmets to connect them with
Asahara's brain waves by means of six-volt electric shocks. Many were

scalded with hot water, hung upside down, or given various hypnotic drugs. A number of Asahara's followers even paid $1,000 to drink his bathwater or $10,000 to drink a small vial of his blood. Cult members who voiced dissent or were uncooperative were drugged, confined, and, in some cases, murdered. Despite these conditions, Aum Shinrikyo grew to include a worldwide membership of approximately 60,000 by the mid-1990s, with total assets of more than $1 billion.

Religious tolerance is a staple of modern Japanese society, and people are exposed to a wide variety of beliefs and practices. In this environment, Aum Shinrikyo drew no special attention. With its foundation in Buddhist teachings, it appeared familiar and benign to Japanese citizens and authorities. In 1989, Aum was officially recognized as a religion by the city of Tokyo and granted special tax status. The cult even appeared to be a productive contributor to Japanese society, running numerous small businesses, including computer stores, restaurants, herbal tea and medicine sales, health clubs, and dating and babysitting services.

Yet out of the public eye, Aum Shinrikyo proved to be a dangerous enterprise. In the fall of 1989, a number of parents of young cult members formed a group called "Concerned Parents of Aum Children." Believing that their children had been kidnapped by the cult, they hired a lawyer, Tsutsumi Sakamoto, to help them confront Aum and find their children. Four days after Sakamoto appeared on television criticizing Aum Shinrikyo, he and his family disappeared. While an Aum lapel badge was found in their ransacked apartment, the cult was not investigated in connection with the family's disappearance. It would be six years before authorities learned that Sakamoto, his wife, and their three-year-old child were murdered by Aum members, on Asahara's orders.

The reluctance of Tokyo police to pursue Aum Shinrikyo after Sakamoto's disappearance stemmed from the cult's status as an official religion and Japanese laws forbidding government interference in religious affairs. Japan had been plagued by centuries of religious persecution. Modern Japanese policy precluded investigation of religious practices or even entering sacred buildings without solid proof of illegal activity.

Unknown to police, however, Aum Shinrikyo's threat as a disruptive force ran well beyond the disappearance of the Sakamoto family. Asahara was obsessed with acquiring the equipment and knowledge necessary to carry out attacks using weapons of mass destruction/effect (WMD/E). As early as 1988, the cult had tried—unsuccessfully—to purchase chemical weapons.

In 1990, 25 Aum members, including Asahara, ran for public office. All lost in landslide decisions. This rejection by Japanese society skewed Asahara's philosophies, and he began drawing more heavily from the Christian idea of Armageddon, the Buddhist idea of anarchy resulting from rejection of Buddha's wisdom, and the writings of Nostradamus on the end of the world. Using these sources of inspiration, the cult leader ordered his followers to arm themselves in preparation for the battle that would accompany the impending apocalypse, promising them that they would prevail as Earth's "super race."

Aum Shinrikyo consequently began plotting to produce or acquire the weapons necessary to wage an apocalyptic war. This strategy included recruiting scientists and technicians experienced in weapons production, along with a largely fruitless worldwide search for advanced and experimental weaponry, such as high-powered lasers and an earthquake-generating device. In 1993, Aum opened a weapons factory and eventually began producing AK-74 assault rifles.

In addition to its quest for mechanized weaponry, the cult also actively pursued biological agents. Some items on Aum's list of desirable agents included botulinum toxin, anthrax, Ebola virus, Q fever bacteria, toxic mushroom spores, and green mamba snake venom. The cult's efforts in this area were largely unsuccessful, however. For instance, Aum's scientists were unable to isolate a toxic strain of botulinum, and an anthrax sample acquired by the cult turned out to be a nonviral strain used for veterinary vaccines. Cult members discovered these facts when, on four separate occasions between 1990 and 1993, their attempts to spray these agents from vans and rooftops resulted in no casualties.

With little success acquiring or producing mechanical and biological weapons, the group turned its focus toward chemical weapons. In 1993, Aum began producing small quantities of the chemical warfare agents VX, tabun, soman, mustard, hydrogen cyanide, and phosgene. The cult chose to focus most of its production capabilities, however, on sarin. This nerve agent is colorless, tasteless, and odorless in its pure form yet so toxic that exposure to less than one-third of an ounce can be fatal. Shortly after producing a test batch of slightly less than one ounce, Aum spent more than $10 million to construct a state-of-the-art production facility, disguised as a temple, to manufacture sarin in larger quantities. By early 1994, the cult was producing 44 pounds of sarin in a single batch.

In the spring of that same year, Aum began carrying out sarin attacks. The first, executed by spraying sarin from a van, targeted the leader of a rival religious sect. During the attack, however, the sprayer malfunctioned, filling the van with sarin vapor and nearly killing a cult member.

On the night of June 27, 1994, Aum carried out its second sarin attack, this time aimed at three judges presiding over a lawsuit filed against the cult in the city of Matsumoto. Again, cult members sprayed the agent from a van, this time releasing 44 pounds of sarin near the judges' homes. Although the intended victims survived, seven people who were asleep with their windows open died, and several hundred others became ill.

The attack was initially ruled an accident. In November 1994, however, police took soil samples from the Aum compound and found evidence of sarin production. Production of such substances was not against the law at the time in Japan, however, so Asahara and his followers went uncharged.

The next month, an Aum member touted the benefits of VX as a weapon during a broadcast on the cult's radio station. From December 1994 to January 1995, the group carried out as many as three attacks on individuals using the chemical, killing one person while causing another to lapse into a coma.

In March 1995, Tokyo police prepared to raid the Aum Shinrikyo compound based on evidence from both the sarin attack in Matsumoto and cult involvement in a recent kidnapping. However, two members of the Japanese Ground Self Defense Force (JGSDF), which had loaned police protective gear for the impending raid, tipped off the cult that the raid would take place on March 22. Asahara and his disciples hastily formulated a plan to prevent the raid, while Aum scientists produced two gallons of low-concentration (one-quarter-strength) sarin for the occasion.

On the night of March 19, Aum members firebombed their own headquarters, hoping to mislead police in the days to come and generate sympathy for the cult. The following morning, two days before the planned police raid, 10 of Asahara's disciples entered the Tokyo subway system at specified locations. Five of them carried a morning newspaper that concealed bags of sarin and closed umbrellas with sharpened tips. They entered the subway and boarded inbound trains (see Exhibit 8.2), while their partners waited farther down the line to drive them from the scene of the crime.

Once on the trains, each attacker placed the newspaper on the floor or in a baggage rack. At coordinated times between 7:46 and 8:01 AM, each attacker used the umbrella tip to puncture the sarin bags. The five then disembarked at designated stations, took antidotes, and rendezvoused with their getaway drivers.

Meanwhile, the trains continued to converge on Kasumigaseki Station, the cult's ultimate target. A major hub of the Tokyo subway system, the station is located within walking distance of the Japanese parliament, several government ministries, and not far from the Imperial Palace. Most important, however, Kasumigaseki is the subway stop for the Tokyo police department, where a shift change was to occur at 8:30 AM. By having the sarin-filled trains meet at Kasumigaseki Station just prior to the shift change, Asahara hoped to cripple the Tokyo police and forestall the impending raid.

Of 11 bags filled with sarin, 8 were successfully penetrated, releasing over a gallon of the chemical agent. Within minutes of the release,

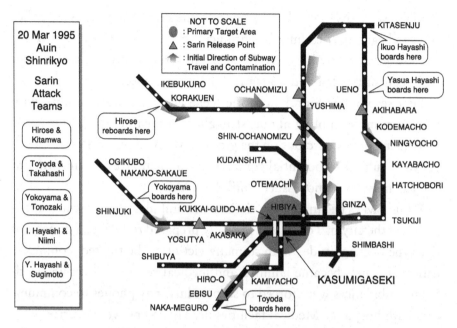

EXHIBIT **8.2** *Diagram of Tokyo subway system indicating sarin release points and location of Kasumigaseki Station*

Source: U.S. Army Training and Doctrine Command, "Terror Operations: Case Studies in Terrorism," U.S. Army Training and Doctrine Command, Fort Leavenworth, KS, 2005.

passengers began feeling the effects of sarin exposure. On one train, riders simply complained of a foul odor, a result of the chemical's poor quality. These complaints prompted subway attendants to clean up the spilled liquid and allow the train to continue in service. Commuters on the other lines were not so fortunate. Passengers on the four remaining contaminated trains began coughing, vomiting, convulsing, and losing consciousness, in some cases even before they could notice the unusual smell. These effects were not limited to passengers on the trains; commuters on train platforms also fell victim to the vaporized chemical.

The first call to emergency services was placed at 8:09 AM. Over the next hour, calls poured in from 15 different subway stations. Several thousand firefighters, police, and emergency medical technicians

(EMTs) were dispatched to respond to the crisis. At 9:00 AM, police officers began barricading the entrances to stations that subway workers had not already blocked. By 9:27, all service on the affected lines had been suspended and 26 stations had been closed.

First responders found a chaotic scene at the subway stations, with some victims stumbling about, struggling to breathe, while others lay convulsing or unconscious on the ground. Many of the earliest responders were subject to potential contamination themselves, as the order to use gas masks was not issued until 8:50 AM.

While EMTs began loading victims into ambulances, it became apparent that the city of Tokyo was not fully prepared to handle a disaster of this type or magnitude. With so many victims to be treated, communication channels became jammed and medical resources overwhelmed. Some ambulances were forced to stop and use pay phones to communicate with hospitals. Medical facilities near the scene were overrun with victims, with the injured being housed in hallways and chapels.

As victims began arriving at local hospitals, there was considerable confusion over what was causing the symptoms that doctors were observing. Hospitals were initially told that there had been a gas explosion, so they made preparations to treat patients suffering from burns and carbon monoxide poisoning. When patients did not display these symptoms, hospital staff relied on the opinions of EMTs, who speculated that tear gas had been released. The fire department then informed hospitals that the cause was acetonitrile poisoning. The reports of several deaths and clinical observations contradicted these theories, though. As doctors began to suspect another form of poisoning, a physician involved in treating victims of the Matsumoto attack suggested the possibility of sarin contamination. Experts from the JGSDF soon agreed. It took roughly two and a half hours after victims began arriving at hospitals for the correct diagnosis to be made, precious time lost to counteract the effects of sarin exposure.

Upon positive identification of the poison, hospitals began decontaminating victims and administering antidote. Only one local hospital had any quantity of the necessary antidote on hand. Fortunately, a company that manufactured the antidote in Osaka had dispatched its product to Tokyo upon first hearing of a chemical poisoning incident, which helped to avert further disaster.

Decontamination teams from the JGSDF, which were called into service at 10:10 AM on the morning of the attack, arrived on scene nearly seven hours later, around 5:00 PM. By early on the morning of March 21, decontamination of trains and stations had been completed and normal subway service had resumed.

Twelve people would eventually die from sarin poisoning, all through direct contact with the liquid agent. Another 5,510 people were injured, although the majority of these were patients suffering from mental and emotional distress. Approximately 10% of rescuers displayed symptoms of sarin exposure, either from firsthand contact with vapors or off-gassing from other victims. Overall, however, the consequences of the disaster could have been much worse. It has been estimated that, given "ideal" circumstances (e.g., pure sarin, effective dissemination method), tens of thousands of commuters could have been killed.

The Tokyo subway sarin attack was prompted by Shoko Asahara's quest for violent confrontation with Japan and the world. His remarkable ability to recruit followers provided him with the expertise, manpower, and funds to carry out attacks. The inherent vulnerability of subways also provided the cult with an ideal environment for devastation. Japanese law and enforcement policies allowed the threat posed by the cult to grow unchecked for nearly a decade. Finally, when the attack occurred, response agencies were unprepared to deal with the situation.

Terrorists throughout the world have chosen subways as a target because of a lack of security and the potential to inflict significant harm. Moreover, attacking such indispensable infrastructure also targets the psychological welfare of a city, a nation, and the international community.

Asahara, like many terrorist leaders, recognized and exploited the increased freedom afforded by certain nations. Aum was able to construct a vast terrorist organization using the protections given to religious institutions in Japan. With Japanese law forbidding enforcement agencies from investigating "religious activities or doctrine," when police found credible evidence that Aum may have been involved in several serious crimes, they were hesitant to confront the cult. Had police investigated the cult after finding an Aum lapel pin at the Sakamoto home or after finding evidence of sarin production at the cult compound following the Matsumoto attack, the Tokyo subway attack may have been averted.

Thorough investigation of Aum's criminal activities would have been difficult, however, as the structure of Japanese law enforcement does not lend itself to criminal investigations beyond the local level. Japan has no national investigative police unit similar to the Federal Bureau of Investigation in the United States. While Tokyo police can assist in investigations outside of its jurisdiction, it may only do so after a formal request has been made by the local government. This independence of local police also hinders the type of communication and information sharing essential to investigating terrorists carrying out operations in more than one location.

Communication also became a problem as the sarin attack unfolded. Subway passengers were the first to become aware of a problem as they began experiencing symptoms of sarin poisoning or noticing others around them falling ill. However, the situation was not immediately reported to train conductors, despite intercom systems located in each subway car, allegedly because passengers were either unaware of the system or were hesitant to be the first to raise an alarm.

Once train operators were notified, they contacted the train control center but were unaware of the extent of the problem. Consequently, trains continued to run on the affected lines for over an hour, further contaminating commuters and infrastructure. Additional casualties resulted from the deployment of response crews who were not trained to deal with the removal and cleanup of such hazardous substances. Moreover, available crews trained in such procedures were stationed 20 miles away in the city of Omiya, constraining the ability to perform rapid and effective decontamination. Further exacerbating the situation was the delay in announcing the attack to the public and a lack of protocols for verifying a chemical attack and quarantining affected areas.

Rendering appropriate medical treatment to contaminated individuals was especially problematic because most of the doctors and EMTs had not been trained to care for chemical warfare victims and did not have ready access to treatment guidelines. Moreover, even if they had been so trained, EMTs were prevented from providing medications or intubating victims of such an attack. Under Japanese law, only physicians, who rarely participate in on-site emergency response, can perform such procedures.

On March 22, 1995, 2,500 police and soldiers, wearing protective gear and carrying chemical detection equipment, raided the Aum Shinrikyo compound and other cult sites throughout Japan. Numerous Aum members were arrested, but Asahara and the members of his inner circle were able to escape and went into hiding.

In the months following the attacks, loyal Aum members carried out a series of new attacks, including the shooting of the Tokyo police commissioner, a mail bomb aimed at the governor of Tokyo, and five separate unsuccessful chemical releases on subways in Tokyo and Yokohama.

Asahara was eventually found and arrested in May 1995. Aum membership quickly plummeted to approximately 700 of Asahara's most loyal followers. Even as cult members were being tried in connection with the Tokyo sarin attack, however, membership began climbing once again. By 1997, Aum had rebounded to 2,700 members and continued growing, due in large part to recruitment seminars the cult held each month. Over the next two years, as new members joined and the cult's computer business continued to thrive, Aum's net worth surpassed $20 million.

In 2000, as Asahara's trial was under way, Aum changed its name to "Aleph" and apologized for its previous actions. Asahara was eventually convicted for his role in the attack and sentenced to death, along with six of the attackers. Of the remaining attackers, three were given life sentences and one remains at large. Aleph continues operating as a religious society today, although it is formally considered a terrorist organization by many nations and has been banned by a number of governments including Canada, the European Union, Russia, and the United States.

The Tokyo sarin attack highlighted numerous deficiencies faced by the Tokyo subway system in the areas of disaster preparedness and management. Japanese transportation authorities have since increased subway security by adding more police and security cameras, developed a protocol for reporting incidents, created a manual for dealing with gas attacks, and attempted to raise public awareness of the threat of attacks through posters and public announcements.

Japanese national disaster response has been augmented in the aftermath of this attack. In order to reduce the effect of secondary contamination, protocols have been developed and equipment has been distributed throughout the country to decontaminate large numbers of victims at the scene of a chemical attack. The Japanese Poison Information Center has begun training doctors and responders in detecting chemical attacks and treating victims, and personal protective equipment has been distributed to responders and hospitals throughout Japan. The JGSDF has been supplied with automated antidote injectors and provided with enhanced chemical response training. The JGSDF has also developed laboratory infrastructure for rapid detection of chemical agents. Similar detection equipment has been distributed to over 70 emergency centers across the country.

The Japanese government has formed a standing committee of experts in chemical incident management to facilitate information flow, should a future chemical attack occur. The national government has also created a model for coordinating on-scene response, one in which the Japanese Poison Information Center provides technical assistance to local coordinators.

In 1999, Japan passed a law enabling police to investigate more easily suspicious activities in religious institutions. The next year, legislation was passed that allowed Japanese police to tap phone and e-mail conversations, a move bolstered largely by public fear of a new terrorist attack. Using these investigative powers, Japanese police have continued to monitor Aleph as well as other terrorist threats. One such cult, which was subsequently compared to the early stages of Aum Shinrikyo, was raided by Japanese police in May 2003.

The Tokyo subway sarin attack awakened the world to the new threat of terrorism involving WMD/E. In the wake of this event, however, a debate has arisen over the likelihood of further chemical and biological attacks. Some experts argue that because supplies and instructions to create such weapons are readily available to terrorists, such attacks like those perpetrated by Aum Shinrikyo will become commonplace in the twenty-first century. Others point out that, despite access to materials and information, construction of such weapons remains difficult, as evidenced by Aum's numerous failed attempts at dispersing biological agents and a number of casualties the cult sustained in attempting to manufacture chemical weapons. They argue that these kinds of weapons should be considered less of a threat than conventional bombs, which are much easier to produce and deploy.

While it remains to be seen if chemical and biological weapons will present a significant threat to society in the near future, the vulnerability of subway and train systems throughout the world continues to pose a risk to commuters and the cities in which they live. Since the time of the Tokyo sarin attack, terrorists have continued to plan and carry out devastating attacks on such targets. These attacks include thwarted attempts to release chemicals on the London and New York City subway systems in 2002 and 2003, respectively; the 2003 bombing of a passenger train in Mumbai; bombings of a subway station in Moscow and a Madrid commuter train in 2004; a bombing and a subsequent failed plot against the London subway in 2005 (see Chapter 11); and three bombings of commuter trains and stations in India during 2006 and 2007.

REFERENCES

ALEPH. http://english.aleph.to.

BBC. "Madrid Attacks Timeline," March 12, 2004. http://news.bbc.co.uk/2/hi/europe/3504912.stm.

CNN. "India: Blasts Caused by 'Sabotage,'" February 19, 2007. www.cnn.com/2007/WORLD/asiapcf/02/18/india.train/index.html.

CNN. "Major Attacks in India," 2007. www.cnn.com/2007/WORLD/asiapcf/02/19/india.attacks.ap/index.html.

CNN. "Moscow Suicide Bomber Kills 9," August 31, 2004. www.cnn.com/2004/WORLD/europe/08/31/russia.carblast/index.html.

CNN. "Murderous' Suicide Bombs Plot," January 15, 2007. www.cnn.com/2007/WORLD/europe/01/15/bombings.trial/index.html.

CNN. "Report: Al Qaeda Planned N.Y. Subway Attack," June 18, 2006. www.cnn.com/2006/US/06/17/subway.plot/index.html.

CNN. "3 Terror Suspects in London Court," November 17, 2002. http://archives.cnn.com/2002/WORLD/europe/11/17/tube.terror/index.html.

Council of the European Union. "Council Decision of 21 December 2005 Implementing Article 2(3) of Regulation (EC) No 2580/2001 on Specific Restrictive Measures Directed Against Certain Persons and Entities with a View to Combating Terrorism and Repealing Decision 2005/848/EC (2005/930/EC)," *Official Journal of the European Union* 240 (2005): 64–66.

French, Howard. "Cult Surveillance Extended," *New York Times*, February 25, 2003.

"In Brief," *New York Times*, February 26, 2007.

Okumura, Testu, et al. "The Tokyo Subway Sarin Attack: Disaster Management, Part 2: Hospital Response," *Academic Emergency Medicine* 5 (1998): 618–624.

Okumura, Testu, Norifumi Ninomiya, and Muneo Ohta. "The Chemical Disaster Response System in Japan," *Prehospital and Disaster Medicine* 18 (2003): 189–192.

"Order Recommending that Each Entity Listed as of July 23, 2006, in the Regulations Establishing a List of Entities Remain a Listed Entity," *Canada Gazette* 140, no. 2 (2006): 1955–1958.

"Police Search Sect's Buildings," *New York Times*, May 15, 2003.

Schuster, Henry. "Transit Systems Are Frequent Targets," July 7, 2005. www.cnn.com/2005/US/07/07/schuster.column.transit/index.html.

Smithson, Amy E. "Rethinking the Lessons of Tokyo." In *Ataxia: The Chemical and Biological Terrorist Threat and the US Response*, ed. Amy E. Smithson and Leslie-Anne Levy. Washington, DC: The Henry L. Stimson Center, 2000.

Suzuki, Kouichiro, et al. "The Tokyo Subway Sarin Attack: Disaster Management, Part 1: Community Emergency Response," *Academic Emergency Medicine* 5 (1998): 613–617

Syle, Murray. "Nerve Gas and the Four Noble Truths," *The New Yorker*, April 1, 1996, 56–71.

U.S. Army Training and Doctrine Command. *Terror Operations: Case Studies in Terrorism*. Fort Leavenworth, KS: U.S. Army Training and Doctrine Command, 2005.

U.S. Department of Heath and Human Services, Agency for Toxic Substances and Disease Registry. "Medical Management Guidelines for Nerve Agents: Tabun (GA); Sarin (GB); Soman (GD); and VX." www.atsdr.cdc.gov/MHMI/mmg166.pdf.

U.S. Department of State. "Foreign Terrorist Organizations," October 11, 2005. www.state.gov/s/ct/rls/fs/37191.htm.

U.S. Department of Transportation. "US-Japan Mass Transit Security Workshop Proceedings and Meetings Summary: January 2002." http://ntl.bts.gov/lib/12000/12100/12190.

U.S. Senate Government Affairs Permanent Subcommittee on Investigations. "Global Proliferation of Weapons of Mass Destruction: A Case Study on the Aum Shinrikyo," October 31, 1995. www.fas.org/irp/congress/1995_rpt/aum/index.html.

Williams, Martyn. "Japan's Police Gain Right to Tap Phones and E-mail," August 16, 2000. http://archives.cnn.com/2000/TECH/computing/08/16/japan.police.idg/index.html.

CHAPTER 9

ATTACK ON THE
USS *COLE*

O n October 12, 2000, while the USS *Cole* was refueling in the harbor of Aden, Yemen, two men in a small boat pulled alongside the vessel and detonated 500 pounds of C-4 explosive (see Exhibit 9.1). The blast blew a large hole into the side of the ship, nearly sinking it, and killing 17 sailors and wounding another 39 in the process. U.S. military intelligence, engagement strategy, force protection measures, and communication efforts were all questioned in the aftermath of the attack.

The Middle East is home to a vast amount of the world's energy resources, some of the busiest international shipping lanes, and a number of key strategic military locations. Consequently, nations outside of the area have long had an interest in engaging Middle Eastern governments to promote stability and ensure access to the region's resources. The United States is one such country, maintaining a presence in the Middle East despite a long-standing terrorist threat.

U.S. citizens and assets in the Middle East have historically been targets of terrorists seeking to expel western influences from the region. In 1979, the U.S. embassy in Tehran, Iran, was attacked by militants. Sixty-six U.S. citizens were taken hostage, 52 of whom were held captive for nearly 15 months. Four years later, 241 U.S. Marines were killed when a truck bomb exploded outside of their barracks in Lebanon.

EXHIBIT **9.1**   USS Cole *following the October 12, 2000 bombing*

Source: Don L. Maes, www.dodmedia.osd.mil/Assets/Still/2003/Navy/DN-SD-03-09092.jpeg.

In the early 1990s, a new age of terrorism in the Middle East dawned with the rise of a militant Islamic group known as al Qaeda ("the Base"). This group was formed after the war between Afghanistan and the Soviet Union, as a headquarters for organizing and funding further jihad (holy war) against societies not subscribing to Islamist ideals. By 1991, the founder and leader of al Qaeda, Osama Bin Ladin, had established a permanent home for his organization under a sympathetic government in the nation of Sudan. From there, Bin Ladin created a network of terrorist cells throughout the world and a myriad of business enterprises to provide operational financing. A year later, al Qaeda issued its first decree, calling for war against the western "occupation" of Islamic lands, specifically singling out U.S. forces. A second decree against U.S. involvement in the region was issued months later when U.S. troops were deployed to Somalia.

Attacks against U.S. personnel and assets followed closely behind al Qaeda's declarations. In December 1992, two hotels in Aden, Yemen, that frequently housed U.S. military en route to Somalia were bombed, killing two people. The following year, fighters trained and supplied by al Qaeda engaged U.S. forces in Mogadishu, Somalia. In the ensuing firefight, two U.S. helicopters were shot down, 18 Americans were killed, and another 73 were wounded. In 1995, a car bomb detonated outside a joint Saudi-U.S. facility in Riyadh killed 5 Americans and 2 Indian nationals. Less than one year later, a massive truck bomb exploded in a complex that housed U.S. military personnel in Dhahran, Saudi Arabia; 19 Americans were killed and 372 were wounded.

Following the attack in Dhahran, Bin Ladin and members of the al Qaeda leadership relocated to Afghanistan, where they continued to issue orders calling on Muslims to drive western forces from the Middle East. From this new, less restrictive headquarters, al Qaeda was able to assume a more active position in its jihad. The organization moved from being motivators, financiers, and trainers, to actually planning and executing the attacks. The first such attack came on August 7, 1998, when al Qaeda operatives detonated two truck bombs minutes apart at U.S. embassies in Nairobi; Kenya; and Dares Salaam, Tanzania, killing 224 people and wounding 5,000.

During the 1990s, terrorism was not the only source of instability in the Middle East. Of particular interest to the U.S. military was Eritrea's war for independence from Ethiopia. The U.S. Navy used the port of Djibouti as its refueling stop in the southern Red Sea, but the nearby war caused an increase in traffic and security risks to its ships. Thus, the decision was made to investigate other options for refueling.

Aden, Yemen, was found to be a suitable alternative (see Exhibit 9.2). Using this port was seen as a means for strengthening U.S. ties with Yemen, a nation that offered a unique geostrategic advantage. Located between the Suez Canal and the mouth of the Persian Gulf, Yemen controls the maritime bottleneck at the southern end of the Red Sea. Additionally, U.S. forces had used the port for operations in the

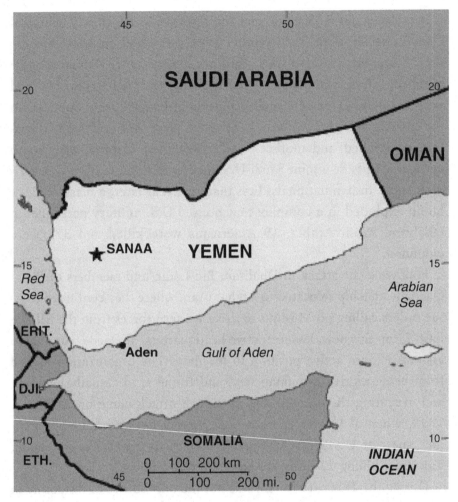

EXHIBIT 9.2   *Map of Yemen indicating the location of Aden along its southern coast*

Source: U.S. Central Intelligence Agency. www.cia.gov/library/publications/the-world-factbook/geos/ym.html.

past and thus had some familiarity with it. In 1998, with these considerations in mind, the U.S. military began making arrangements for refueling ships in the port of Aden, starting the following January.

It was around this time that an al Qaeda operative named Abd al Rahim al Nashiri suggested the idea of attacking a U.S. vessel. Nashiri, who had originally been recruited to al Qaeda by Bin Ladin himself, was given authorization to plan the attack and to report directly to the al Qaeda chief. When Nashiri had difficulty finding a U.S. oil tanker along the western coast of Yemen to serve as a suitable target, Bin Ladin directed him to focus his efforts on U.S. warships in the port of Aden.

In January 2000, Nashiri's team loaded a small boat full of explosives with the intent of attacking the USS *Sullivans*. After the terrorists' overloaded boat sank under the weight of the explosives, however, preventing the attack, the bombers retrieved their equipment undetected from the sea floor and waited for the next window of opportunity. That opportunity came when the USS *Cole* arrived in the port nine months later.

The *Cole*, a $1 billion navy guided missile destroyer, had deployed from Norfolk, Virginia, on August 8, 2000, with orders to reinforce a naval battle group in the Persian Gulf. After crossing the Atlantic and conducting operations in the Mediterranean Sea, the *Cole* transited through the Suez Canal on October 9. In order to cover the 3,300-mile distance around the Arabian Peninsula to the northern Persian Gulf, the *Cole* had to stop for refueling. Preparations were made for this stop in the port of Aden, and the *Cole* arrived on the morning of October 12. The ship was moored in the harbor just before 9:00 AM, and refueling began 90 minutes later.

Upon observing the ship's arrival, two Al Qaeda operatives launched a small boat and began piloting it toward the vessel. From the deck of the ship, the terrorist craft appeared to be just another of the many small boats involved in the refueling activity. In the boat, however, was over 500 pounds of a military explosive known as C-4, which was capable of penetrating the steel skin of the *Cole*. As their boat approached the warship, the terrorists stood, saluted the sailors onboard, and detonated the charge. The resulting explosion ripped a 40-by-45-foot hole in the side of the *Cole*, knocking out the ship's communications and damaging one of its engines (see Exhibit 9.3). Seventeen sailors died and 38 were wounded. Among the casualties were the first two female sailors ever killed in an attack on a U.S. Navy vessel.

EXHIBIT 9.3   *USS* Cole *being transported to the United States after the*
bombing

Source: U.S. Navy, Military Sealift Command. *www.msc.navy*
.mil/N00p/graphics/bluemarlin3.jpg.

The Yemeni government quickly mobilized to provide medical support for the bombing victims and, in the days that followed, security for
U.S. officials arriving on the scene. Other nations, such as Djibouti,
France, and the United Kingdom, offered response resources, while U.S.
allies in the region offered the use of transportation facilities and expedited fly-over clearance for U.S. aircraft.

Within 24 hours of the attack, the wounded sailors were being
airlifted to a U.S. military hospital in Germany. Meanwhile, two
navy ships, the USS *Hawes* and the USS *Donald Cook*, arrived to
assess blast damage and help keep the distressed vessel afloat. Two
weeks later, the *Cole* was towed from the port of Aden and loaded
onto a heavy-lift ship for a return trip to the United States (see Exhibit 9.3). Since terrorist threats had been made against U.S. warships transiting the Suez Canal, the *Cole* returned home by sailing
around the southern tip of Africa, extending its trip by a week. Once
home, it took a year and $250 million to repair the damage caused
by the attack.

The bombing of the USS *Cole* resulted from a terrorist group's agenda of removing the United States from the Middle East. A lack of resources, a questionable U.S. policy of engagement with a high-threat nation, poor understanding and communication of the threat being faced, and an absence of preparation for sea-based attacks all placed the ship at high risk, providing al Qaeda with an accessible and vulnerable target.

Military downsizing in the years preceding the *Cole* attack had left the U.S. Navy with a smaller fleet to meet an increasing number of operational demands. Under these circumstances, often it was necessary to shuffle individual vessels from one region to another to bolster defenses wherever the current threat dictated. Because ships traveling alone do not have the same access to refueling boats that support a larger operation, strategic refueling sites had become increasingly more important. Therefore, when refueling in Djibouti was deemed undesirable, it became essential for the U.S. Navy to locate another port within the region.

For years prior to the *Cole* bombing, the United States had sought to strengthen its ties with Yemen. Moving refueling operations to the port of Aden presented a unique opportunity to pursue this policy of engagement. U.S. officials hoped that an American presence in Yemen would be a stabilizing force in a country recently emerging from a bloody civil war. Moreover, it would provide an excellent location for the navy to carry out its mission of ensuring access to Middle East resources and waterways.

The decision to become more actively engaged with Yemen by refueling in Aden was made despite the country's connection to terrorists and its history of anti-American sentiment. Until Yemen's reunification in 1990, South Yemen was listed as a state sponsor of terrorism by the U.S. government. During the first Gulf War, the newly reunited country openly supported the Iraqi regime that was opposing the United States. Anti-American agendas in Yemen ran well beyond those officially sanctioned by the state, however. In 1992, terrorists targeted U.S. military forces in a pair of hotel bombings in Aden. Subsequently, workers under a U.S. military humanitarian program were threatened as they attempted to remove land mines left behind from the Yemeni civil war. Perhaps most significantly, in 1998, information was uncovered by the Federal Bureau of Investigation (FBI) that pointed toward a possible terrorist attack on a U.S. Navy ship.

Although U.S. officials were well aware of the dangerous environment in Yemen, they believed that the benefits of increased engagement outweighed the risks. Thus, despite an environment labeled as "high threat" and a "safe haven for terrorist groups" by the U.S. military and Department of State, respectively, the navy began making routine refueling stops in the port of Aden in January 1999.

While acknowledging the hazardous environment in Yemen, the U.S. military believed that its naval warships were relatively safe from terrorist attacks. This notion was so ingrained within the U.S. military that four separate vulnerability assessments of Aden were conducted without mention of the possibility of waterborne attacks on navy ships. Such misunderstanding of the terrorist threat in Aden, or perhaps arrogance, led U.S. officials to underestimate the risk of using the port for refueling. The discounting of waterborne threats also led to a lack of preparedness, as navy defense personnel were focused almost exclusively on protecting the ship from land-based attacks. While these forces were highly competent in defending the ship from a truck bomb on a pier, they were unable to recognize or impede an attack from a small boat.

Underestimation of the terrorist threat in Aden can be attributed, in part, to difficulty in obtaining quality intelligence on terrorist groups. These organizations are typically small, tightly knit, security conscious, and wary of outsiders, making gathering of detailed intelligence extremely challenging. Thus, even with the 1998 FBI report indicating the general possibility of an attack against a U.S. Navy ship, there was no concrete or actionable evidence indicating that terrorists were planning an attack on the *Cole*. Obtaining this kind of information was so problematic that the attempted bombing of the USS *Sullivans* was not discovered until after the bombing of the *Cole,* almost a year after the *Sullivans* plot had failed.

A lack of resources compounded the difficulty in obtaining quality intelligence. The U.S. military did not have enough analyst personnel to review the quantity of information received each day. As a result, a flood of vague intelligence often overshadowed higher-quality or more detailed information. Thus, when accurate intelligence was circulated, it was often discounted or ignored. One day after the *Cole* attack, a U.S. Department of Defense (DoD) intelligence analyst resigned his post because he felt that his repeated warnings about an impending terrorist attack in the Middle East had been ignored by military officials.

Lapses in the communication of threat levels added to a false sense of security felt by military personnel operating in the port of Aden. In one such instance, on October 1, 2000, DoD revised its threat level ranking system. The new system consisted of four risk categories: high, significant, moderate, and low. The system used prior to this scheme was nearly identical, except that it contained a fifth category, negligible, which was used to represent the lowest possible threat level. Under the new four-category system, Yemen was shifted from "high" to "significant," even though the actual magnitude of risk had not changed. The commander of the *Cole* misinterpreted the new designation to be a lowering of the threat level for the region and thus underestimated the risk faced by his ship and crew. A lack of communication between DoD and the U.S. Department of State, which oversees U.S. embassies, added to the confusion. DoD, and thus the *Cole*'s commander, was not informed that the U.S. embassy in Yemen had been operating under an elevated threat level and even had been forced to suspend operations for several days prior to the ship's arrival because of security concerns.

The commander's misperception of the risk present in Aden likely played a role in his decision not to invoke all of the ship protection measures called for under the threat condition (THREATCON). At the time of the *Cole* bombing, U.S. military officials decided that the threat level in Yemen called for "TREATCON Bravo" force protection measures. The second lowest level of four force protection categories, "Bravo" requires that 62 specific protection measures be implemented beyond the 25 already in place under THREATCON Alpha. In accordance with standard U.S. Navy procedure, the commander of the *Cole* filed a force protection plan stating that all 62 of the "Bravo" measures would be operational while the ship was in the Middle East. Of these measures, however, 19 were waived and another 12 were never implemented. Among the 31 force protection measures not executed were coordinating security measures with local agents and keeping small unauthorized vessels away from the ship.

In the investigation that followed the attack on the USS *Cole,* circumstantial evidence emerged that connected al Qaeda and Bin Ladin to the bombing but with no definitive link. Consequently, the U.S. refrained from military retaliation, opting instead for increased antiterrorism funding and a more aggressive stance toward al Qaeda.

Elsewhere in the world, however, al Qaeda was recognized as the architect of the bombing. The terrorist organization and its members received praise from those with similar anti-American agendas. Iran, for example, began seeking closer ties and offering support to Bin Ladin. Al Qaeda even reenacted the attack for use in a widely distributed recruiting video. This propaganda helped al Qaeda to emerge as the preeminent Islamist movement and convinced many extremists to undertake terrorism training and jihad.

Within al Qaeda, those involved in the plot were honored and promoted. Nashiri became well known within the organization and was eventually installed as the group's head of operations in the Arabian peninsula. In 2002, he supervised a second ship bombing, targeting the French tanker *Limburg,* as well as a failed plot to bomb U.S. and British warships in the Strait of Gibraltar. Shortly after the *Limburg* attack, Nashiri was captured in Yemen and later sentenced to death.

Five other *Cole* conspirators have been captured since the bombing and were given sentences ranging from 5 to 15 years in prison. One of the convicted, however, remains at large after escaping from a Yemeni prison in 2006. A sixth conspirator, the former head of al Qaeda in Yemen, was killed there by a 2002 U.S. missile strike.

At least two of the *Cole* conspirators, Tawfiq bin Attash and Fahd al Quso, played a part in a larger-scale al Qaeda attack carried out less than a year after the bombing: the 2001 airline attacks on U.S. soil. Bin Ladin had suggested carrying out these attacks on the seven-month anniversary of the *Cole* bombing, but preparations were not yet complete. The plot eventually unfolded on September 11 of that year, vastly overshadowing the relaunching of the *Cole* just five days later.

Shortly after the *Cole* bombing, the commander of U.S. armed forces in the Middle East, General Tommy Franks, declared a renewed commitment to engagement with Yemen. "Terrorists have declared war on us," General Franks said. ". . . I will never recommend disengagement." Despite General Franks's commitment to engagement with Yemen, the United States suspended all refueling operations after the attack. By 2006, however, Germany and Great Britain had begun sending ships into Aden harbor and the U.S. Navy began weighing the possibility of returning.

Issues that precipitated the *Cole* bombing remain unresolved. Terrorism and anti-American sentiment continue to thrive in Yemen. In 2002, three U.S. doctors were killed and one was wounded when a Yemeni Islamic militant attacked the hospital where they worked. In 2006, Yemeni officials thwarted two suicide car bombings of the country's oil infrastructure. More recently, anti-American protests flared in the Yemeni capital during the Israeli–Hezbollah war, stemming from a perceived U.S. bias toward Israel. Additionally, al Qaeda continues to call for Muslims to attack U.S. interests in the Middle East.

In spite of these threats and the *Cole* incident, U.S. warships remain vulnerable to a sea-based terrorist attack. In July 2004, the aircraft carrier USS *John F. Kennedy* collided with a small boat in the Persian Gulf. Although the collision was most likely an accident, it demonstrated that nearly four years after the *Cole* bombing, standard ship protection measures remained inadequate.

REFERENCES

BBC. "New al-Qaeda Tape Is Released," October 2, 2004. http://news.bbc.co.uk/2/hi/middle_east/3707550.stm.

BBC. "US Missionaries Murdered in Yemen," December 30, 2002. http://news.bbc.co.uk/1/hi/world/middle_east/2614091.stm.

CNN. "Casualties of USS *Cole* Blast Airlifted to Germany," October 13, 2000. http://archives.cnn.com/2000/US/10/13/uss.cole.04/index.html.

CNN. "C-4 Explosive Used in USS *Cole* Attack," November 1, 2000. http://archives.cnn.com/2000/US/11/01/cole.investigation/index.html.

CNN. "*Cole* Attack Was Terrorists' Second Try, U.S. Officials Say," November 9, 2000. http://archives.cnn.com/2000/US/11/09/uss.cole.02/index.html.

CNN. "Court Upholds Death Sentence in USS *Cole* Bombing," February 28, 2005. www.cnn.com/2005/WORLD/meast/02/26/yemen.cole/index.html.

CNN. "Defense Official Resigned After *Cole* Attack, Says Warnings Were Ignored," October 25, 2000. http://archives.cnn.com/2000/ALLPOLITICS/stories/10/25/cole.hearing/index.html.

CNN. "U.S. Carrier Collides with Boat," July 23, 2004. www.cnn.com/2004/WORLD/meast/07/23/gulf.collision/index.html.

CNN. "U.S. Military Vessels Avoid Suez Canal in Wake of Increased Threats," October 31, 2000. http://archives.cnn.com/2000/US/10/30/uss.cole.02/index.html.

CNN. "U.S. Missile Strike Kills al Qaeda Chief," November 5, 2002. http://archives.cnn.com/2002/WORLD/meast/11/05/yemen.blast/index.html.

CNN. "U.S. Officials: No Ships Going to Yemen," March 20, 2002. http://archives.cnn.com/2002/US/03/20/ret.us.yemen/index.html?related.

CNN. "U.S.: Top al Qaeda Operative Arrested," November 22, 2002. http://edition.cnn.com/2002/US/11/21/alqaeda.capture/index.html.

CNN. "U.S. Warships Ordered to Steer Clear of Suez Canal over Threat of Terrorism," *WorldView,* October 30, 2000. http://transcripts.cnn.com/TRANSCRIPTS/0010/30/wv.01.html.

CNN. "USS *Cole* Relaunched with Little Fanfare," September 16, 2001. http://archives.cnn.com/2001/US/09/16/gen.cole.repairs/index.html.

CNN. "Yemen Foils Two Suicide Attacks," September 15, 2006. www.cnn.com/2006/WORLD/meast/09/15/yemen.attacksfoiled/index.html.

Daugherty, William J. Testimony before a Hearing on Iran: A Quarter-Century of State-Sponsored Terror, given to the U.S. House of Representative Committee on International Relations, 109th Congress, 1st session, February 16, 2005.

Franks, Tommy R. Testimony before the U.S. Senate Armed Services Committee, 106th Congress, 2nd session, October 25, 2000.

Jaffe, Greg. "U.S. Navy Weighs Refueling Ships in Yemen," *Wall Street Journal,* August 9, 2006. http://blogs.wsj.com/washwire/2006/08/09/us-navy-weighs-refueling-ships-in-yemen.

National Commission on Terrorist Attacks upon the United States. *The 9/11 Commission Report.* New York: W.W. Norton & Company, 2004.

U.S. Central Intelligence Agency. *Yemen.* www.cia.gov/cia/publications/factbook/geos/ym.html.

U.S. Department of Defense. "USS *Cole* Casualty Update," October 20, 2000. www.defenselink.mil/releases/release.aspx?releaseid=2721.

U.S. Department of State. *Patterns of Global Terrorism: 1999.* Washington, DC: Author, 2000.

U.S. Federal Bureau of Investigation. "Most Wanted Terrorist—Jamel Ahmed Mohammed Ali Al-Badai." www.fbi.gov/wanted/terrorists/terbadawi.htm.

U.S. House of Representatives Armed Services Committee Staff. "The Investigation into the Attack on the USS *Cole,*" House Armed Services Committee, Washington DC, 2001.

CHAPTER 10

SEPTEMBER 11: THE WORLD TRADE CENTER

On the morning of September 11, 2001, terrorists affiliated with the al Qaeda international terrorist organization hijacked two commercial airliners, crashing the planes minutes apart into the World Trade Center in New York City (see Exhibit 10.1). Each aircraft was directed into a different tower, resulting in the eventual collapse of both buildings and destruction of other infrastructure in the immediate vicinity. Nearly 3,000 people died in the towers and on the ground, including over 400 firefighters and police officers. The terrorists successfully exploited weaknesses in U.S. aviation security and communication gaps in the U.S. intelligence system.

The World Trade Center (WTC), a complex of seven buildings spread over 16 acres in lower Manhattan, embodied the symbol of New York City as major hub of world commerce. Collectively, WTC buildings housed large and small businesses, hotels, and federal, state, and local government agencies. However, the center was best known for its 110-story twin towers (WTC 1 and 2), which were, at the time of their construction in the early 1970s, the tallest buildings in the world (see Exhibit 10.2).

The economic importance and symbolic status of the World Trade Center, combined with the reputation of its tenants, made the complex a prime target for terrorists with an anti-American agenda. As early as 1977, the center had begun receiving bomb threats. These threats were

EXHIBIT **10.1**   *Smoke rising from the twin towers of the World Trade Center as seen from Ellis Island on the morning of September 11, 2001*

Source: U.S. National Park Service, 2001.
www.nps.gov/remembrance/statue/index.html.

realized on February 26, 1993, when a tremendous explosion rocked the North Tower (WTC 1), ushering in a new era of terrorism in which militants became intent on killing indiscriminately and without limit.

The explosion resulted from the detonation of a 1,500-pound truck bomb in the basement of the WTC garage. The blast created a hole seven stories tall, damaging communications systems, rupturing coolant pipes to emergency generators, and filling the stairwells of WTC 1 with smoke. Six people were killed and 1,042 were wounded as a result. Notably, these totals fell well short of the goal set by the bomber, a Sunni extremist who later confessed that he had hoped to kill 250,000 people.

The disaster highlighted a number of deficiencies in emergency preparedness that plagued the World Trade Center in the early 1990s. At

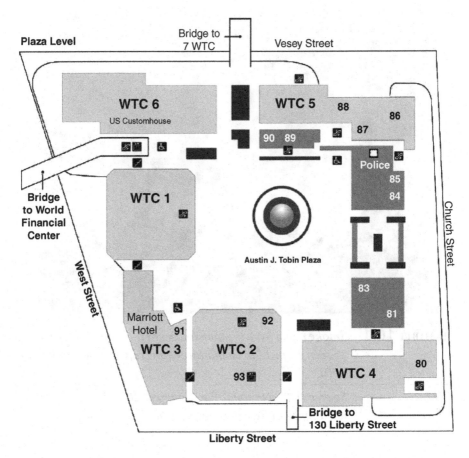

EXHIBIT 10.2   *Layout of World Trade Center complex. The 110-story North and South Towers are indicated as WTC 1 and WTC 2, respectively.*

Source: National Institute of Standards and Technology, Occupant Behavior, Egress, and Emergency Communications (Washington, DC: U.S. Department of Commerce, 2005).

the time of the attack, approximately 150,000 occupants had to be evacuated from the complex, a process that took four hours to complete. This lengthy procedure began with workers gathering at assigned fire drill locations to receive emergency instructions. Instructions never came, however, as the emergency communications system was damaged in the blast and the fire alarms did not sound. Occupants attempting to seek information from the 911 emergency dispatch center were stymied by a system that was overwhelmed by calls.

Once the evacuation began, a number of obstacles were encountered. Without operational elevators, the only exit was through stairwells, which had no lighting and were rapidly filling with smoke. Responders, who typically relied on elevators for rescues in skyscrapers, were forced to enter the same crowded, smoke-filled stairwells and climb more than 100 stories. Firefighters' jobs were further complicated by their reliance on radios that were not powerful enough to operate effectively in such large buildings. Additionally, so many firefighters were attempting to use the same channel at one time that communications became unintelligible.

In the years following the 1993 bombing, the Port Authority of New York and New Jersey, which managed the operation of the World Trade Center, spent $100 million on structural improvements, power systems, emergency preparedness, and safety and security systems. Included in these improvements were elements meant to decrease evacuation times, including biannual fire drills, the formation of employee "fire teams" to facilitate evacuations, and additional lighting in stairwells. A radio repeater tower was also erected on top of WTC 5, aimed at increasing the effectiveness of firefighter communication within the building complex. Additionally, New York City established the Office of Emergency Management (OEM), located in WTC 7, to coordinate responses to major disasters.

Sadly, the 1993 bombing would not be the last attack by Sunni militants on the World Trade Center. Osama Bin Ladin, leader of the al Qaeda international terrorist group, admired the bombing's mastermind, Omar Abdel Rahman, and shared his desire to attack U.S. citizens and interests. Throughout the 1990s, Bin Ladin's organization had carried out a number of bombings against U.S. facilities and personnel in the Middle East, in an attempt to combat U.S. influence in the region. In a 1998 interview, Bin Ladin suggested that if what he saw as "American injustice" against Muslims was to continue, he would move "the battle to American soil," just as the WTC bombers had done. He further declared that the best thing a Muslim could do was to kill an American and that there should be no distinction between military and civilians in this slaughter.

At the time of the interview, Bin Ladin had already started formulating plans for an attack of massive proportions within the United States. The plan, referred to as the "Planes Operation" within al Qaeda, was initially conceived in 1995 by Khalid Sheik Mohammed, one of the conspirators of the 1993 WTC bombing. In 1996, Mohammed, who was not affiliated with al Qaeda at the time, pitched his idea to Bin Ladin and the al Qaeda leadership. His proposal involved hijacking 10 planes simultaneously and crashing them into skyscrapers and strategic targets throughout the United States. By early 1999, Mohammed had joined al Qaeda and Bin Ladin had not only approved the attack but also promised to finance it.

Bin Ladin scaled back the operation to include four planes and began selecting operatives for the mission. By January 2000, the terrorists who would serve as pilots began arriving in the United States. Once in America, they found apartments to rent, established bank accounts, and enrolled in flight schools. As the "pilots" neared the end of their training, additional operatives, known as "muscle" hijackers, charged with the actual takeover of the jets, began arriving in the United States. By early July 2001, the entire team of 19 hijackers was assembled within the United States, awaiting the day of the attack.

That day arrived on September 11, 2001. Two of the hijackers checked in for a 6:00 AM flight from Portland, Maine, to Boston's Logan International Airport. One was randomly selected by the airport's Computer Assisted Passenger Prescreening System (CAPPS) as a passenger requiring additional security screening. The only consequence of being selected, however, was that the passenger's checked bags were held off of the airplane until he was confirmed to have boarded.

Once in Boston, the two terrorists checked in for American Airlines Flight 11 to Los Angeles, scheduled for a 7:45 AM departure. They were joined by three other members of their team. Elsewhere, other hijacking squads were checking in for flights to Los Angeles: five as passengers at another Logan terminal to board United Flight 175, five others as passengers on American Airlines Flight 77 leaving Dulles International (near Washington, D.C.), and a group of four at the Newark, New Jersey, airport on United Flight 93. All 14 of these men passed through security despite 5 of them being selected by CAPPS or customer service for increased security screening, 2 setting off metal detectors, 1 having no photo identification, and 1 having trouble giving acceptable responses to standard security questions.

American Flight 11 departed Logan at 7:59 AM. Over the next 15 minutes, the flight crew piloted the aircraft to 26,000 feet and the attendants began preparations for serving breakfast. At 8:14, the crew responded to flight instructions from Boston's air traffic control, but a second set of instructions 16 seconds later went unanswered. Authorities believe that this moment marked the beginning of the worst hostile attack ever committed on U.S. territory.

The hijacking began as two terrorists seated in the second row of the first-class section left their seats and stabbed two members of the cabin crew. They then gained access to the cockpit, possibly by using a key from one of the injured attendants or by force. The "pilot" hijacker and one other member of the attack team then moved forward from their seats in the business section to take control of the plane. A passenger seated directly behind them, who may have tried to intervene, was stabbed by the fifth attacker, seated one row farther back. The hijackers then subdued the passengers by spraying mace and claiming that a bomb was onboard.

During the ordeal, one of the flight attendants was able to reach an American Airlines call center via air phone to report the situation. At 8:24 AM, the hijackers themselves notified air traffic controllers, when they mistakenly broadcast a radio message they had meant to announce over the cabin public address system.

At 8:27, the jet made an unexpected turn to the south and started descending soon thereafter (see Exhibit 10.3). The plane continued flying erratically over the next 18 minutes, until it suddenly began to dive.

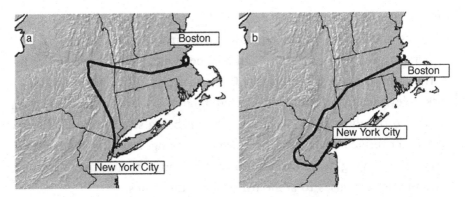

EXHIBIT 10.3   *Flight paths of American Flight 11 (a) and United Flight 175 (b)*

Source: National Commission on Terrorist Attacks upon the United States, The 9/11 Commission Report (New York: W.W. Norton & Company, 2004).

The flight attendant speaking with the American Airlines call center became distraught as she noticed how low the plane had dropped. Then, suddenly, at 8:46, the call went dead. At that moment, all 92 people on board were killed instantly as the airliner slammed into the North Tower of the World Trade Center.

The plane cut through the ninety-second to ninety-ninth floors of WTC 1, killing an unknown number of people within the building. Immediately, a jet fuel fireball exploded from the plane, shooting down elevator shafts as far as four levels below ground. Fires ignited throughout the building, and the tops of both towers were soon engulfed in smoke. On and above the impacted floors, over 1,300 people remained alive with no means of escape, as elevators had been knocked out of service and all three stairwells had been destroyed.

The Fire Department of New York (FDNY) began responding almost immediately, and members of the Port Authority Police Department (PAPD) on scene began making their way toward those trapped on floors above and in the subway station below. While FDNY chiefs immediately determined that the building should be evacuated, occupants remained unsure of whether to leave, as the tower's emergency communications system had been damaged during impact. Many of those in WTC 1 tried contacting 911, but were unable to get through as all circuits were busy. Callers able to establish a connection learned that operators knew little about the situation and could not advise how best to escape the fire.

Even without emergency information, the evacuation of both towers began soon after the crash. The quick start to the evacuation can be attributed partially to the many building occupants who had been present during the 1993 bombing. Many of them recalled the length and difficulty of the previous evacuation and began exiting the building immediately.

Unknown to those in WTC 1, who were only beginning to realize the magnitude of the disaster, the plot continued to unfold some 31,000 feet above. Sometime between 8:42 and 8:46 AM, a second set of terrorists took control of United Flight 175. These hijackers used tactics similar to those of the attackers aboard American Flight 11 to gain control of the plane, before turning it eastward toward New York City (see Exhibit 10.3).

Meanwhile, at 8:48, from WTC 7, OEM activated the Emergency Operations Center and, in doing so, requested the involvement of the FDNY, New York Police Department (NYPD), and the Department of Health and Greater Hospital Association. OEM then contacted the Federal Emergency Management Agency to request the dispatch of no fewer than five Urban Search and Rescue Teams stationed throughout the country.

As response operations were getting under way for the North Tower, many tenants in the South Tower remained uncertain of what action to take. At 8:49 AM, an announcement was broadcast over the public address system in WTC 2 telling occupants to remain in their offices. About this time, two NYPD helicopters began investigating the possibility of a rooftop rescue for occupants stranded on the upper floors of WTC 1. The pilots found that smoke and flames from the fire precluded such a maneuver. 911 and FDNY dispatch operators were not informed of this assessment, however, which resulted in some people trapped in the North Tower climbing the stairs toward the roof in a futile attempt to escape the flames.

At 8:57 AM, FDNY chiefs, while not expecting WTC 1 to collapse, judged the damage to the structure sufficient to order the evacuation of the South Tower. As this order was relayed to PAPD, Emergency Medical Services personnel began establishing triage areas at the base of WTC 1 and the first two companies of firefighters began climbing the stairs toward the impact zone. As in the 1993 bombing, the stairs had become the only significant means for vertical movement within the building, forcing firefighters to fight against the flow of evacuees for a potential 100-story climb.

FDNY quickly determined that their role would involve only rescue operations. With each floor of the building equal to approximately one acre in size, several stories of fire would have outstripped the firefighting capabilities of the responders on hand. Even with this reduction in responsibility, firefighters faced a dangerous and seemingly insurmountable task. One FDNY division chief later remarked:

> We had a very strong sense we would lose firefighters and that we were in deep trouble, but we had estimates of 25,000 to 50,000 civilians, and we had to try to rescue them.[1]

By 9:02 AM, more than 1,000 emergency responders had arrived on the scene and the evacuation announcement for WTC 2 was sounding over the building's public address system. One minute later, United Flight 175 slammed into the South Tower. What was already the largest disaster in New York City's history had immediately intensified.

The jet cut through the seventy-seventh to eighty-fifth floors of WTC 2 and exploded into a massive fireball. The collision rendered elevators inoperable and stairs on the impacted floors unusable, with the exception of the stairway farthest from the point of impact. As in the case of WTC 1, 911 and FDNY dispatch operators had little information to provide. Thus, these operators advised victims from the upper floors of the South Tower to remain where they were and wait for help to arrive, even though there was a potential route for escape. Of the more than

600 occupants on or above the impacted floors, only 18 would ever take this escape route to safety.

Immediately following the impact, the NYPD chief increased the number of responders to 2,000 police officers. He additionally set in motion Operation Omega, a response plan for protecting police stations, government buildings, and other critical or sensitive locations throughout the city. FDNY chiefs also called more crews into action, and numerous off-duty fire fighters volunteered to join the response. PAPD officers quickly began ascending the South Tower stairs, despite their lack of proper protective equipment.

The impact of the second plane damaged the public address system in WTC 2, but an evacuation signal still rang throughout the building. As in the case of WTC 1, occupants evacuating the tower by the stairways created an obstacle for the firefighters attempting to ascend. Such impediments, combined with 100 pounds of equipment carried by each firefighter, made the climb extremely difficult, and many firefighters succumbed to exhaustion.

By this point, the response to the two crashes had grown so large that it was nearly unmanageable. FDNY officials could not keep track of its responders, and FDNY field commanders were unable to relay information among responders because their communication system was incapable of handling so many users at one time. To complicate matters, OEM headquarters was evacuated at 9:30 AM when it became apparent that other airliners (American Airlines 77 and United 93) were missing. The fate of these planes, which subsequently crashed in Arlington, Virginia, and Shanksville, Pennsylvania, respectively, are not discussed in this narrative.

Throughout the ordeal, NYPD helicopters had been investigating the possibility of rooftop rescues from WTC 2. Unfortunately, pilots found the situation to be similar to that on the North Tower rooftop, negating this option. However, as with the situation with WTC 1, this assessment was not conveyed to emergency dispatchers.

At 9:51 ~AM, an indication of the South Tower's instability came when a helicopter pilot reported that large pieces of the building appeared ready to fall. Seven minutes later, the entire structure collapsed, killing everyone left inside, people on the street below, and others in adjacent buildings. The victims included well over 600 civilians and more than 100 emergency workers. The collapse of this enormous structure generated an immense cloud of dust that spread over lower Manhattan.

NYPD helicopter teams were also filing reports chronicling the decay of the North Tower. At 10:04 AM, one pilot reported that the top 15 stories of the tower "were glowing red" from the fire. Within the next 18 minutes, various pilots reported that the tower would not be able to stand much longer. Suddenly, at 10:28, WTC 1 collapsed, killing nearly everyone inside. Miraculously, a group of 16 responders and civilians who were descending one of the building's three stairways survived the collapse.

Over the course of two hours and 14 minutes, from the beginning of the first hijacking to the collapse of the North Tower, 2,750 people perished at the World Trade Center. The FDNY lost more people (343) than any other response agency in history, while the PAPD (37) and NYPD (23) lost the most and second most officers of any police force.

The September 11, 2001, plot against the United States was the latest in a string of attacks by militant Sunni extremists that included the 1993 World Trade Center and 2000 USS *Cole* bombings. Such terrorists view Israel and western society as inherently evil forces oppressing Muslims. In 1996, Bin Ladin delivered a speech in which he declared that the United States was the leader of this oppression, the "head of the snake," and that Muslims should focus their efforts on destroying it. Khalid Sheik Mohammed, who had long been violently opposed to what he viewed as America's pro-Israel foreign policy, agreed with Bin Ladin's assessment. Mohammed saw an attack on the World Trade Center, the conspicuous landmark he viewed as the heart of the U.S. economy, as the best way to impact American foreign policy. With a shared hatred of the United States, the two terrorists joined together; Mohammed sought financing and manpower from al Qaeda, while Bin Ladin saw the opportunity for credibility and propaganda from Mohammed's plot. Once the plan was adopted, Bin Ladin had no trouble finding operatives willing to become martyrs for his Islamist ideology.

Although blame for the attacks rests squarely on the shoulders of the terrorists and the ideology they represented, numerous safety and security failures allowed their plot to reach fruition. Susceptible areas included intelligence, transportation and airport security, building design, and emergency preparedness.

In the aftermath of September 11, it became apparent that numerous intelligence shortcomings played a role in the disaster. The U.S. intelligence community, which included the Federal Bureau of Investigation (FBI), Central Intelligence Agency (CIA), and National Security Administration (NSA), suffered from resource deficit and mismanagement issues. With the end of the Cold War in the late 1980s, the United States slashed its intelligence funding. As a result, the number of essential intelligence personnel, such as translators and analysts, had dwindled. Consequently, the intelligence community faced a backlog of untranslated documents in addition to the inherent difficulty of gathering information on terrorist organizations. For example, the NSA intercepted a number of communications indicating an impending attack on September 8 to 10, 2001, but was unable to translate them until after the September 11 attacks had occurred.

Communication among various agencies involved with U.S. intelligence also suffered from lack of a unifying strategy against terrorism prior to the September 11 attacks. Each agency essentially operated independently with regard to counterterrorism, a situation largely stemming from differences in their respective mission, legal authority, and culture. To make matters worse, there was no established interagency database for sharing counterterrorism data. Further rifts in communication resulted from U.S. Justice Department procedures governing information sharing between intelligence and law enforcement officials. Such obstacles not only stifled communication among federal intelligence agencies but also suppressed information sharing among federal, state, and local officials.

Despite these difficulties, the U.S. intelligence community was relatively well informed of the threat posed by Sunni extremists, al Qaeda in particular, and plots potentially directed against the country. As far back as 1994, intelligence indicated the possible use of airliners as weapons, but this information did little to convince federal officials that such an attack could be carried out successfully within the United States. Consequently, a federal response to the threat was never formulated.

Beginning in 1998, there was a modest but steady flow of information indicating that a terrorist attack within the borders of the United States was a possibility. The prevailing opinion of the intelligence community, however, held that attacks against U.S. interests would remain overseas. By May 2001, counterterrorism officials received several tips describing various attacks planned to take place in the United States. This intelligence began increasing two months later, yet the FBI informed federal, state, and local law enforcement agencies that it had "no information indicating a credible threat of terrorist attack in the United States." As a result, federal officials did not issue a public warning, increase domestic intelligence gathering, or bolster security at borders and airports in the days prior to the attack.

Critical clues went overlooked in a number of instances. For example, on July 10, 2001, an FBI agent in Phoenix, Arizona, issued a memo to the agency's Radical Fundamentalist Unit, the Osama Bin Ladin Unit, and the International Terrorism team at the FBI's New York field office. The agent described his firsthand knowledge of an ongoing effort by Bin Ladin to have students train as pilots within the United States. The agent went on to recommend that the FBI begin working with aviation schools and gathering visa information for flight school students to guard against future aviation-related terrorism. These recommendations went unheeded.

The mind-set that discounted the possibility of attacks on U.S. soil continued in the month of August, when a foreign aviation student was arrested by the FBI's Minneapolis field office under suspicion of participating in a hijacking plot. Although the student was connected to al Qaeda, this incident was never linked to the July 10 warning, the increased flow of threatening intelligence, or the recent entry to the United States of two suspected terrorists who later took part in the hijackings. On August 6, two CIA analysts, convinced of an immediate threat against the U.S. homeland, prepared a presidential briefing entitled "Bin Ladin Determined to Strike in U.S." This warning inspired no action among members of the executive branch and was not discussed again before the September 11 attacks. Federal officials closer to the aviation threat were similarly unaware of intelligence reports. Neither the administrator of the Federal Aviation Administration (FAA) nor her deputy reviewed FAA intelligence reports with regularity, and they lacked knowledge of a considerable amount of hijacking information compiled by the agency's own intelligence unit.

The disconnect between the FAA administration and its intelligence operation is just one manifestation of the agency's misunderstanding of the threat it faced. This situation was substantiated by the failure of FAA security measures to thwart the 19 terrorists. CAPPS, one of these security elements, was based on the premise that terrorists would not be willing to die with their victims. Therefore, CAPPS only ensured that selected passengers were on the plane before their baggage was loaded onboard. CAPPS was also not well suited to profiling high-risk passengers, as its selection algorithm did not account for attributes such as national origin, ethnicity, or religion. This flawed system, however, was the best tool for screening passengers that the FAA had at the time of the attacks, since there had been no coordinated effort among federal agencies to produce a comprehensive no-fly list. In fact, at the time of the attacks, the FAA's no-fly list contained the names of just 12 of the 60,000 known or suspected terrorists identified by the U.S. State Department.

Another gap in FAA security involved the ability of passengers to carry knives of less than four inches onboard planes. The FAA had considered banning all knives from flights in 1993, but rejected the idea because such weapons would be difficult to detect with standard screening equipment. Furthermore, since no commercial U.S. airliner had been hijacked since 1986, FAA believed that the prospect of bombings overshadowed the potential for hijackings using small knives. This flaw allowed the September 11 hijackers to carry box cutters and knives onto planes without suspicion.

Once the terrorists had boarded, their mission probably was made easier by the FAA's misunderstanding of the modern terrorist threat. The FAA "Common Strategy" for managing hijackings did not consider the possibility of a suicide hijacking and directed flight crews to accede to terrorists' demands until military or law enforcement officials could handle the situation. Such a strategy meant that terrorists would have only to ask to gain entry to the cockpit through its reinforced door. The September 11 hijackers knew that they would likely not need to make such a demand, as their reconnaissance flights had taught them that cockpit doors routinely remained open or unlocked. The attackers relied on easy entry into the cockpit; in fact, they had no backup plan for being locked out.

Misjudgment of the terrorist threat to aviation was further evidenced in FAA and North American Air Defense protocols for hijackings. Several assumptions of these plans proved faulty on the morning of September 11, 2001: (1) hijackers would not attempt to conceal a plane's location, (2) there would be adequate time to react to the hijacking, and (3) the hijacking would not include a suicide-style attack. Due to these preconceived notions, air traffic controllers had difficulty recognizing the hijacking scenario. For example, controllers monitoring American Flight 11 did not recognize that the plane had been hijacked until 10 minutes after the takeover had occurred. Even then, the attack was positively confirmed only because of the terrorists' accidental radio transmissions.

As each hijacking was identified, little could be done to mitigate the situation. The hijackers disguised the location of each plane, making it difficult to dispatch military interceptor aircraft. Even if the planes' transponders had not been altered, there would not have been enough time for military jets to reach them before they were crashed.

The collapse of both buildings was attributable only in part to the impact of the planes, however. The towers had actually been designed beyond local code requirements to withstand potential impact damage. Unfortunately, the insulation used to protect the structural steel of the towers was dislodged when the planes cut through the buildings. With no protective insulation, the tower frames were exposed to extreme heat from the fires, eventually causing them to fail.

Fire suppression in large buildings often is achieved by firefighting personnel with access to functioning elevators. Such was the case in 1945, when a U.S. Army Air Force bomber accidentally collided with the seventy-eighth and seventy-ninth floors of the Empire State Building. While the resulting fire was much smaller than those ignited within WTC 1 and 2, firefighters were able to extinguish the blaze quickly, in part because of elevator service to the sixty-fifth floor. In the case of the WTC towers, however, elevators and the buildings' sprinkler systems were damaged during the plane crashes, removing this option from consideration.

The lack of elevator access was just one of the many obstacles responders faced. Rescuers rushing into the towers faced hazards such as falling debris and victims who had jumped or fallen from the buildings. As mentioned, the flow of evacuees coming in the opposite direction also slowed responders climbing the stairs.

However, these problems were overshadowed by the lack of effective communication, as firefighters had difficulty operating their radios in the building complex. Although a repeater tower had been erected to address this issue following the 1993 bombing, on September 11, 2001, many firefighters did not use the repeater channel. Furthermore, the repeater's transmission function was never engaged during the operation, meaning that while firefighters could use the channel to communicate among themselves, fire chiefs were not able to disseminate information to their companies from the tower's master handset.

The size of the response itself added to communication and coordination problems. Responders often found it difficult to communicate with one another or with field commanders because radio communication channels were overloaded. Additionally, different groups of responders operated on different radio frequencies. In the resulting confusion, critical information was lost. For example, an NYPD helicopter and an FDNY boat both witnessed and reported the collapse of the South Tower. Due to communication breakdowns, however, this information did not reach fire chiefs or firefighters within the North Tower in a timely manner. Therefore, when the order came for responders to evacuate WTC 1, many firefighters refused to leave or did not rush to escape. There were even instances in which the rivalry between NYPD and FDNY short-circuited critical attempts at communication. In one instance, NYPD officers exiting the North Tower relayed evacuation orders to firefighters, who refused to take an order from police officers.

Communication from response authorities to the buildings' occupants was also problematic, with announcements not made in a timely manner and instructions issued and then contradicted. Moreover, 911 and fire dispatch were unable to offer additional advice to workers in either tower, as operators were not receiving information from responders at the site.

The evacuation itself can be viewed as both a success and a failure. The WTC evacuation time decreased from four hours in 1993 to less than one hour in 2001. Moreover, 87% of all occupants successfully exited the building, including 99% of those located below the impacted floors. These achievements were attributed in large part to building improvements since the 1993 bombing and the regularity of fire drills.

The single largest factor limiting the number of casualties on September 11, 2001, however, was likely the fortunate circumstance that the towers were filled to less than half of their capacity at the time of the attacks. The U.S. National Institute of Standards and Technology estimated that if the buildings had been filled to capacity, a full evacuation would have taken three hours to complete and 14,000 people would have perished.

It is interesting to note that each of the towers had only three stairwells for emergency exit, despite a local building code that required four. This was allowed because the Port Authority had been created under a clause in the U.S. Constitution that exempted its buildings from being subject to local building codes. Had there been a fourth stairway in each building, it is possible that one extra escape route may have provided victims trapped on upper floors with a means of escape. That possibility would have depended on the location of the fourth stairwell. In WTC 1, because all three stairways were clustered at the building's core, they were simultaneously destroyed, trapping workers above the ninety-second floor. In contrast, the design of WTC 2 spaced the stairwells more widely throughout the building, allowing one to remain passable, as evidenced by at least one survivor making it to safety from the ninety-first floor.

With the loss of stairs and elevators, occupants of the towers' upper floors had no means of escape. The Port Authority had not developed plans for rescuing victims trapped above a fire or for rooftop rescues, despite the presence of a helipad on the South Tower. However, even if rooftop evacuation had been possible, it would not have helped the victims on the upper floors. The doors to the roof were locked, and damage to security software during the attacks prevented them from opening.

The September 11 attacks resulted in nearly 3,000 deaths and an estimated $120 billion in damage. In the months following the disaster, airlines were unable to fill planes, even with 30% fewer flights, as Americans fearful of further attacks began traveling less. The already fragile U.S. economy suffered through the loss of 1.1 million jobs over the last quarter of 2001. Seventy percent of all major layoffs during this period came from the transportation industry.

The federal government implemented a number of changes as a direct result of the attacks. Little more than a month after September 11, the Patriot Act was enacted. This law was directed at bolstering counterterrorism resources, improving border security, and undermining terrorist funding sources. The Homeland Security Act of 2002 was passed one year later, establishing the Department of Homeland Security (DHS) within the executive branch of the federal government. DHS was charged with preventing terrorism against the United States, making America less vulnerable to terrorist attacks, and assisting in the recovery from such events.

In the weeks following the attacks, U.S. authorities identified the hijackers and connected them to al Qaeda and Bin Ladin. Al Qaeda had been operating out of Afghanistan since the mid-1990s, with the blessing of the ruling political party there, the Taliban. President Bush issued an ultimatum to the Taliban requiring, among other things, that it shut down al Qaeda camps and extradite the terrorist organization's leaders. On October 7, 2001, when these requests were not met, U.S. and international military forces launched attacks on al Qaeda and Taliban strongholds, beginning what has become known as the Global War on Terrorism. While these operations have resulted in the death or detainment of a number of key al Qaeda operatives, including Khalid Sheik Mohammed, Bin Ladin has yet to be found, despite offers of $27 million in potential rewards for information leading to his capture. A new front of the Global War on Terrorism was launched in March 2003, when a military coalition led by U.S. troops invaded Iraq, based in part on alleged connections between the Iraqi government and international terrorists, including al Qaeda.

Since September 2001, there have been numerous attempts by terrorists to carry out large-scale attacks against the United States, all of which have been disrupted by U.S. and allied efforts. These failed plots include at least two plans in which commercial airliners would be flown into large buildings within the United States and another plot to bomb three planes in flight between the United States and the United Kingdom. There is also evidence that al Qaeda, in particular, has sought to acquire weapons of mass destruction, including chemical, biological, radiological, and nuclear weaponry. Terrorism experts suggest that incidents such as the September 11 attacks demonstrate that al Qaeda would not hesitate to unleash such horrific instruments on western cities.

A July 2007 report of the terrorist threat to the United States indicates that al Qaeda is adapting to counterterrorism and security improvements implemented after September 11 and is increasing its efforts to plant operatives within U.S. borders. The report also concludes that al Qaeda is continuing to plan large-scale attacks against U.S. cities and that the overall threat from Islamic militants is growing as terrorist cells become more numerous and cohesive. Shortly after the release of this threat estimate, U.S. intelligence revealed that a high-ranking al Qaeda member vowed not to rest until he had attacked the U.S. capital.

The continued threat of terrorism has not deterred the Port Authority or developers from rebuilding on the site of the World Trade Center. A new WTC 7 building was completed in 2006, five years after the attack. Architectural plans for the remainder of the site call for the construction of a mammoth, 1,776-foot-tall building to be known as Freedom Tower, standing roughly 400 feet higher than the previous North and South towers. This building will be situated among five other large skyscrapers, ranging in height from 42 to 78 stories.

REFERENCES

Bagli, Charles V. "Chase Bank Set to Build Tower by Ground Zero," *New York Times*, June 14, 2007.

BBC. "'Airlines Terror Plot' Disrupted," 2006. http://news.bbc.co.uk/2/hi/uk_news/4778575.stm.

BBC. "Investigating al-Qaeda: Overview," 2003. http://newsvote.bbc.co.uk/2/hi/south_asia/2816381.stm.

Breasted, Mary. "100,000 Leave Offices as Bomb Threats Disrupt City; Blasts Kill One and Hurt Seven," *New York Times*, August 4, 1977.

Bush, George W. Presidential Address to the Nation, October 7, 2001. www.whitehouse.gov/news/releases/2001/10/20011007-8.html.

CNN. "Bush Defends Iraq War; Details Al Qaeda Threat," July 24, 2007. www.cnn.com/2007/POLITICS/07/24/bush.

CNN. "New York: 9/11 Toxins Caused Death," May 24, 2007. www.cnn.com/2007/US/05/24/wtc.dust/index.html.

CNN. "White House Lists 10 Foiled Attacks," 2006. www.cnn.com/2006/US/02/09/whitehouse.plots/index.html.

Fahy, Rita F., and Guylène Proulx. "Human Behavior in the World Trade Center Evacuation," Fire Safety Science, Fifth International Symposium Proceedings, Melbourne, Australia, March 3–7, 1997.

Gregory, Frank, and Paul Wilkinson. "Riding Pillion for Tackling Terrorism is a High-risk Policy." In Security, Terrorism, and the UK, ISP/NSC Briefing Paper 05/01. London: The Royal Institute of International Affairs, 2005.

Homeland Security Act of 2002. 107th Congress, 2nd session, 2002.

"Hunting Bin Ladin," PBS Frontline, 1998. www.pbs.org/wgbh/pages/frontline/shows/binladin/who/interview.html.

Joint Resolution to Authorize the Use of United States Armed Forces against Iraq. 107th Congress, 2nd session, 2002.

MSNBC. "9/11 Panel Sees No Link Between Iraq, al-Qaida," 2004. www.msnbc.msn.com/id/5223932.

National Commission on Terrorist Attacks upon the United States. The 9/11 Commission Report. New York: W.W. Norton & Company, 2004.

National Institute of Standards and Technology. Final Report on the Collapse of the World Trade Center Towers. Washington, DC: U.S. Department of Commerce, 2005.

National Institute of Standards and Technology. Occupant Behavior, Egress, and Emergency Communications. Washington, DC: U.S. Department of Commerce, 2005.

Office of the Director of National Intelligence, U.S. National Intelligence Council. The Terrorist Threat to the US Homeland, National Intelligence Estimate. July 2007. www.dni.gov/press_releases/20070717_rel-ease.pdf.

U.S. Federal Bureau of Investigation. "Most Wanted Terrorist—Osama Bin Ladin." www.fbi.gov/wanted/terrorists/terbinladen.htm.

U.S. Fire Administration. The World Trade Center Bombing: Report and Analysis. Emmitsburg, MD: Author, 1993.

U.S. House of Representatives Armed Services Committee Staff. *The Investigation into the Attack on the* USS *Cole*. Washington, DC: House Armed Services Committee, 2001.

U.S. Senate Select Committee on Intelligence and U.S. House Permanent Select Committee on Intelligence. *Report of the Joint Inquiry Into the Terrorist Attacks of September 11, 2001* (redacted version). 107th Congress, 2nd session, 2002.

USA PATRIOT Act of 2001. 107th Congress, 1st session, 2001.

Wesbury, Brian S. "The Economic Cost of Terrorism. September 11, One Year Later." *International Information Programs*, September 2002, Washington, DC: U.S. Department of State. http://usinfo.state.gov/journals/itgic/0902/ijge/ijge0902.pdf.

World Trade Center. www.wtc.com.

NOTE

1. National Commission on Terrorist Attacks upon the United States, *The 9/11 Commission Report* (New York: W.W. Norton & Company, 2004).

CHAPTER II

LONDON TRANSIT BOMBINGS

On July 7, 2005, during the morning commute, four separate bombs were detonated on the London mass transit system, killing 56 people (including the 4 suicide bombers) and injuring over 700 others. It marked the deadliest attack on British soil since World War II. The coordinated attack was carried out by four British citizens, allegedly in retaliation for British involvement in the U.S. invasions of Iraq and Afghanistan. Lack of effective intelligence and insufficient deterrence and detection strategies were blamed for allowing this disaster to occur.

By the end of the twentieth century, the United Kingdom and the city of London had become familiar with the threat of terrorism from decades of violence over the political status of Northern Ireland. The attacks against the United States on September 11, 2001, however, presented British authorities with the prospect of internationally based, mass-casualty terrorism, a threat encountered only once before in the United Kingdom, with the 1988 bombing of Pan Am Flight 103 over Lockerbie, Scotland.

British officials quickly began altering the nation's intelligence, law enforcement, and emergency response systems in an effort to ensure the safety of its citizens under the new paradigm of Islamist terrorism. Several pieces of legislation were ratified by the British Parliament and members of the British intelligence community, such as the Security

Service, Secret Intelligence Service, and Government Communications Headquarters, allocated additional resources to Islamist counterterrorism. Communication and coordination among these agencies were also strengthened with the formation of the Joint Terrorism Analysis Centre (JTAC).

In London, emergency response capabilities were bolstered, as was law enforcement. The London Metropolitan Police Service added nearly 800 officers to its counterterrorism program and arrested more than 500 suspected terrorists in the four years following the September 11 attacks. Metropolitan police increased their presence and organized disaster drills near high-risk targets throughout the city. Security around Parliament buildings was tightened with the addition of police officers and installation of barriers to guard against a boat or truck bomb.

Even as officials enhanced security and prepared for a mass-casualty event, the danger of militant Islamic extremism continued to grow in and around London. In 2001, two Islamist British nationals attempted to detonate shoe bombs aboard transatlantic flights. The following year, a reporter investigating one of these attempts was kidnapped and murdered by another British-born Islamic militant in Pakistan. Also in 2002, British authorities thwarted an Islamic terror cell's plan to release cyanide gas in the London Underground. In 2003, men from Britain were involved in a suicide bombing in Tel Aviv, Israel. One year later, authorities broke up two terrorist operations in London, one involving a massive fertilizer bomb, the other involving attacks against financial targets within the United States. Meanwhile, in the years following September 11, a number of British nationals were taken prisoner from the battlefield in Afghanistan under suspicion of aiding the Taliban, and at least two more died in suicide attacks against coalition forces in Iraq.

The death of 26 Britons in an attack on a Bali nightclub in 2002 and bombings of the British Consulate and a British bank in Istanbul in 2003 further demonstrated that the United Kingdom, its citizens, and assets were principal targets for Islamic militants. The bombing of a commuter train in Madrid on March 11, 2004, not only claimed the lives of more Britons, but also demonstrated that targets in Europe, particularly "soft targets" such as elements of the transportation system, were particularly vulnerable to Islamic terrorism.

As British authorities concentrated on preventing terrorism, they also acknowledged the difficulty and magnitude of the task at hand. In a 2003 speech, the director general of the Security Service remarked:

> the reality is that we can never stop all [terrorist] attacks and no security intelligence organization in the world could do so. An attack may get through our defenses.[1]

The commissioner of the Metropolitan Police went one step further in 2004 by echoing the sentiments of two high-level British officials, remarking that a terrorist attack in London was "inevitable" and that it would be "inconceivable" and "miraculous" for the city to avoid such a fate. The following year, the British Joint Intelligence Committee (JIC), a board of intelligence agency heads, predicted that a successful attack would be carried out in the United Kingdom within the next five years.

Despite the ever-looming threat of terrorist attacks, security within the United Kingdom was seen as improving. In the spring of 2005, the JTAC prepared a confidential report stating that, at the time, there was no terrorist organization with the intent and the ability to attack within the United Kingdom. The JTAC used this assessment as a justification for lowering the nation's threat level by one category out of a seven-category system, from "severe general" to "substantial." This sense of relative safety seemed to be confirmed when, on July 6, 2005, London was selected to host the 2012 Olympic Games.

The following day, the United Kingdom was rocked by its largest mass casualty event since World War II.

Just before 7:00 AM on July 7, 2005, three men arrived by car at the train station in Luton, approximately 30 miles north of London. They parked the car and greeted a fourth man, who had been waiting for them in a nearby auto. Each man, ranging in age from 18 to 30 years, carried a backpack, giving the appearance of a group of friends setting out on a camping trip. The men then entered the train station and boarded a train destined for the King's Cross station in London. Three members of the group knew this trip well, as they had practiced it a week and a half earlier. Although their luggage and casual dress attracted some attention, it was not enough to raise suspicion during the start of the summer tourist season.

The train arrived at King's Cross just before 8:30 AM (see Exhibit 11.1). The men disembarked, embraced one another, and exchanged what appeared to be euphoric farewells. They then went separate ways into the London Underground system, also known as the Tube.

Rush hour proceeded that morning as heavy showers fell throughout the city, delaying a number of Underground trains. At 8:50 AM, commuters rushed to board a train that had just pulled into the Liverpool Street station. Among them was one of the four men from Luton. Seconds later, the bomb he was carrying exploded, killing him and 7 other people while injuring 171 others.

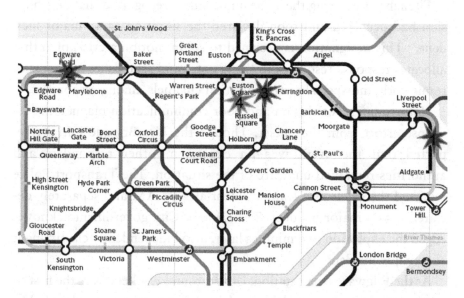

EXHIBIT 11.1   *Map of the central London Underground with the approximate locations of the bombings. Note that the fourth explosion took place on a bus at street level.*

Source: Adapted from London Transport Standard Tube map. www.tfl.gov.uk/assets/downloads/colourmap.pdf.

Less than one minute later, a second member of the group detonated his explosive aboard a train at the Edgware Road station, nearly four miles away. This blast killed 7 people, including the bomber, and left an additional 163 people injured. Another minute later, a third explosion occurred on a train traveling between the King's Cross and Russell Square stations, killing 26 people, in addition to the bomber, and injuring 340 others.

Response to the first bombing, between Liverpool Street and Aldgate stations, came quickly. The first emergency call received by authorities was to the Transport Police, one minute after the explosion. The Ambulance Service began receiving calls around the same time. The Transport Police arrived at the Aldgate station four minutes later, followed closely by the Fire Brigade, which reported to both the Aldgate and Liverpool platforms. The first ambulance on the scene reached the Liverpool Street station minutes later.

Firefighters entering the Tube immediately recognized that an explosion had occurred and soon declared the situation as a "major incident." This designation is designed to set in motion a crisis plan that allocates response resources to the disaster and establishes a command framework and special communication channels among responders.

Unfortunately, confusion and poor communication plagued the response effort from the outset. Though the Fire Brigade initially reported that the event was an explosion, other responders and authorities remained unaware of the situation. The Transport Police reported the event as a train accident at 9:08 AM and separately declared it as a major incident. The London City government acknowledged the explosion two minutes later, also independently classifying it as a major incident.

At the Edgware Road station, Underground workers were the first to reach the incident scene. On the basis of initial reports, the Underground Network Control Center notified emergency services at 8:59 AM. One minute later, the Fire Brigade had mobilized five units, but confusion surrounding the event caused the fire teams to be dispatched to the wrong location.

The first ambulance arrived at Edgware Road station at 9:12 AM. Within minutes, the paramedic crew established that an explosion had taken place and requested more ambulances for what appeared to be a mass-casualty situation. The Metropolitan Police arrived on the scene simultaneously with the first ambulance crew. Twenty minutes later, and nearly 40 minutes after the explosion, the Metropolitan Police declared a major incident at Edgware Road station. The Fire Brigade declared a major incident two minutes later.

As rescue crews raced to the scenes of the first two explosions, victims of the third explosion struggled to find a way to safety in total darkness as smoke billowed into the rail cars. Very few emergency (999) calls were placed regarding this incident initially, because the train was belowground, between two stations, and passengers were unable to make a connection via cellular phone. The first indication that a third explosion had occurred was from closed-caption television footage at 8:56 AM, six minutes before the first call was received by 999 emergency dispatch. At 9:04, four fire engines were dispatched, one to the King's Cross station and three to an erroneous location. Metropolitan Police and the Ambulance Service declared a major incident at 9:15 and 9:21 AM, respectively. Difficulties were encountered in relaying information to the Fire Brigade, however, as their hand-held radios were not operable in the isolated location of the explosion. Thus, firefighters were forced to use runners to transmit information from the site, through the Tube, and up the escalators to command posts at the street level.

Because the third bombing took place at the front of the train, which was closer to the Russell Square station, the most seriously injured passengers began emerging there, rather than at King's Cross. The first calls to 999 from Russell Square came in at 9:18 AM, 25 minutes after the explosion. Emergency medical crews began arriving 12 minutes later and the Ambulance Service declared a major incident at 9:38, 45 minutes after the explosion.

No fire crews were sent to the Russell Square station during the first hour of the response. In the absence of the Fire Brigade, the evacuation of passengers was carried out by two Underground drivers and members of the London Underground Emergency Response Unit, a small and relatively unknown quick response unit for Tube emergencies.

Meanwhile, unknown to British authorities or London residents, the fourth bomber had yet to carry out his suicide attack. Just minutes after the three initial bombings, the fourth terrorist had exited the King's Cross station and tried to call his three recently deceased partners. After failing to make contact, he reentered the Tube station and purchased a 9-volt battery, which suggests that his delay may have stemmed from technical difficulties.

After this purchase, the lone remaining terrorist visited a fast-food store and then boarded the Number 91 bus from King's Cross to Euston station. At Euston station, he switched to the Number 30 bus, traveling east. He took a seat on the lower deck of the bus, then began rummaging in his backpack before moving to the rear of the upper deck. Suddenly, at 9:47 AM, his bomb exploded, peeling back the roof of the bus and showering the streets with debris. The blast killed 13 people besides the bomber and injured at least 110 others.

In contrast to the first three bombings, this final explosion occurred aboveground, on the crowded streets of London, making it quite visible. Calls to the 999 dispatch poured in immediately. Metro police were nearby at the time of the explosion, and ambulances and firefighters began arriving within 10 minutes.

The individual response efforts to the four bombings began to take shape as a single, organized endeavor at 10:30 AM, when the Gold Coordinating Group, a committee of senior representatives from emergency services and response agencies, first gathered. The response continued to be plagued by communications issues, however, as many on-scene managers relied on cellular phones to communicate with their respective Gold commander. Cellular phone networks were inundated with calls from the public attempting to verify the status of loved ones, with carriers experiencing up to a 250% increase in calls and a 200% increase in text messages. As a result, many response managers were unable to communicate with the Gold Group.

At 11:15 AM, the commissioner of the Metropolitan Police Service gave the first public address regarding the event and advised the residents of London to stay off the streets and public transportation until further notice. Ten minutes later, all bus service was stopped. Ambulances would continue transporting victims from the bomb sites for the next hour, eventually evacuating more than 400 people. City workers then worked to restore bus and Tube service as the largest criminal investigation in London's history began to take shape. Investigators found themselves at an immediate disadvantage as hundreds of witnesses had been allowed to walk away from the crime scenes in the midst of the ensuing chaos. Consequently, less than one-quarter of those directly affected by the bombings ever gave testimony to police about their experience.

Since the attacks, a number of organizations have claimed responsibility. The first group to do so was the previously unknown Secret Organisation Group of al-Qaida in Europe. Later, Osama Bin Ladin's second in command, Ayman al-Zawaheri, issued a series of video messages in which he claimed responsibility and praised the attacks for bringing the "blessed battle" to the "enemy's land." While the targets and methods of the bombings are consistent with previous attacks by al Qaeda and those inspired by the terrorist network, investigators have been unable to verify any group's claim of responsibility for the event.

Although the specific group responsible for the attacks remains unknown, militant Islamism clearly played a role. In a video message produced before the bombings, one of the four terrorists described himself as a soldier for Islam. He went on to say that the attacks were acts of vengeance for atrocities against Muslims and that civilians are acceptable targets because they support the governments that perpetrate such oppression. The bomber's message also praised Bin Ladin and al-Zawaheri, both of whom had previously singled out the United Kingdom as a target.

While the July 7, 2005, attacks were rooted in the long-standing Islamist war against western society, the potential for such attacks within the United Kingdom was heightened by the British role in the wars in Afghanistan and Iraq. Following the September 11, 2001, attacks, the United Kingdom became part of a U.S.-led coalition of forces that toppled the Taliban regime in Afghanistan and ousted Saddam Hussein in Iraq. These military actions in predominantly Muslim lands served as a source of motivation and propaganda for Islamist terrorist organizations. As a result, these organizations increased their efforts against the United Kingdom because of its alliance with the United States and its leading role in global counterterrorism. Months before the July 7 bombings, the JTAC prepared a confidential report noting an increase in terrorist activity within the United Kingdom as a result of the country's involvement in Iraq. This assessment was later supported by statements from groups claiming responsibility for the bombings and issuing warnings to those governments involved in Iraq and Afghanistan.

Despite JTAC's awareness of increased Islamist activity within the United Kingdom, shortcomings in counterterrorism intelligence contributed to the terrorists' ability to carry out their attack. At the time of the bombings, the U.K. intelligence community was well versed in counterterrorism from its experience with Northern Ireland. While this experience strengthened communication and collaboration among intelligence agencies and departments, it also served to divert attention from the rising threat of Islamic militants. The British intelligence community became preoccupied with the threat posed by Irish hard-liners opposed to the 1998 Good Friday peace agreement between Ireland and the United Kingdom. Even in the late 1990s, British intelligence and law enforcement, which had became aware of London's growing status as a base for Islamic terrorist organizations, did not view these groups as a threat to national security. Consequently, Islamist organizations were placed low on the British authorities' list of priorities.

Following the events of September 11, 2001, Islamic terrorism grew in importance as a target of British intelligence. A continued lack of resources hampered the intelligence community's ability to identify and monitor targets, however. Trained agents were scarce, both within the United Kingdom and abroad. Intelligence agencies were overwhelmed with monitoring current targets, leaving few resources for developing new leads. Consequently, difficult decisions often had to be made regarding which intelligence sources would be investigated further and which would be have to be ignored.

None of the four bombers had ever been labeled as a potential threat. Ironically, the Security Service had encountered two of these men years before due to their apparent connection with training and insurgency in Pakistan; however, neither was considered an immediate threat to the United Kingdom. Months before the July 7 attacks, an intelligence report describing the travels of one of these men to and from Pakistan with a Muslim extremist was brought to the attention of the Security Service. It was not until after the bombings that the Security Service was able to identify him, however.

The ability of the bombers to evade identification before the attacks was further facilitated by the British mischaracterization of terrorists within the United Kingdom. All four bombers were British nationals, three of whom were born and raised in the United Kingdom. The recruitment of such terrorists within the country was made possible, in part, by increased liberties and the nurturing of diversity in British society. Like Shoko Asahara, whose cult exploited Japanese civil liberties to conduct attacks against the Tokyo subway system in 1995, Islamists had taken note of this opportunity and exploited it to attract recruits and funding.

The fact that the July 7 attacks were suicide bombings was equally unexpected. British intelligence recognized that such acts of terrorism were a possibility as early as 2002 but did not consider them to be a domestic threat. Prior to July 2005, Britons had carried out suicide bombings in Israel and Iraq, but never within the United Kingdom. Traditionally, authorities believed that Islamist suicide bombers would not come from Europe because the ideological culture and extremist population required for long-term indoctrination of recruits was not present in the West. The July 7 bombings demonstrated that this radicalization

can occur relatively quickly, however, as one of the bombers was a recent convert to Islam.

As the terrorists began preparations for the attack, they found materials and information readily available. Each device was constructed
with inexpensive, commercially available chemicals using guidance
from Internet sources and possibly advice from someone with bomb-
making experience.

The damage caused by the bombs was largely a result of the selected
targets. With such a dense population, the Tube trains at rush hour and
a crowded bus created opportunities for mass casualties. Additionally,
damaging the infrastructure familiar to and heavily utilized by London
residents would cause widespread psychological impact. Moreover, the
public transportation system provided the terrorists with easy access to
carry out their attacks.

In the hours after the attacks, the response effort suffered from confusion surrounding the four explosions, communications problems, and
gaps in predisaster planning. The confusion brought about by the blasts
is evidenced by the conflicting calls received by 999 operators that resulted in fire engines being dispatched to the wrong locations. This dis-
order resulted in the breakdown of emergency procedures, such as the
failure of the emergency services to work cooperatively. At each bombing site, each response agency made its own declaration of a major incident, despite guidance in the London Emergency Service Procedures
Manual implying that one service make the initial call on behalf of all
others at the scene.

The temporal and spatial proximity of the bombings served to further complicate matters, as responders struggled to handle numerous
incidents simultaneously. For instance, the response to the second
bombing was delayed, in part, because emergency services were already
consumed by the first bombing, which had been reported only minutes
before. Additionally, response to the Russell Square Underground station and the bus bombing were impeded because the two locations were
in such close proximity that ambulances attending to each site inter-
fered with one another.

Communication problems among emergency workers, local authorities, and the public were another impediment to the response effort. These difficulties began with the first explosion, as Tube passengers were unable to alert authorities or receive instructions. The trains contained no means for passengers to communicate with the driver or with any other information source. Since the targeted trains were underground, cellular phones were ineffective. Furthermore, the drivers had no way of communicating with the control center or emergency services, as the radios on all three bombed trains were antiquated and did not work properly.

Communication within the tunnels was similarly problematic for responding authorities. The British Transport Police was the only emergency service that had radios capable of communicating underground. Even the London Underground Emergency Response Unit, whose primary responsibility is emergencies on the Tube network, did not have this capability. Furthermore, at the Russell Square station, none of the response agencies could communicate using radios, as the blast damaged the Transport Police's local antenna. Responders encountered these issues despite a formal review of a Tube fire in 1988 that highlighted the lack of underground communications and called for the development of a system to alleviate the problem.

Communication between ambulance crews and dispatchers was equally problematic. The Ambulance Service normally employs two-radio channels during emergency events, with the control room instructing employees as to which channel to use by means of an initial cellular phone call. On July 7, ambulance managers found both channels overloaded, owing to the massive number users and the fact that both channels were being routed through a single operator. As a result, only 10 to 15% of radio calls were successful, and requests for additional supplies and paramedics often fell through the cracks. Before long, ambulances at all four sites began running out of the most basic supplies, such as tourniquets and fluids.

The overloaded cellular network created numerous problems for emergency services that relied on mobile phones. Ironically, a measure known as the Access Overload Control (ACCOLC) was developed to allow emergency responders to use cellular phones in just such a situation. ACCOLC is designed to free mobile networks for emergency use by blocking all nonauthorized users within a given geographical area. The Gold Coordinating Group decided not to use this technology, however, due to the potential for increasing panic among the public and because many responders in the field were not equipped with AC-COLC-enabled phones.

The lack of contingency plans for communications issues was but one of several gaps in emergency planning that came to light on July 7, 2005. Another such oversight became evident when ambulances and fire engines were not on hand for the victims emerging from the Russell Square station. Emergency plans did not call for responders to be deployed to each end of an Underground link during a disaster. Consequently, all fire and medical personnel responding to the third bombing were initially dispatched only to the King's Cross station. Another planning issue involved the London Underground Emergency Response Unit, which was required to rapidly attend disaster scenes while obeying standard traffic laws, using no flashing emergency lights, and even paying tolls. Finally, emergency plans did not include provisions for utilizing all available medical resources. The plans called for distributing victims evenly to each of the 11 local hospitals with large emergency departments. This specification did not account for the assistance of a number of smaller hospitals located throughout the city. In one instance, a smaller hospital adjacent to Russell Square was not called on for medical assistance. Fortunately, when hospital staff discovered the crisis in close proximity, they responded swiftly by establishing a field hospital for the wounded.

London recovered quickly following the July 7 bombings. Bus service was restored to the city by 5:00 AM the following day, and most of the Tube trains began running by the next morning. For two weeks, the city made steady progress in dealing with the aftermath of the attacks.

Then, on July 21, 2005, the transit system was again disrupted by terrorism. Several men attempted to stage an attack mimicking the July 7 bombings. Fortunately, none of the four explosive devices placed on three trains and one bus detonated completely, and no one was injured. Six men eventually were arrested, and by July 2007, four had been convicted of conspiracy to murder. At least one of these felons cited the British role in the Iraqi War as motivation for the attempted attack.

The July 7, 2005, bombings were the first successful suicide bombings in Western Europe. Experts predict that these attacks will continue and possibly spread throughout Europe and the United States as Islamist extremists attempt to combat western influences and spread their ideology. This theory is supported by a June 2007 episode in which Islamic militants carried out a suicide bombing on the Glasgow airport one day after their failed attempt to detonate two car bombs in west London. The lack of a large radical population in the West remains an impediment to terrorist recruitment, though, which suggests that such attacks are unlikely to become commonplace.

Since the London transit attacks, the United Kingdom has taken additional steps to prevent future terrorist acts. In August 2005, the British government passed legislation permitting increased surveillance of suspected terrorists and refusal of asylum to religious radicals and those with connections to terrorism. Among the thousands of people deported under this new law was a militant Muslim cleric who had influenced one of the July 7 bombers. The British government has been further preparing for the threat of new terrorist attacks by developing an underground communications infrastructure, working more closely with local police and emergency services, and reallocating resources to counterterrorism intelligence.

REFERENCES

Aylwin, Christopher J., et al. "Reduction in Critical Mortality in Urban Mass Casualty Incidents: Analysis of Triage, Surge, and Resource Use After the London Bombings on July 7, 2005," *Lancet* 368 (2006): 2219–2225.

BBC. "Bali Death Toll Set at 202," February 19 2003. http://news
.bbc.co.uk/1/hi/world/asia-pacific/2778923.stm.

BBC. "Race Hate Cleric Faisal Deported," May 25, 2007. http://news
.bbc.co.uk/2/hi/uk_news/6691701.stm.

BBC. "7 July: The Investigation." http://news.bbc.co.uk/1/shared/spl/hi/
uk/05/london_blasts/investigation/html/introduction.stm.

BBC. "Three on London Terror Charges," November 17, 2002. http://
news.bbc.co.uk/1/hi/england/2198228.stm.

Britten, Nick. "Locals Shun the Tipton Taliban," *Daily Telegraph*,
January 27, 2005.

CNN. "4 Found Guilty in London Bomb Plot," July 10, 2007. www.cnn
.com/2007/WORLD/europe/07/09/britain.july21/index.html.

CNN. "U.S. Journalist Daniel Pearl Is Dead, Officials Confirm,"
February 22, 2002. http://archives.cnn.com/2002/WORLD/asiapcf/
south/02/21/missing.reporter/index.html.

Cowan, Rosie. "Attack on London Is Inevitable," *The Guardian*, March
17, 2004.

"Deporting Hatred," *The Times* (London), August 6, 2005.

Giles, Jim, and Michael Hopkin. "Psychologists Warn of More Suicide
Attacks in the Wake of London Bombs," *Nature* 436 (2005): 308–309.

Gregory, Frank, and Paul Wilkinson."Riding Pillion for Tackling Ter-
rorism Is a High-Risk Policy." In *Security, Terrorism, and the UK, ISP/
NSC* Briefing Paper 05/01. London: Royal Institute of International
Affairs, 2005.

Harrison, David, Andrew Alderson, and Bruce Johnston. "Forceful,
Persistent, Patient: Unraveling the Bombing Plot," *Daily Telegraph*,
August 17, 2005.

Hughes, G. "The London Bombings of 7 July 2005: What Is the Main
Lesson?" *Emergency Medicine Journal* 23 (2006): 666.

Jones, David Martin, and M. L. R. Smith. "Greetings from the
Cybercaliphate: Some Notes on Homeland Insecurity," *International
Affairs* 81 (2005): 925–950.

Leppard, David. "Britain Under Attack as Bombers Strike at Airport,"
The Times (London), July 1, 2007.

London Assembly 7 July Review Committee. "Report of the 7 July Review Committee." London: Greater London Authority, 2006.

Manningham-Buller, Eliza. Lecture, City of London Police Headquarters, October 16, 2003.

Office of the President of the United States. "Progress Report on the Global War on Terrorism." Washington, DC: US Department of State, 2003.

McGrory, Daniel, and Zahid Hussain. "New Wave of British Terrorists Are Taught at Schools, Not in the Mountains," *The Times* (London), July 14, 2005.

Page, Jeremy, David Lister, and Patrick Foster. "Airport Bomb Suspects Left Behind Suicide Note Detailing Their Motives," *The Times* (London), July 5, 2007.

Ressa, Maria. "Sources: Reid Is al Qaeda Operative," CNN, December 6, 2003. www.cnn.com/2003/WORLD/asiapcf/southeast/01/30/reid.alqaeda.

Schuster, Henry. "Transit Systems Are Frequent Targets," July 7, 2005. www.cnn.com/2005/US/07/07/schuster.column.transit/index.html.

Sciolino, Elaine, Don Van Natta Jr., and Héléne Fouquet. "June Report Led Britain to Lower Its Terror Alert," *New York Times*, July 19, 2005.

Syle, Murray. "Nerve Gas and the Four Noble Truths," *The New Yorker*, April 1, 1996, pp. 56–71.

U.K. House of Commons. *Report of the Official Account of the Bombings in London on 7th July 2005*. London: The Stationery Office, 2006.

U.K. Intelligence and Security Committee. *Report into the London Terrorist Attacks on 7 July 2005*(redacted version). London: The Stationery Office, 2006.

NOTE

1. Manningham-Buller, Eliza. Lecture at the City of London Police Headquarters, October 16, 2003.

PART THREE

NATURAL DISASTERS

Natural disasters occur every day, throughout the world. They come in many different forms, including avalanches, droughts, earthquakes, floods, hurricanes, landslides, tornadoes, tsunamis, wildfires, and volcanic eruptions. While every geographical area is susceptible to multiple types of natural disasters, it would be rare for a single location to experience the entire range of possibilities. Coastal communities are particularly prone to hurricanes, tsunamis, and flooding of low-lying areas. Seismically active areas face greater risk of earthquake and volcanic eruption. Less inhabited areas, particularly those faced with drought conditions, are at risk for wildfires, while steep terrain provides ideal conditions for landslides, including avalanches in locations where severe winter weather is prevalent. Tornadoes tend to be more random in terms of where they touch down, although there are "alleys" where the climate and topography make these sites a more likely target.

Unlike man-made accidents, natural disasters generally are considered acts of God and therefore not preventable. Consequently, our sole means of minimizing the risk of natural disasters is through the way in which we respond to these events before, during, and after they occur. Our response can dramatically affect the associated consequences in terms of fatalities, injuries, property damage, and environmental degradation.

In many instances, we are forewarned about an impending natural disaster and can employ measures to stave off the worst effects. Advances in weather forecasting have been a particularly important development in this regard. Monitoring of earth movement and moisture content have also helped, although this information provides more of a general indication of a developing hazard rather than a precise prediction of when a problem might occur. Unfortunately, even with these improvements, the human element creeps in, with people either ignoring the warning signs or authorities underestimating the amount of planning and resources required to mitigate the wrath of these events when they do occur.

The case studies that you are about to read span a period of 30 years. They represent various types of natural disasters occurring in different geographical locations. Some were localized in terms of their impact while others inflicted massive and widespread damage. All are notable in terms of human failure in response to the event and the types of corrective actions that were taken in the aftermath of the tragedy.

CHAPTER 12

WRECK OF THE
EDMUND FITZGERALD

O n November 10, 1975, the SS *Edmund Fitzgerald* (see Exhibit 12 .1) sank in Lake Superior during a freak early-winter storm. Of the 29 crew members aboard, none was ever found, motivating Gordon Lightfoot to memorialize the tragedy in a famous song. A variety of risk factors have been cited as contributing to the *Fitzgerald*'s loss, including greedy economic policies and captain's pride.

Powerful autumn storms have long wreaked havoc on Great Lakes shipping vessels, destroying countless ships since the late seventeenth century. In early November 1975, a weather disturbance began taking shape over the plains of the central United States. This storm would strengthen as it moved northward over the course of three days, eventually crossing over Lake Superior and precipitating one of the worst shipping disasters in modern history.

The SS *Edmund Fitzgerald* was introduced into operation in 1958. Measuring 729 feet long, 75 feet wide, and 39 feet deep, it was the largest vessel on the Great Lakes until the early 1970s. On the morning of November 9, 1975, the *Fitzgerald* was being loaded with iron ore pellets for a trip from Superior, Wisconsin, to Detroit, Michigan. Like many other Great Lakes ships during that time of year, the *Fitzgerald* was attempting to make a late-season voyage to supply factories with stockpiles of raw materials for the winter. There seemed to be no major problems encountered in loading the massive amount of iron ore onto

EXHIBIT 12.1   *SS* Edmund Fitzgerald

Source: National Oceanic and Atmospheric Administration, "NOAA Scientists Re-Analyze Weather Conditions During Wreck of the Edmund Fitzgerald." *www.noaanews .noaa.gov/stories2006/s2633.htm.*

the ship that morning, though personnel on the shore would later claim to have seen the ship's crew working on the hatch covers after loading.

Just after 2:00 PM on November 9, the *Fitzgerald,* under the command of 37-year veteran captain Ernest McSorley, embarked on its journey. Two hours into the trip, the ship encountered the SS *Arthur M. Anderson,* a cargo vessel with Captain Jesse Cooper at the helm, traveling to Gary, Indiana, along a route similar to the *Fitzgerald*'s.

An hour before the *Fitzgerald*'s departure, the National Weather Service (NWS) predicted storms in the Lake Superior area for the next day. By early evening on November 9, the NWS issued gale warnings (winds of 39 to 54 mph) for the entirety of Lake Superior. The winds were predicted to be easterly during the night, southeasterly the following morning, and west to southwest by the afternoon of November 10. The NWS further advised that there would be rain, thunderstorms, and waves of 8 to 15 feet. Early on November 10, the NWS upgraded its forecast to a storm warning (winds of 55 mph or more) and predicted northeast winds eventually becoming northwesterly for the following day.

Upon receiving the storm warning, Captains McSorley and Cooper conferred and decided to change their course. The new course would take them northward along the Canadian coast, offering greater protection from the wind blowing out of the northeast and the waves it would produce. This maneuver was a widely accepted practice among Great Lakes vessels under such conditions. The two vessels continued along this course until the early afternoon.

Just before 2:00 PM on November 10, Captain Cooper decided to change the *Anderson's* course slightly to account for the changing direction of the wind, which was starting to blow out of the northwest (see Exhibit 12.2). This shift in wind direction left the two vessels exposed to large waves caused by the high winds, which were now blowing over open Superior waters rather than land. The *Fitzgerald* radioed the *Anderson* that she would stay on her current course, though she was "rolling some."

At 3:00 PM, Captain Cooper radioed to Captain McSorley that he thought the *Fitzgerald* might be too close to an area of shallow water known as the Six Fathom Shoal. Thirty minutes later, Captain McSorley notified the *Anderson* that "I have a fence rail down, have lost a couple of vents and have a list [the ship had begun to lean to one side]." He further informed Captain Cooper that both of the *Fitzgerald's* pumps were working to remove water that had begun to flood the ship. About 4:10, Captain McSorley radioed the *Anderson* that his ship had lost the use of both of its radars and asked Captain Cooper to help him navigate to an area known as Whitefish Point on the Michigan coast (see Exhibit 12.2).

Captain McSorley attempted to determine his position using a radio indicator from a beacon stationed at Whitefish Point, but he could not

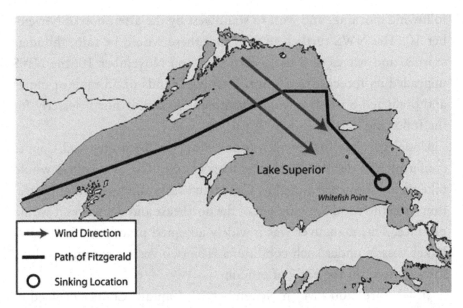

EXHIBIT 12.2   *Map of Lake Superior depicting the approximate route of the* Fitzgerald. *Winds from the northwest direction blew over a large area of water creating big waves for the* Fitzgerald.

Source: Adapted from Steve Ackerman and John Knox, "The Sinking of the SS Edmund Fitzgerald—November 10, 1975." *http://cimss.ssec.wisc.edu/wxwise/fitz.html.*

locate the signal. At 4:39, the coast guard notified the *Fitzgerald* that the beacon was not operating. About 20 minutes later, Captain McSorley contacted another ship in the area, the Swedish vessel *Avafors*, at which time he was informed that the radio beacon at Whitefish Point was still not operating. During the conversation, Captain McSorley remarked that his ship had a "bad list," was taking on heavy seas over the ship's deck, and was in one of the worst seas he had ever encountered.

At 7:00 PM, the *Anderson* contacted the *Fitzgerald* and asked about its situation. Captain McSorley replied, "We're holding our own." Twenty minutes later, the *Fitzgerald* could not be found on the *Anderson*'s radar. Even though the latter ship's crew could see the shore 20 miles away, they could not find the *Fitzgerald* on the horizon.

From 7:20 to 8:30 PM, the *Anderson* attempted to contact the *Fitzgerald* on VHF-FM radio-telephone, but did not receive a response. At 8:32 PM, Captain Cooper notified the coast guard that the *Fitzgerald* might have been lost.

A search for the ship and any survivors was launched immediately. The *Anderson* and two other nearby ships, the *William Clay Ford* and the *Hilda Marjanne*, scoured the area where the *Fitzgerald* was thought to have gone down. A lifeboat, raft, life preserver, and various pieces of debris were found, but no survivors or bodies of any of the 29 officers and crew were ever recovered. After three days, the search was called off.

Since that time, there have been numerous expeditions to the bottom of Lake Superior to survey the ship's wreckage and determine the cause of its sinking. When initially discovered, the ship was found torn in two, with much of the lifesaving equipment still in place.

In 1995, 20 years after the sinking, the ship's bell was recovered during the final expedition to the *Fitzgerald* wreckage. The bell has since been restored and is now on permanent display at the Great Lakes Shipwreck Museum on Whitefish Point. It is rung each November 10 in memory of the 29 officers and crewmen who perished that day on board the *Fitzgerald*.

While the actual cause of the *Fitzgerald*'s disappearance is shrouded in mystery, a number of reasons have been given as to why the ship sank so abruptly. As is the case in all major disasters, multiple risk factors were at work that collectively doomed the *Fitzgerald* and its crew.

A popular theory is that the hatch covers on the ship's cargo hold were not weathertight and allowed water to flood the ship (see Exhibit 12.3). As waves crashed across the *Fitzgerald*, water was held on deck by the 15-inch wall that surrounded it. The unsealed hatch covers allowed this water to drain down into the cargo area, where it was partially absorbed by the cargo of iron ore. The weight of the water in

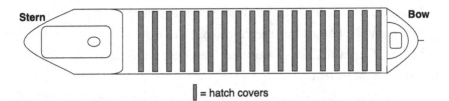

EXHIBIT 12.3   *Schematic aerial view of the* Fitzgerald *depicting locations of the hatch covers*

the hold caused the ship to sit progressively lower, allowing more water from waves to reach the deck and pour down into the hold. Since bulk cargo like iron ore tends to clog pumping systems, the pumps working to drain the cargo hold would have been unable to remove water from the compartment quickly enough to overcome the rate of flooding by the waves. The crew remained unaware of the rising water level in the hold because the only way to check was through visual observation. The crew would have seen the water only once it had submerged the cargo. It was equally difficult to know if the ship was sitting lower in the water, since the *Fitzgerald* carried no instruments to detect a change in the ship's list or its height in the water. The increased weight in the cargo eventually caused the vessel to sit dangerously low in the water, at which time it was struck by a large wave. The *Fitzgerald*, no longer buoyant, was unable to recover and sank instantly.

Several explanations have been offered as to why the hatch covers were unable to seal out water. One theory suggests that the initial source of flooding was through hatch cover damage that occurred during the event that caused the *Fitzgerald* to lose its fence rail and vent covers. The National Transportation Safety Board (NTSB), in its post-accident investigation, concluded that the force of the water on deck would have been sufficient to damage or collapse the hatch covers.

A second argument is that the hatch covers were already damaged at the outset of the voyage, bringing into question deferred maintenance as a risk factor. The last coast guard inspection of the *Fitzgerald* found four minor structural defects to hatch covers that were to be repaired at the conclusion of the 1975 shipping season. The decision to defer repair until the end of the season indicates how schedule constraints may have played a role in this disaster. With such a short shipping season on the Great Lakes, there was constant pressure to make the next shipment as soon as possible in order to maximize the amount of product moved. Beyond pressure to defer what was believed to be nonurgent maintenance, a tight schedule may have pushed crews to ignore the warning signs of an impending storm or be willing to accept the risks associated with sailing under those conditions.

A third hypothesis is that the crew of the *Fitzgerald* did not properly seal the hatch covers after loading the vessel in Superior. In not following standard procedures, the seals were not verified as watertight. Hence, water entry into the cargo hold became more likely, as did the resulting destructive chain of events.

Whatever the reason for seepage of water through the hatch covers, the rate at which flooding occurred clearly was exacerbated by the lowering of the ship's assigned freeboard. "Freeboard" is the distance between the water and the height of the ship deck (see Exhibit 12.4). When first built, the *Fitzgerald* had been assigned a minimum freeboard of 14 feet 9 ¼ inches by the coast guard. From 1969 to 1973, however, the *Fitzgerald* was granted three reductions in its minimum freeboard, eventually lowering it to 11½ feet. This new minimum height meant that the *Fitzgerald*'s deck would be more than three feet closer to the water, a situation that further exposed the deck and hatch covers to flooding from waves.

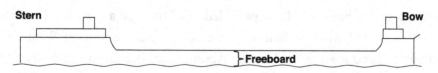

EXHIBIT **12.4**   *Schematic profile of the* Fitzgerald *depicting freeboard*

These freeboard reductions bring into question the role of economic pressure as a risk factor. In order to maximize profit in the shipping industry, priority is placed on moving the most cargo possible at the least expense. Therefore, in addition to a demanding schedule, there is a desire to maximize the load on each shipment. One way to achieve greater capacity is by lowering the freeboard.

Another theory posed to explain the sinking of the *Fitzgerald* is the grounding of the ship on Six Fathom Shoals. Captain McSorley reported damage to the ship's fence rail and vents as it sailed near the shoals, only minutes after Captain Cooper of the *Anderson* had expressed concern about the *Fitzgerald*'s position with respect to shallow water. The *Fitzgerald*, like many Great Lakes vessels at the time, was thought to be particularly vulnerable to damage from groundings because of decreased freeboard. Concern for such groundings had been validated by a reported increase in the number of groundings during docking operations due to decreased freeboard. Moreover, repeated groundings tend to reduce the thickness of the ship's hull, decreasing its strength. As vessels typically were dry docked only once every five years, there would be ample time for the effects of these incidents to accumulate before being discovered and repaired.

The lack of detail on charts used by most Great Lakes vessels for navigation at the time would have made a severe grounding more probable. Lake Survey Chart Number 9, which was most likely the chart used by Captain McSorley, made no mention of Six Fathoms Shoals. The *Fitzgerald* was also not equipped with a fathometer, a device for determining the depth of water when other instruments fail.

The *Fitzgerald*'s ability to survive the storm was also hampered by poor communication. Even though contact with the *Anderson* was steady, the *Fitzgerald* was not able to communicate with other information sources that could have provided much-needed assistance. Notable in this regard was the failure of the coast guard station at Whitefish Point to produce a signal beacon. Absent radar detection capability and needing to rely on more conventional means, the *Fitzgerald* was heavily dependent on visual landmarks.

It is also hypothesized that the *Fitzgerald* may have been a victim of poor design. At the time, Great Lakes vessels, typically thought to operate in relatively calm waters, were built with fewer structural constraints than oceangoing vessels. This translated into reduced hull thickness and less overall structural integrity in terms of the vessel's ability to withstand the pressure induced by large storm waves. The low strength of the *Fitzgerald*, combined with the unusually large waves produced by the storm, may have caused the vessel to break in two, causing it to sink rapidly.

One factor over which there was little control was the accuracy of weather forecasting at the time. Most significantly, the NWS was unable to accurately predict wave height for Lake Superior on November 10. At 4:39 PM, the NWS predicted wave heights from 8 to 16 feet, considerably lower than the actual 18- to 25-foot swells observed by the *Anderson*. Knowledge of the actual condition of the seas during the voyage may have prompted Captain McSorley to delay his departure time or alter his course.

This raises the question of whether arrogance played a role as a relevant risk factor. One could argue that Captain McSorley's 37 years of experience might have created a mind-set that there was no circumstance on the Great Lakes that he could not handle. Not to say that he relished the opportunity to defeat an early-winter storm, but one can speculate that it did little to deter him from proceeding. This may also explain why Captain McSorley did not alter course to the extent that the *Anderson* did and why he did not call for help, even though it was clear for several hours that the *Fitzgerald* was in serious trouble.

Finally, a lack of planning and preparedness may have contributed to the *Fitzgerald*'s demise. The ship's lifesaving and distress signaling methods were seemingly inadequate to allow for any hope of rescuing the crew. They had been supplied with an adequate number of life rafts, boats, and vests, and had conducted frequent fire and lifeboat drills. Even during drills when the ship was docked and in good weather, however, it was impossible to launch a lifeboat in less than 10 minutes. Also, a device known as an emergency position indicating radio beacon

(EPIRB), designed to float free from the ship and transmit an emergency signal, was available at the time. This signal could have notified local vessels and coast guard stations of an accident and provided responding vessels with a well-defined area to search for survivors. The *Fitzgerald*, unfortunately, was not required to carry an EPIRB and did not have one. Without a distress signal, the *Anderson* did not contact the coast guard about the *Fitzgerald*'s possible sinking for over an hour after its disappearance from the radar screen.

Regardless, the coast guard would have been of little use in this instance. Even if it had been contacted promptly after the sinking of the *Fitzgerald*, the only coast guard vessel in the area capable of withstanding the conditions on Lake Superior that night was the cutter *Woodrush*, stationed 300 miles away. If notified immediately and responding at top speed, it would have taken the *Woodrush* nearly 20 hours to reach the accident site.

The NTSB officially concluded that the primary cause of the accident was flooding of the ship's cargo hold through non-weathertight hatch covers. The board ruled out snapping of the ship's hull based on a structural analysis and concluded that the ship most likely broke in two when it hit the seafloor. The NTSB also discarded grounding as a possibility, based on a reconstruction of the *Fitzgerald*'s most probable path and a lack of visual damage on the hull. Not everyone agreed with this finding, however. For some, the *Fitzgerald*'s first reported damage in the vicinity of the shoals and its subsequent deterioration remains too much of a coincidence.

As is often the case, if one or more of the cited risk factors had been mitigated due to better risk management, the incident might have been prevented or the consequences might have been less severe. One is left to ponder whether maintenance on the hatch covers while in port would have prevented water from entering the cargo hold or delayed it sufficiently for the crew to survive. If the freeboard had not been reduced, how much less water would have crossed the deck and into the holds and how much less force would have been applied to the radar equipment?

There have been numerous changes in maritime regulations, industry practice, and technology since the time of the *Fitzgerald*'s sinking, much of it in response to the wake-up call delivered by this catastrophe. Within two years of the disaster, all large commercial vessels were required to have fathometers on board. Other communication and tracking technology advances were also implemented on Great Lakes ships, including use of Long Range Aid to Navigation (Loran-C) systems that were previously employed only by oceangoing vessels and, more recently, the introduction of global positioning systems (GPS). Emergency preparedness also has been upgraded, with the coast guard having larger rescue vessels permanently stationed in the region and improved maintenance procedures in place to ensure that a sufficient number of vessels are on hand for rescue procedures during the Lake Superior storm season. Personal lifesaving equipment has evolved to better insulate sailors from the icy waters of the Great Lakes; personal radio position beacons and flashing lights are also available to transmit the location of individual survivors. Finally, weather prediction has made significant advances in the areas of improved understanding of low-pressure systems and wave growth, use of more sophisticated weather models, enhanced radar technology, a network of observation buoys on the Great Lakes, and better methods for communicating weather information to vessels.

It is a testament to the effectiveness of these developments that in 1998, 23 years after the disaster, a strong autumn storm, similar to the one that sank the *Fitzgerald*, crossed the western Great Lakes without causing a single casualty. An unfortunate but cruel reality is that it may have taken a disaster of *Fitzgerald*-like proportions to bring proper attention to the management of shipping risks on the Great Lakes.

REFERENCES

Bishop, Hugh E. "*Edmund Fitzgerald*, 25 Years of Speculation, Fascination and Grieving," *Lake Superior Magazine* 22 (2000): 18–24.

Lombardy, Kirk. "Great Lakes Storm November 9–11, 1998: *Edmund Fitzgerald* Remembered," *Mariners Weather Log* 46 (2002): 4–10.

McCall, Timothy Craig. "S.S. *Edmond Fitzgerald* Online." www.ssefo .com.

National Transportation Safety Board. "Marine Accident Report: SS *Edmund Fitzgerald* Sinking in Lake Superior on November 10, 1975." Report No. NTSB-MAR-78-3. Washington, DC: Author, 1978.

National Weather Service. "Storm Warning: Advancements in Marine Forecasting Since the *Edmund Fitzgerald*." www.crh.noaa.gov/mqt/ Fitzgerald.

Noland, Jenny. "The Fateful Voyage of the *Edmund Fitzgerald*," *Detroit News.* http://info.detnews.com/history/story/index.cfm?id= 114&category=events.

CHAPTER 13

ERUPTION OF MOUNT ST. HELENS

Following two months of increasing seismic activity, Mount St. Helens (see Exhibit 13.1) erupted in full fury on May 18, 1980, leaving a path of destruction that completely changed the landscape of the mountain and the region. The blast and ensuing landslides, mudflows, and eruption cloud killed 57 people and over 7,000 large game animals, destroyed 27 bridges, ruined 200 homes, and toppled 4 billion board-feet of timber. While seemingly prepared for this eruption, authorities were caught off guard by the type of eruption that occurred, communication required to notify the public, and resources necessary to respond to such a widespread disaster.

Off the northwest coast of the U.S. mainland, the floor of the Pacific Ocean is sliding underneath North America under the forces of plate tectonics. For 37 million years, this collision has led to the formation of volcanoes in the area now occupied by the modern Cascade Range in Washington state and British Columbia (see Exhibit 13.2). More than 40,000 years ago, in what is now southern Washington, a new volcano began forming in this chain. Later named for a British diplomat by eighteenth-century explorers, Mount St. Helens has grown to become the most active and violent volcano in the continental United States over the past 4,500 years.

Since 2,500 BC, Mount St. Helens has not been dormant for more than 500 years at a time, often with gaps of only a couple of hundred

EXHIBIT 13.1   *Mount St. Helens on March 17, 1980, the day before eruption*

Source: *Harry Glicken, U.S. Geological Survey, March 17, 1980. http://vulcan.wr.usgs.gov/Imgs/Jpg/MSH/Images/MSH80_st_helens_from_johnston_ridge_05-17-80.jpg.*

years between major eruptions. During the mid-1800s, a series of eruptions took place, with a dozen or more reported by explorers, such as Lewis and Clarke, and early pioneers. After an eruption in 1857, however, the volcano entered a period of dormancy.

With little to no activity coming from the mountain, Mount St. Helens sat in relative obscurity for more than a century. The once-explosive volcano became better known for its beauty than the hazard it presented to the surrounding region. By the late 1960s, however, a small number of scientists began to realize the potential for an impending disaster. An article by three of these researchers in 1975 warned that the volcano would awaken, "perhaps before the end of the century." Three years later, another publication outlined the type and extent of the hazards that the volcano presented and called for increased monitoring and emergency preparedness. On the morning of March 18, 1980, these

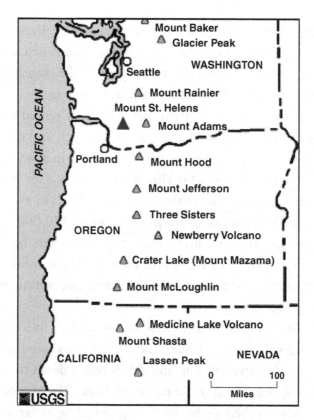

EXHIBIT 13.2　*Location of major Cascade Range volcanoes*

Source: Lyn Topinka, U.S. Geological Survey. *http://vulcan
.wr.usgs.gov/Imgs/Gif/MSH/SlideSet/1.gif.*

warnings proved to be one of the most accurate predictions of a destructive geologic event in history.

According to witnesses, the morning of March 18 was exceptionally
quiet on Mount St. Helens. The usual sound of birdsong was noticeably
absent as a handful of geologists, hikers, and campers started their
day. Just after 8:30 AM, the silence was suddenly broken by the rum-
bling of the ground.

A 5.1-magnitude earthquake shook the mountain, causing its north
side to collapse. David Johnston, a geologist monitoring the volcano at
a distance of five miles from the snowcapped peak, sent out a frantic

radio transmission as the tremor began: "Vancouver, Vancouver, this is it!" In an instant, 3 billion cubic yards of rock slid down the mountain at speeds of up to 155 miles per hour, forming the largest landslide in recorded history. Johnston was never heard from again.

The north side of the mountain had essentially served as the volcano's "cork," holding back an eruption of hot rock and gas. With this obstruction removed, the mountain's pressurized magma chamber exploded with the energy of 500 Hiroshima bombs. Hot gas and rock were thrown out of the side of the volcano at speeds in excess of 2,200 miles per hour, instantly destroying or damaging 150,000 acres of forest. At nearly the same instant, vertical eruptions began, belching a column of ash more than 15 miles into the sky. The combined effect of these explosions ripped the top from the mountain, cutting its height by more than 1,300 feet.

The heat of the eruption melted the snow and ice covering the volcano, triggering volcanic mudslides known as lahars (see Exhibit 13.3). Waves of mixed snowmelt, ash, and debris rolled down the smoldering mountain at speeds of up to 50 miles per hour. The lahars wiped out millions of trees in their paths, eventually traveling as far as 120 miles down the North Fork Toutle River to the Cowlitz and Columbia rivers, knocking out bridges and altering river channels along the way.

A cloud of ash continued to rise from the newly formed crater until early the next morning. Particles ejected during the eruption were eventually found over an area of 22,000 square miles. The ash drifted across the United States in the three days following the initial eruption and circled the globe over a two-week period.

As the eruption waned on March 19, the dangers did not. Debris shed by the volcano had created a 200-foot-tall dam, cutting off nearby Spirit Lake from the Toutle River. As water began backing up in the lake, 50,000 downstream residents feared that the blockage would give way, unleashing a deluge on their towns. Within days, however, the water slowly began seeping through the mud and ash, relieving pressure on the dam and reducing the chances of a catastrophic flood.

EXHIBIT 13.3   *Lahar flowing from the crater of Mount St. Helens following an eruption in 1982*

Source: John Casadevall, U.S. Geological Survey, March 21, 1982. *http://vulcan.wr.usgs.gov/Imgs/Jpg/MSH/Images/ MSH82_lahar_from_march_82_eruption_03-21-82.jpg.*

The eruption had a devastating effect on the people and infrastructure surrounding the once-quiet mountain. Fifty-seven people died, most succumbing to inhalation of volcanic ash. Another 130 people had to be airlifted to safety by the U.S. Army National Guard. Two hundred homes were destroyed along with 15 miles of railway, 27 bridges, and over 185 miles of roads. Thousands more miles of roadway were covered by ash, requiring an extensive cleanup effort. Hundreds of millions of dollars' worth of lumber and agriculture were destroyed. Many of the trees were swept off of the mountain and deposited in local rivers (see Exhibit 13.4), blocking major shipping lanes and stranding dozens of ships. Alternate means of shipping and travel were also impacted, as airports and roads throughout the region had to be closed because of reduced visibility.

EXHIBIT 13.4   *Blown-down trees, sediment, and other debris clogged local rivers after the eruption.*

Source: *U.S. Army Corps of Engineers. www .historycooperative.org/journals/ohq/106.2/images/ willingham_fig02b.jpg.*

The environment and local wildlife suffered immense damage beyond the complete alteration of the landscape. Nearly all wildlife within a 15-mile radius was wiped out, including all birds, most small mammals, and 7,000 large animals, such as bear, elk, and mountain lion. Furthermore, an estimated 70 million trout and salmon perished in local lakes and rivers.

The eruption of Mount St. Helens was the worst volcanic disaster in U.S. history. Although the devastation caused by the event was tremendous, the human toll was relatively low. In contrast, a much smaller eruption of a Colombian volcano in 1985 resulted in the deaths of more than 23,000 people. Such stunning loss of life was avoided in the case of Mount St. Helens, primarily due to the volcano's remote location and a two-month warning in the form of tremors and small eruptions of steam. The U.S. Geological Survey (USGS) reacted to the seismic precursors on April 1, 1980, by producing a map of the various hazards posed by a possible eruption. This map became an integral part of the formulation of the Mount St. Helens Contingency Plan created by the U.S. Forest Service eight days later. Using the contingency plan, the Forest Service, Washington state, and local officials were able to restrict access to the mountain prior to the explosive eruption of May 18, thereby saving numerous lives. Additionally, although the USGS was unable to predict the volcano's explosion, the agency did recognize the possibility of such an event and briefed local emergency officials on the situation by May 1.

While the short-term response by federal, state, and local officials to the possibility of an eruption has been credited with saving lives, these agencies appear to have been remarkably unprepared and underfunded when one considers that the USGS had been aware of the threat posed by Mount St. Helens since at least the late 1960s. In a 1968 interview, a former director of the USGS described being "especially worried about snow-covered Mt. St. Helens." Scholarly publications in the mid- to late 1970s supported this idea, yet when the mountain began to awaken, officials found themselves scrambling to prepare for an impending disaster.

Concerns over Mount St. Helens and other peaks within the Cascade Range had caused the USGS to request additional funding for volcano monitoring and hazards studies before the tragic events of 1980. When these requests went unfulfilled, the agency decided to focus its limited resources on Hawaiian volcanoes, which were thought to present a greater threat. This attention shift away from the Cascades was justified by the absence of a major eruption in the continental United States since 1915. The lack of activity had caused scientists and the U.S. public to overlook the threat posed by these volcanoes. Thus, when evidence pointing toward an eruption of Mount St. Helens began to surface, federal and state officials showed little urgency for increasing volcanic hazards studies or emergency preparedness.

With resources and attention diverted from the mainland, the USGS lost nearly a month of time before it was able to closely monitor a bulge that had begun growing on Mount St. Helens' north side at the onset of early seismic activity in March 1980. While this physical change eventually became recognizable to all scientists, they were unable to link it definitively to an impending eruption. A limited understanding of the behavior of volcanoes combined with Mount St. Helens' lack of recent eruptive history made such prediction rather difficult. Furthermore, available monitoring technology was not able to predict the type, magnitude, or affected areas of an eruption, leaving geologists unaware that a massive explosion was about to take place. Consequently, the USGS issued no predictions in the two months prior to the eruption, despite seismic activity and ground deformation that would today be seen as obvious warning signs.

Though the USGS made no specific prediction, it did develop a number of forecasts and prepared a report describing a wide range of possible scenarios for volcanic activity. The USGS, a highly technical organization placed in a relatively new role of informing the public of volcanic hazards, saw the distribution of this report to local officials as fulfillment of its public information duties. Local officials, however, found the information difficult to decipher and were therefore limited in their ability to convey critical hazard information to the general public. Thus, the people who would be affected never understood important information about volcanic threats, such as the deadly ash falls.

Following the eruption of Mount St. Helens, the federal government dramatically increased funding for volcano monitoring and research. The USGS strengthened and expanded hazard assessments, volcano research, and emergency planning within all levels of government. The agency also established the David A. Johnston Cascades Volcano Observatory in Vancouver, Washington, in order to closely observe ongoing activity at Mount St. Helens and to study other peaks in the Cascade Range.

With the establishment of the observatory and availability of new monitoring resources, such as tools for detecting changes in the slope of the volcano's surface, the USGS was able to successfully predict each of the 13 relatively small eruptions of Mount St. Helens that occurred between June 1980 and August 1983. Initially these eruptions were predicted hours in advance, but by April 1983, USGS scientists were predicting volcanic activity days to weeks before the events took place. Just as importantly, the agency did not issue any predictions for eruptions that failed to occur. Additionally, new techniques and better monitoring of volcanic gases allowed researchers to predict whether the type of eruption would be explosive or nonexplosive.

In 1982, President Reagan and the U.S. Congress created the 110,000-acre Mount St. Helens National Volcanic Monument, designated for research, recreation, and education. Under the management of the U.S. Forest Service, the environment within the monument has been allowed to rebound naturally from the disaster.

Geologic hazards persisted while the land began its long process of recovery, however. The mountain's bare landscape continued to threaten the area with mudslides and flooding. This situation, combined with the volcanically dammed Spirit Lake and reshaped stream system, created the possibility of further destruction. To mitigate these new hazards, the USGS and the National Weather Service created flood-warning systems for the Toutle and Cowlitz rivers. In addition, the U.S. Army Corps of Engineers constructed a diversionary tunnel to drain excess water from Spirit Lake and maintain the water level at a safe height.

In the mid- to late 1980s, Mount St. Helens slipped into a period of relative quiet, with only periodic increases in seismicity. By 2004, a new glacier had even formed in the mountain's crater. On September 23 of that year, however, a number of small earthquakes began occurring beneath the lava dome that had formed during the 1980s. By October 1, the tremors had become nearly continuous, prompting scientists and emergency management officials to issue volcanic hazard warnings. Later that day, an explosion of steam and ash shot through the newly formed glacier, several thousand feet into the air. Four more eruptions followed over the next four days. Then, on October 6, as the volcano began to settle down, a new mound of solid, but still hot, lava began pushing its way to the surface in the crater. Over time, such periodic episodes of volcanism and growth may restore the shape of the mountain to what it was before the cataclysmic eruption of March 18, 1980.

Today, monitoring of Mount St. Helens and other Cascade volcanoes has been greatly improved thanks to advances in technology. A network of seismic stations, a lahar detection system, and tools such as global positioning system (GPS) receivers dot the mountain's surface, helping scientists provide more timely and accurate warnings to the public. The communication of such warnings has become more efficient, as well, with the introduction of the USGS alert notification system. This system simplifies complex geologic data into four standardized terms (normal, advisory, watch, and warning), making critical volcanic hazard information easier to understand and disseminate.

While improvements in funding, monitoring, research, and communication have led to better predictions of volcanic activity, this improved forecasting has yet to be tested by any large, explosive eruptions. Of the 170 volcanoes active within the United States over the past 10,000 years, approximately 50 are thought to be capable of erupting in modern times, and several may have the capacity to produce catastrophic explosive eruptions of a magnitude unprecedented in recorded history. The possibility of such an occurrence, combined with continued population growth, economic development, and urbanization, will make effective volcano observation and hazard communication critical in the years to come.

REFERENCES

Boyle, Alan. "High-Tech Tools of the Volcano Trade," May 17, 2000, MSNBC. www.msnbc.msn.com/id/3077291.

Burke Museum of Natural History and Culture, University of Washington. "The Cascade Episode." www.washington.edu/burkemuseum/geo_history_wa/Cascade%20Episode.htm.

Casadevall, T., et al. "Gas Emissions and the Eruptions of Mount St. Helens through 1982," *Science* 221 (1983): 1383–1385.

Crandell, Dwight R., and Donal R. Mullineaux. *Potential Hazards from Future Eruptions of Mount St. Helens Volcano, Washington.* U.S. Geological Survey Bulletin 1383-C. Reston, VA: USGS, 1978.

Crandell, Dwight R., Donal R. Mullineaux and Meyer Robin. "Mount St. Helens Volcano: Recent and Future Behavior," *Science* 187 (1975): 438–441.

Foxworthy, B. L., and M. Hill. *Volcanic Eruptions of 1980 at Mount St. Helens: The First 100 Days.* U.S. Geological Survey Professional Paper 1249. Reston, VA: USGS, 1982.

Gardner, Cynthia A., and Marianne C. Guffanti. "U.S. Geological Survey's Alert Notification System for Volcanic Activity." U.S. Geological Survey Fact Sheet FS2006-3139. Reston, VA: USGS, 2006.

Major, Jon J., et al. "Mount St. Helens Erupts Again." U. S. Geological Survey Fact Sheet FS2005-3036 Reston, VA: USGS, 2005.

Merchant, James, A., et al. "Health Implications of the Mount St. Helens' Eruption: Epidemiological Considerations," *Annals of Occupational Hygiene* 26 (1982): 911–919.

Mileti, Dennis S., and John H. Sorensen. "Communication of Emergency Public Warnings," Oak Ridge, TN: Oak Ridge National Laboratory, 1990.

Nania, Jim, and Timothy E. Bruya. "In the Wake of Mount St. Helens," *Annals of Emergency Medicine* 11 (1982): 184–191.

Saarinen, Thomas F., and James L. Sell. *Warning and Response to the Mount St. Helens Eruption.* Albany: State University of New York Press, 1985.

Swanson, D. A., et al. "Predicting Eruptions at Mount St. Helens, June 1980 through December 1982," *Science* 221 (1983): 1369–1376.

Tilling, Robert I. "Mount St. Helens 20 Years Later: What We've Learned," *Geotimes* (May 2000).

Tilling, Robert I., and Roy A. Bailey. "Volcano Hazards Program in the United States," *Journal of Geodynamics* 3 (1985): 425–446.

Tilling, Robert I., Lyn Topinka, and Donald A. Swanson. *Eruptions of Mount St. Helens: Past, Present, and Future.* Reston, VA: USGS, 1990.

U.S. Forest Service. "Mount St. Helens National Volcanic Monument." www.fs.fed.us/gpnf/mshnvm.

U.S. Geological Survey, Cascades Volcano Observatory. "Mount St. Helens, Washington May 18, 1980 Eruption Summary.", 1997, http://vulcan.wr.usgs.gov/Volcanoes/MSH/May18/summary_may18 _eruption.html.

CHAPTER 14

SOUTH CANYON FIRE

A relatively small wildfire, first reported on July 3, 1994, in South Canyon (see Exhibit 14.1), located seven miles west of Glenwood Springs, Colorado, grew into a dangerous blaze over the next two days, while firefighting resources were allocated to other fires in the district. Once fragmented resources began to arrive, the fire could not be easily contained, and firefighters found themselves in a position where no escape routes existed if there was a sudden reverse in the direction of the blaze. Unfortunately, a cold front blew through on the afternoon of July 6, creating a wind shift and subsequent "blowup" that trapped and killed 14 firefighters. Management, leadership, and communication within the firefighting community were directly to blame for this tragedy.

Each year in the United States, wildfires burn several million acres of land, destroying communities, natural resources, wildlife habitats, and watersheds while leaving behind a scorched earth susceptible to floods, landslides, and debris flows. Beyond destruction caused by flames, the accompanying smoke contains pollutants that can damage human health. For these reasons, the federal government spends billions of dollars annually to combat wildfires. One such battle started rather innocently on July 3, 1994, when the Bureau of Land Management (BLM) began tracking a relatively small fire in South Canyon, located seven miles west of Glenwood Springs, Colorado (see Exhibit 14.2).

The Glenwood Springs area was experiencing high temperatures and drought during the summer of 1994, so when dry lightning storms

EXHIBIT **14.1**   *South Canyon fire late in the afternoon on July 6, 1994*

Source: South Canyon Fire Accident Investigation Team, Report of the South Canyon Fire Accident Investigation Team *(Washington, DC: U.S. Government Printing Office, 1994).*

moved into the region in early July, authorities quickly issued a fire warning. During this warning, more than 40 lightning-induced fires popped up in the region. The South Canyon fire was one of these, igniting on July 2.

The South Canyon fire was first reported by the local sheriff to the BLM Grand Junction District Dispatch Center at 11:00 AM on July 3. At this point, the fire was situated on a hilltop above Interstate 70 and was slowly spreading downhill. It burned with a relatively low intensity, consuming dry grass, leaf litter, and twigs that covered the ground.

A BLM engine crew was dispatched to the scene. Upon arrival, the crew foreman assessed the situation and recommended that the fire be observed until additional firefighting resources became available. At the time, 90% of the Grand Junction District's firefighting capabilities had

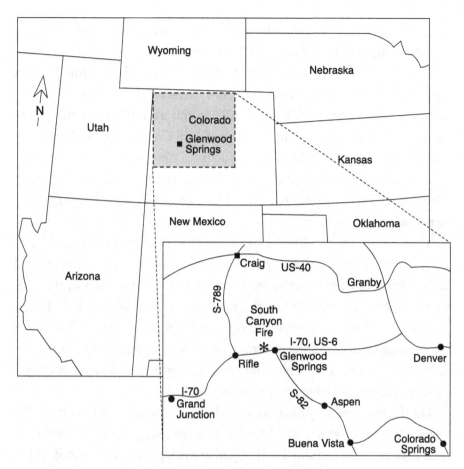

EXHIBIT 14.2 *Location of the South Canyon Fire*

Source: Bret W. Butler et al., "Fire Behavior Associated with the 1994 South Canyon Fire on Storm King Mountain, Colorado," Research Paper RMRS-RP-9 (Ogden, UT: U.S. Department of Agriculture, Forest Service, Rocky Mountain Research Station, 1998.

been allocated to other fires in the jurisdiction. Since the South Canyon fire appeared to be rather routine, it was assigned a low priority. This was due primarily to its remote, inaccessible location, meaning that it did not present an immediate threat to life or property. Moreover, the fire was not expected to spread rapidly. When the district fire control officer arrived on the scene, he agreed with the foreman's assessment and requested that resources be released from other fires in anticipation of attacking the South Canyon fire the next day.

By the morning of July 4, 31 fires in the Grand Junction District remained out of control and 5 new ones had started, 2 of which covered areas of greater than 100 acres. All "initial attack" firefighters were occupied fighting blazes other than the South Canyon fire, and the number of fires had constrained the capacity of the communications infrastructure, making safe and effective aircraft use problematic. The South Canyon fire, meanwhile, continued its slow spread, growing to three acres in size by midday.

That afternoon, the BLM Grand Junction District increased the priority given to the South Canyon fire in response to concerns expressed by residents of Glenwood Springs. At 6:30 PM, Butch Blanco, the incident commander assigned to the fire, met with BLM and U.S. Forest Service firefighters at the bottom of the hill below the blaze. With darkness setting in over the steep terrain, he decided to wait until morning to commence operations. That night, the fire quietly spread to occupy a 29-acre region, 10 times its previous size.

On the morning of July 5, an initial attempt was made to control the blaze. A crew of seven BLM firefighters approached the fire from the east drainage (see Exhibit 14.3). Upon arrival, the crew prepared a helicopter landing site, designated Helispot 1, for the delivery of personnel and supplies. They then began constructing a fireline (a line cleared of flammable materials) along the fire's edge on the downhill side.

While the clearing was taking place, Blanco called for additional resources, including another engine crew, a helicopter, and a 20-person ground ("hotshot") crew. These resources were subsequently delivered except for the hotshot crew; instead, 8 smokejumpers (parachuting firefighters) were sent in their place. Support from air tankers was also requested, but strong winds and the rugged terrain made aerial drops of fire retardant ineffective as well as dangerous.

At 5:30 PM, Blanco and the BLM crew left the fire to repair equipment. The smokejumper crew arrived on scene shortly thereafter and began assisting with fireline construction. Unfortunately, this fireline

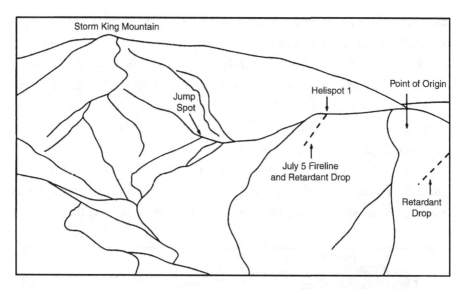

EXHIBIT **14.3**   *South Canyon fire site map*

Source: South Canyon Fire Accident Investigation Team, Report of the South Canyon Fire Accident Investigation Team (Washington, DC: U.S. Government Printing Office, 1994).

was unable to contain the flames. Don Mackey, the jumper in charge, then ordered his crew to construct a new line. He also called the Grand Junction District dispatcher and ordered two more hotshot crews.

By 8:00 PM, the fire had steadily grown to encompass 50 acres. At this point, however, it was still considered to be low intensity, leaving many islands of unburned vegetation behind as flames moved downhill toward I-70.

Shortly after midnight, the smokejumpers were forced to discontinue their work on the second fireline because of darkness and rolling rocks. As the night wore on, the fire continued to grow, threatening both the jump site and equipment at that location. Early in the morning on July 6, Mackey was forced to order a helicopter to remove this gear. He further requested that a hotshot crew recently assigned to the fire be ferried to the site by helicopter to speed their arrival.

As dawn broke, 36 other fires continued to burn in the region and the South Canyon fire had grown to encompass 127 acres. The forecast for the day called for strong, shifting winds resulting from a passing cold front. As a consequence, new fire warnings were issued for the region.

BLM and U.S. Forest Service firefighters arrived back at the fire scene at 8:00 AM and began working on a new helicopter landing site, Helispot 2 (see Exhibit 14.4). The plan formulated by Mackey and Blanco then called for the smokejumpers and reinforcements, once they arrived, to begin working on firelines.

At 9:30 AM, an observation helicopter flew over the blaze. Due to the high demand for the helicopter, its aerial observation period was purposely cut short. The observer did, however, note that the fire area

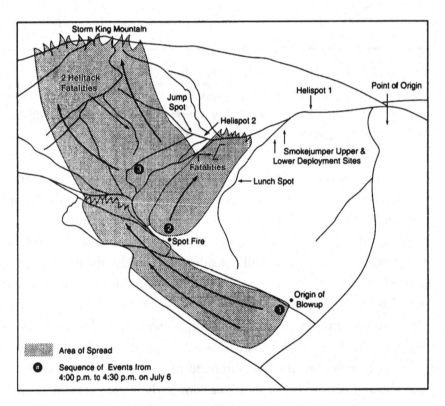

EXHIBIT 14.4   *Map of South Canyon "blowup," July 6, 1994*

Source: South Canyon Fire Accident Investigation Team, Report of the South Canyon Fire Accident Investigation Team *(Washington, DC: U.S. Government Printing Office, 1994).*

contained no safe havens in which firefighters could seek refuge. Despite this warning, Mackey felt that it was best to continue fighting the fire as originally planned.

Another eight-person smokejumper crew arrived about an hour later and began working on firelines along the west flank. Because of difficulties in finding the necessary equipment, the hotshot crew did not arrive until 12:30 PM. Even then, in order to make space on the helicopter for transporting equipment and water to other fire sites, only half of the 20-person crew was sent. It was then that Mackey, Blanco, and the hotshot crew superintendent, Tom Sheppard, discussed strategy and decided to reinforce the west flank.

At 3:00 PM, the other half of the hotshot crew arrived via helicopter. Within the next 30 minutes, a cold front began passing over the fire site, accompanied by winds in excess of 40 miles per hour, blowing northeasterly up the west drainage. The strong winds caused the fire to make several quick runs upslope, moving at speeds of up to six miles per hour with flames reaching 100 feet in height. Helicopter water drops proved futile because of the high winds and fire intensity. Minutes later, the fire "blew up."

A "blowup" is a sudden change in a wildfire from a slowly spreading, low-intensity surface fire to a rapidly spreading, high-intensity inferno that burns all vegetation, from the ground to the treetops. At 4:00 PM on July 6, the South Canyon fire blew up as it crossed the western drainage and began rolling rapidly uphill (see Exhibit 14.4). The blaze quickly worked its way up the drainage, moving as fast as 11 miles per hour.

At 4:04, Blanco ordered all firefighters on the ridgeline east of the western drainage to retreat to a safety area near Helispot 1. Before they could reach the spot, they were cut off by flames but were able to escape by reversing direction and heading toward the interstate below. Seven minutes later, Blanco notified the dispatch center that he was losing control of the fire and requested air support.

About that time, Mackey encountered a smokejumper crew and directed them to the safety area. As the smokejumpers climbed the hill, the flames began to close in, prompting the firefighters to drop their chainsaws and supplies in order to run. Upon reaching the designated safety area, they began, with some degree of difficulty, given the strong winds, setting up their protective shelters. Glowing ashes blew into the shelters as temperatures inside rose to 110°F.

Meanwhile, Mackey had hiked downhill to direct members of the hotshot crew to safety. He and the hotshots then hiked uphill toward the safety area, walking slowly in a line, carrying all of their equipment. They were completely unaware that an inferno was racing up the hill. Suddenly the fire exploded behind them. The firefighters began to run, but only 3 made it to safety, suffering burns in process. They were the lucky ones, however; the 12 men following them all perished.

At Helispot 2, two firefighters had been directing helicopter operations. As the fire grew closer, they were told to seek refuge in the east drainage. Believing that area to be unsafe, the firefighters ran along a ridge top above the western drainage, where they were trapped and killed by the flames.

The South Canyon fire burned out of control for another five days. It eventually destroyed 2,115 acres and caused a debris slide of 91,000 cubic yards of rocks and mud. It is the loss of 14 firefighters on July 6, 1994, however, that marked this fire as one of the most tragic U.S. blazes of the twentieth century.

The evolution of the South Canyon fire was a consequence of its location. The heat and drought experienced around Glenwood Springs that summer created excellent fuel for starting and sustaining a fire. Steep slopes at the fire site and the presence of flames at the bottom of these slopes on the day of the blowup made rapid uphill movement of the blaze possible. Strong winds, funneling up through the drainage, then helped to spread the fire more quickly. As the flames grew, live vegetation began to burn, providing a new fuel source and further intensifying the fire.

That the South Canyon fire evolved into an immense inferno was not considered abnormal for the setting in which it occurred. It is for this reason alone that the loss of so many firefighters cannot be considered simply a result of the blaze itself. Rather, the work environment and management decision making associated with the response effort are culpable.

Obtaining firefighting resources was a constant problem through-out the duration of the South Canyon fire. The large number of si-multaneously burning blazes in the Grand Junction District stretched local resources to a breaking point. For this reason, the South Can-yon fire was not attacked when it was initially spotted but was al-lowed to grow until July 5, when the district first requested external assistance. Once firefighting activities were initiated, additional fire-fighters were scarce and sufficient air support was not available. Without essential response resources, the fire continued to spread, making containment more difficult and increasing the risk to those on the scene.

Coupled with lack of support was the absence of information that the firefighters could have used to better protect themselves. For example, firefighters were not informed of the potentially dangerous wind condi-tions forecast for July 6 or of the fire's behavior as it grew. Perhaps most important, they were not given adequate information on the location of escape routes, leading to confusion when the blowup occurred. In ac-tuality, adequate safety zones and escape routes were never established for the fire site, and the few routes that did exist were too long and rugged to allow for a quick escape.

The management structure of firefighting crews on site added to the high-risk environment. Leadership roles among smokejumper crews were chosen somewhat arbitrarily by designating the first experienced team member out of the airplane as the jumper in charge. Thus, the two smokejumper crews on scene did not have well-established leaders. This leadership problem was compounded by the addition of fragments of a hotshot crew to assist with fireline construction. The new patchwork crews did not have time to gel as a single, cohesive unit before the blowup, and were characterized by poor communication and questioning of leadership.

Management inattention to safety concerns further increased the risk to firefighters at South Canyon. Beyond neglecting to establish safety areas and escape routes, there was a failure to follow standard procedures in preparing for blowup conditions. No inspections were conducted to ensure that firefighters were using safe practices in the field. Moreover, management was unable to establish a rigid chain of command or modify strategy to deal with limited resources.

With inadequate oversight in the field, firefighters paid little attention to the 10 "Standard Fire Fighting Orders" and 18 "Watch Out Situations" that are designed to ensure safety, and which each firefighter is required to memorize. The postfire investigation concluded that crews working in South Canyon disregarded 20 of these combined 28 rules. While adherence to these rules is considered effective in ensuring safety, many firefighters at the time considered them to be only general guidelines for flexible decision making and thought nothing of working around them. Those firefighters who did realize that the situation was potentially disastrous, however, did not voice their concerns to those in charge. Any report of a dangerous situation likely would have been difficult, at any rate, since there was no established procedure for making such reports and because many firefighters did not know the identity of the incident commander.

A greater deterrent, perhaps, was a "can-do" culture that causes many firefighters to accept any challenge and refuse to admit defeat. This can spawn a somewhat arrogant way of thinking, where anyone who complains about unsafe situations is viewed as weak. It is perhaps for this reason that, when the blowup occurred, some firefighters held on to their equipment rather than dropping it and running while others refused to deploy their fire shelters. Given that the firefighters were not trained in making decisions under conditions of extreme stress, confusion likely exacerbated the situation.

In the months following the South Canyon fire, the U.S. Occupational Safety and Health Administration conducted a review of the incident and cited both the BLM and the U.S. Forest Service for not providing adequate oversight of the response effort to ensure the safety of their personnel. The BLM and the U.S. Forest Service each conducted their own investigations, focusing largely on environmental factors, organizational processes, and safety failures while largely ignoring human factors and the "can-do" culture.

The years following the disaster brought a new focus on firefighter behavior, with an emphasis on safe decision making under stress. This culminated in 2005, when the U.S. Forest Service adopted a new doctrine intended to provide firefighters with the essential knowledge for escaping from fires without having to memorize a lengthy list of rules. Firefighters also are now better trained in dropping their gear to escape a fire, setting up fire shelters, and avoiding unnecessarily hazardous situations.

Despite these changes, there continue to be fatalities among firefighters combating wildfires. However, the situation is definitely improving. A 10-year review since the South Canyon disaster concluded that entrapment fatalities had decreased by more than 40%.

In the fall of 1994 and spring of 1995, members of the BLM and U.S. Forest Service, along with 160 volunteers, created a memorial trail that winds through South Canyon to the area where the firefighters died. Its purpose is to honor firefighters everywhere, promote an understanding of the events that led to the July 6, 1994, catastrophe, and communicate lessons learned from the South Canyon fire that can be used to prevent future disasters.

REFERENCES

Banda, P. Solomon, "Lessons on the Line—How the Storm King Fire Helped Reshape the Way We Fight Wildfires," *The Missoulian*, July 6, 2004.

Butler, Bret W., et al. "Fire Behavior Associated with the 1994 South Canyon Fire on Storm King Mountain, Colorado," Research Paper

RMRS-RP-9. Ogden, UT: U.S. Department of Agriculture, Forest Service, Rocky Mountain Research Station, 1998.

Cannon, Susan H., et al. "1995 Preliminary Evaluation of the Fire-Related Debris Flows on Storm King Mountain, Glenwood Springs, Colorado." 1995, U.S. Geological Survey Open-File Report 95-508.

National Interagency Fire Center. "Total Wildland Fires and Acres (1960–2005)." www.nifc.gov/stats/fires_acres.html.

Putnam, Ted. "The Collapse of Decision-Making and Organizational Structure on Storm King Mountain," Missoula, MT: U.S. Department of Agriculture Forest Service, Missoula Technology and Development Center, 1995.

Rhoades, Quentin. "Effective Fire-Fighting Calls for Bending Rules Sometimes," *The Missoulian*, August 26, 1994.

Rogers, Don. "Lessons Repeated by the Harshest of Teachers," *Vail Daily*, January 24, 2000.

Safe Fire Programs and Forest Stewardship Concepts. "South Canyon Fire, Ten Year Review of the Effectiveness of Planned Actions." Report prepared for the U.S. Forest Service. June 23, 2004, www.mcsolutions .com/resources/South_Canyon_10Year_Review.pdf.

South Canyon Fire Accident Investigation Team. *Report of the South Canyon Fire Accident Investigation Team.* Washington, DC: U.S. Government Printing Office, 1994.

U.S. Bureau of Land Management. "Storm King Mountain Memorial Trail." www.co.blm.gov/gsra/stormkingtr.htm.

U.S. Geological Survey. "Wildfire Hazards—A National Threat. U.S. Geological Survey Fact Sheet 2006-3015." Reston, VA: Author, 2006.

U.S. Occupational Safety and Health Administration. South Canyon Fire. July 12, 2001, www.coloradofirecamp.com/Cramer/osha-south-canyon.htm.

Webb, Dennis. "Latest Storm King Lessons Focus on Human Behavior," *Glenwood Springs Post Independent*, July 6, 2005.

CHAPTER 15

SUMATRA–ANDAMAN TSUNAMI

The second largest earthquake ever recorded occurred in the Indian Ocean on December 26, 2004. The force of the earthquake spawned a massive tsunami that struck the coasts of Indonesia, Thailand, Sri Lanka, India, and several African nations. The damage from the earthquake and tsunami resulted in over 300,000 people declared dead or missing and more than 1 million people left homeless (see Exhibit 15.1). Many believe that a reasonable disaster preparedness plan and early-warning system would have averted the vast majority of these consequences.

The surface of Earth is composed of a network of massive, rigid plates that are constantly in motion (see Exhibit 15.2). These plates move away from one another only to collide with other plates, ultimately fitting together like the pieces of a puzzle, to form the globe. For millions of years, two of these plates, the ones containing India and Australia, have been moving northeastward, toward Eurasia. As these plates continue their migration, they are being forced under the Eurasian plate. Such strain eventually creates enough force to generate a reaction that is commonly referred to as an earthquake.

Earthquakes formed by this process are typical along the southern coast of Indonesia, where the Indian and Australian plates collide with the Eurasian plate. Three times in recorded history (1797, 1833, and 1861), this region has produced what are referred to as "giant"

EXHIBIT 15.1   *Freighter containing 10,000 tons of cement lies capsized by the tsunami in Lhoknga, Indonesia. In the foreground, stumps from trees snapped by the enormous waves dot the beach.*

Source: *Hermann Fritz, Georgia Institute of Technology, Jose Borrero and Costas Synolakis, University of Southern California. 2005. www.gtsav.gatech.edu/cee/groups/tsunami /sumatra/lhoknga/index_html.html.*

earthquakes with magnitudes greater than 9.0. More than 143 years would pass before another massive quake would strike, with devastating effects seldom seen on a global scale.

At 7:59 AM on December 26, 2004, a 750-mile section of the Eurasian plate overcame the friction that kept it from sliding freely over the Indian and Australian plates. The edge of the Eurasian plate sprang upward more than 66 feet in some places, releasing an amount of energy equivalent to 100 billion tons of TNT. The resulting 9.3-magnitude earthquake lasted eight and one-half minutes, making it the longest and second most powerful quake ever recorded by instruments.

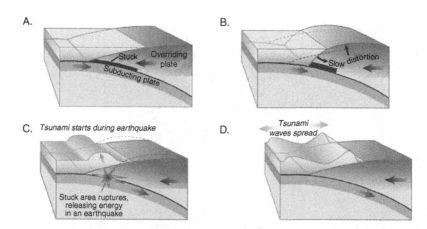

A.

B.

C. *Tsunami starts during earthquake*

D.

EXHIBIT 15.2 *Formation of an earthquake and tsunami as plates collide*

Source: *U.S. Geological Survey, "Surviving a Tsunami— Lessons from Chile, Hawaii, and Japan," USGS Circular 1187 (Reston, VA: U.S. Geological Survey, 2005).*

The enormous power of the quake was enough to cause the entire globe to vibrate by at least half an inch and to slightly shift the position of the North Pole. On a smaller scale, the earthquake reshaped shipping channels and the ocean floor. In one of the world's busiest maritime shipping locations, off the coast of Indonesia, water depths changed from 4,000 feet to 100 feet.

By far the most destructive effect of the earthquake, however, was the massive tsunami it unleashed on coasts throughout the Indian Ocean. Tsunamis (a Japanese term meaning "harbor wave") are enormous, fast-moving waves created when seismic activity displaces large volumes of water. The December 26, 2004, tsunami was created when the Eurasian plate jumped upward, disturbing trillions of tons of water, sending mammoth waves racing across the sea (see Exhibit 15.3). In less than 20 minutes, the tsunami had traveled the 100-mile distance that separated the earthquake's epicenter from the northern coast of the island of Sumatra.

Local Indonesian fishermen noticed the water retreat suddenly from the shore, leaving fish flopping on the dry sand. What they did not realize was that they had just witnessed the trough of the first wave of the

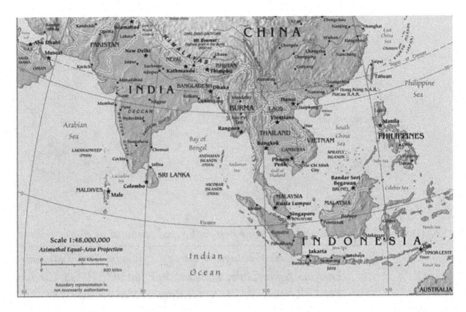

EXHIBIT 15.3   *Southern Asia*

*Source: U.S. Central Intelligence Agency, Asia, 2007.
www.cia.gov/library/publications/the-world-factbook/
reference_maps/asia.html.*

approaching tsunami. The wave's crest, up to 160 feet high in some locations, arrived soon thereafter.

A loud roar filled the air as the enormous wave crashed onshore, toss-
ing fishing boats like toys. The wave hit the coast with tremendous
force, uprooting trees, cars, and buildings. Almost instantly, more than
100,000 people perished.

At 9:04 AM, the Pacific Tsunami Warning Center (PTWC) issued a
bulletin describing earthquake recordings it had received and the possibility that a tsunami had formed near the source of the tremor.
Although this message was dispatched to Indonesia, it came too late for
the inhabitants of Sumatra.

Forty minutes after the PTWC warning, the tsunami hit the mainland
coasts of southern Asia. While at least some of these countries received
the PTWC bulletin ahead of time, they were ill prepared to deal with
the situation. Just as in Indonesia, the coastal population remained

unaware of the danger and made no attempt to evacuate to higher ground. Villages were destroyed and thousands of people were washed away or drowned in Sri Lanka, India, and Thailand. In India, the waves crashed with such force that a 1,200-year-old city, unknown and buried for centuries in the sand, was revealed.

As several massive aftershocks shook the earth near the original epicenter, the giant waves continued on their destructive paths. At 11:30 AM, the tsunami struck the Maldives. An hour later, the PTWC issued further warnings to international organizations. Around 3:00 PM, the U.S. State Department coordinated with the PTWC to communicate information about the disaster to its embassies in the western Indian Ocean and Africa. It was at about this time, however, that the waves began crashing on the shores of Mauritius, Madagascar, and northeastern Africa. More than seven hours after the initial earthquake and more than 3,000 miles away, the tsunami claimed the lives of several hundred unsuspecting victims in Somalia, Tanzania, and Kenya.

All told, the earthquake and tsunami killed nearly 300,000 people and caused $10 billion of damage. The exact number of deceased will never be known, however, as entire villages were destroyed, leaving no survivors behind to count the dead.

Survivors of the catastrophe found themselves facing new dangers as they searched for loved ones and began the recovery process. In the immediate aftermath of the disaster, the potential for epidemics of malaria and an array of other diseases loomed, with bodies littering the landscape and pools of standing water. In Indonesia, Islamic leaders issued an edict allowing Muslims to bury the dead without traditional burial rites, in an attempt to avoid the spread of disease. The threat of disease was compounded, however, by sewage system failures, which were widespread throughout the tsunami region and served to contaminate drinking water supplies.

Debris left behind by receding water further threatened the safety of survivors and rescue workers. Fragmented local governments were incapable of handling the enormous volume and dangerous nature of the waste. Much of the debris from sources such as collapsed buildings was mixed with hazardous substances, such as asbestos, oil, and chemicals, making removal unsafe.

The tsunami, which flooded some coastal areas nearly two miles inland, caused salinization of aquifers and agricultural lands. This contamination is predicted to cause a long-term decrease in agricultural productivity. Seafood production and tourism also have been impacted.

Many affected countries were further damaged by the loss of rare ecosystems. Mangroves, coral reefs, beaches, coastal wetlands, and forests were among the many environments degraded by this event. For example, 90% of the mangrove forests in the tsunami-affected region of Indonesia were heavily damaged. This destruction now allows river contamination, normally filtered out by the mangroves, to flow directly into the sea.

The devastation of the earthquake and resulting tsunami, although almost beyond imagination, is not unparalleled in recent history. A storm surge in coastal Bangladesh in 1970 killed 300,000 people, and as many as 750,000 people died in Tangshan, China, as a result of an earthquake in 1976. What sets the Sumatra–Andaman tsunami apart from others in history, however, is the widespread nature of the destruction, impacting a variety of countries and cultures. This situation, combined with extensive media coverage, inspired the donation of an unprecedented amount of rescue and humanitarian aid resources by governments and private citizens throughout the world. By late January 2005, over $7 billion had been pledged or donated by nations and international organizations, in addition to the deployment of response resources in the form of rescue workers, medical supplies, helicopters, and forensics teams.

The immense human toll of the disaster was due, in large part, to the victims' lack of education and warning about tsunamis. Tsunamis have been fairly unusual throughout recent history in the Indian Ocean, with the last major occurrence having been more than 120 years ago. As a result, countries bordering that ocean do not have advance warning systems in place or educational programs, such as those found in Pacific Ocean nations.

In the early 1990s, Indonesia, the country most affected by the tsunami, began plans for developing an early-warning system for such disasters. With few financial resources to draw upon, the nation sought international aid to help fund the $2 million project. Unfortunately, this request went unfulfilled.

Other countries were unable to recognize the potential hazard posed by the earthquake, in some cases despite hours of advance warning. For example, officials in Thailand were well aware that a massive quake had occurred, but having never experienced a tsunami before, they felt that it was unreasonable to issue a public warning. Even without an official warning, many victims could have saved themselves had they been taught the warning signs of a tsunami and the urgency of evacuating to higher ground.

The demographics of affected areas also contributed to the extent of the disaster. In the decade leading up to the catastrophe, the coasts of developing Asian countries had become more urbanized, putting a higher population at risk from flooding caused by tsunamis, storm surges, and heavy rains. Along the public beachfronts of India, the at-risk population was particularly high, as squatters had settled there. Moreover, the tsunami struck during peak tourist season, when thousands of foreign visitors had flocked to Indian Ocean beaches.

In more rural settings, while the affected population may have been lower, access to aid was extremely difficult. For example, it took relief workers three days to reach the sparsely populated northern tip of Sumatra. After this first contact, relief supplies still were slow to arrive, as the closest airport could accommodate only two planes at a time.

Soon after this incident, countries bordering the Indian Ocean began working with the United Nations on early-detection and public education systems to avert future disasters. As these programs ramp up to full functionality, the PTWC and the Japanese tsunami center will be forwarding alerts to Indian Ocean nations in the event of an earthquake. Plans call for the eventual installation of a vast network of tide and seismic gauges throughout the region, monitored by regional alert centers. These centers will be able to disburse warnings and information to the public through national and local governments as well as via media outlets.

By July 2006, portions of the early-warning system had been implemented. At least two high-tech seismic buoys and more than 20 tide gauges had been installed. Yet, on July 17, 2007, when a magnitude 7.7 quake struck off of the coast of Indonesia near the island of Java, 664 people died and more than 6,500 were injured when a resulting tsunami caught them by surprise. While the partially assembled warning system did not yet cover Java, Indonesian officials had been aware of the potential for a tsunami from alerts issued by the PTWC and the Japanese tsunami center. Yet they were unable to disseminate the information to coastal areas in time to allow for safe evacuation.

Indian Ocean nations continue to face a serious threat of tsunamis. Because giant earthquakes often occur in groups (7 of the 10 occurring in the twentieth century happened in a 15-year span, and 5 of those were clustered in one geographical region), it is reasonable to expect that other major quakes will take place in southern Asia in the near future. This belief is further bolstered by the fact that many of the major faults in the area have been dormant for an exceptionally long period of time, causing the buildup of stress that could lead to an eventual earthquake. With the populations of the countries affected by the Sumatra–Andaman tsunami expected to increase sharply over the next half century (e.g., India by 45%, Maldives by 80%, Somalia by over 180%), the next major quake and tsunami could cause an even greater toll.

REFERENCES

Associated Press. "Tsunami Redrew Ship Channels, Ocean Floor," January 5, 2005. www.msnbc.msn.com/id/6791600.

BBC News. "Indian Ocean Tsunami Warning System," December 23, 2005. http://news.bbc.co.uk/1/hi/sci/tech/4524642.stm.

BBC News. "Indonesia Death Toll Passes 500," July 19, 2006. http://news.bbc.co.uk/2/hi/asia-pacific/5192716.stm.

BBC News. "Tsunami Aid: Who's Giving What," January 27, 2005. http://news.bbc.co.uk/2/hi/asia-pacific/4145259.stm.

Campbell, Matthew, et al. "Focus: Nature's Timebomb," *Sunday Times* (London), January 2, 2005.

CNN. "High-Tech Buoys to Warn of Disaster," December 21, 2005. http://edition.cnn.com/2005/TECH/11/25/spark.banda.aceh/index.html.

Darcy, James. *The Indian Ocean Tsunami Crisis: Humanitarian Dimensions*. London: Overseas Development Institute, 2005.

Elliot, Michael. "Sea of Sorrow," *Time Magazine*, January 2, 2005.

Fritz, Hermann M., and Jose C. Borrero. "Somalia Field Survey after the December 2004 Indian Ocean Tsunami," *Earthquake Spectra* 22 (2006): S219–S233. 2006.

"Girl, 10, Used Geography Lesson to Save Lives," *Telegraph*, January 2, 2005.

Horack, John M. "How the Earthquake Affected Earth," U.S. National Aeronautics and Space Administration, January 10, 2005. http://science.nasa.gov/headlines/y2005/10jan_earthquake.htm.

Kawata, Yoshiaki, et al. "Comprehensive Analysis of the Damage and its Impact on Coastal Zones by the 2004 Indian Ocean Tsunami Disaster." www.tsunami.civil.tohoku.ac.jp/sumatra2004/report.html.

Knubel, Fred. "Geologists Find: An Earth Plate Is Breaking in Two," 1995. www.columbia.edu/cu/pr/95/18688.html.

Korf, Benedikt. "Antinomies of Generosity: Moral Geographies and Post-Tsunami Aid in Southeast Asia," *Geoforum* 38 (2007): 366–378.

Ni, Sidao, Hiroo Kanamori, and Don Helmberger. "Energy Radiation from the Sumatra Earthquake," *Nature* 434 (2005): 582.

Oberle, Mark. "Tsunami, December 26, 2004 at Patong Beach, Phuket, Thailand," 2005. http://faculty.washington.edu/moberle/Tsunami/Tsunami.htm.

Population Reference Bureau. "2006 World Population Data Sheet." Washington, DC: Author, 2006.

Sieh, Kerry. "What Happened and What's Next?" *Nature* 434 (2005): 573–574.

Srinivas, Hari. "The Indian Ocean Tsunami and Its Environmental Impacts," Global Development Research Center. www.gdrc.org/uem/disasters/disenvi/tsunami.html

Stein, Seth, and Emile A. Okal. "Speed and Size of the Sumatra Earthquake," *Nature* 434 (2005): 581–582.

Subaryal, Cecep, et al. "Plate-Boundary Deformation Associated With the Great Sumatra–Andaman Earthquake," *Nature* 440 (2006): 46–51.

Thomas, Evan, and George Wehrfritz. "Tide of Grief," *Newsweek*, January 10, 2005.

"Tsunami Waves Exposed Remnants of Lost City," *New Scientist*, February 26, 2005.

UN Office of the Special Envoy for Tsunami Recovery. "Human Toll." www.tsunamispecialenvoy.org/country/humantoll.asp.

U.S. Geological Survey. "Surviving a Tsunami—Lessons from Chile, Hawaii, and Japan," USGS Circular 1187. Reston, VA: US Geological Survey, 2005.

U.S. National Oceanographic and Atmospheric Administration. "Indian Ocean Tsunami Model, December 26, 2004," *Science on a Sphere*. http://sos.noaa.gov/datasets/Ocean/indiantsunami.html.

U.S. National Oceanographic and Atmospheric Administration, National Geophysical Data Center. NGDC Tsunami Event Database. www.ngdc.noaa.gov/nndc/struts/form?t=101650&s=70&d=7.

U.S. National Oceanographic and Atmospheric Administration. "NOAA and the Indian Ocean Tsunami," 2005. www.noaanews.noaa.gov/stories2004/s2358.htm.

Walton, Marsha. "Scientists: Sumatra Quake Longest Ever Recorded," CNN, May 20, 2005. http://edition.cnn.com/2005/TECH/science/05/19/sumatra.quake/index.html.

CHAPTER 16

HURRICANE KATRINA

During August 2005, Hurricane Katrina slammed into the United States, hitting the coastal areas of Florida, Louisiana, and Mississippi. A combination of storm surge, wave action, and high winds resulted in the destruction of buildings and roads in the affected areas. The impact of Katrina on New Orleans was unusually severe; portions of the city were left under 20 feet of water due to failure of the earthen levees and floodwalls that had been constructed to safeguard the city from this type of event (see Exhibit 16.1). Hurricane Katrina caused nearly 2,000 fatalities and an estimated economic loss of $125 billion, in addition to displacing hundreds of thousands of people from their homes and workplaces. The aftermath of Katrina has resulted in considerable speculation about the causes of levee failure and the parties responsible for the disastrous consequences.

New Orleans, the thirty-fifth largest city in the United States, has long been subject to severe flooding. The city is almost entirely surrounded by water, the Mississippi River to the south, Lake Pontchartrain to the north, and Lake Borgne to the east. To complicate matters, much of New Orleans sits below sea level, while these water bodies average an annual high-water mark of 14 feet above sea level. To deal with this chronic problem, residents began constructing levees around the city soon after its establishment in 1718. In the nearly 300 years that have followed, the people of New Orleans have been locked in a continuous struggle to hold back the waters.

EXHIBIT 16.1   *Aerial view of New Orleans, the day after Hurricane Katrina, showing houses covered in water up to roof level. In the background, water continues to flow through a breach in the city's levee system.*

Source: Jocelyn Augustino, U.S. Federal Emergency Management Agency. www.photolibrary.fema.gov/photodata/original/15022.jpg.

Hurricanes have proven to be a constant threat to New Orleans, having flooded the city 38 times since 1759. Hurricane Betsy, in 1965, caused such damage that a roughly 50-year levee improvement plan was enacted to protect the city from future hurricanes. Forty years later, the still-incomplete 350-mile levee system proved inadequate for this task.

Although Category 3 hurricanes (winds between 111 and 130 miles per hour, with surges between 9 and 12 feet) have made landfall in the United States roughly once every two years since the mid-1800s, none has come close to the destruction caused by Hurricane Katrina. The August 2005 hurricane overpowered New Orleans' flood protection system, precipitating what has been called "the single most costly catastrophic failure of an engineered system in the history of the United States."[1]

Hurricane Katrina began forming as a tropical depression over the southeastern Bahamas on August 23, 2005 (see Exhibit 16.2). The storm migrated westward and began strengthening the following day. On August 25, Katrina moved over southern Florida and started to weaken as it traveled across land. By the morning of August 26, however, the storm had entered the warm waters of the Gulf of Mexico and quickly gathered energy. Over the next two days, Katrina grew to Category 5 status (winds of greater than 155 miles per hour with surges of greater than 18 feet). It had also become enormous in size, with tropical-storm-force winds extending 230 miles from its center.

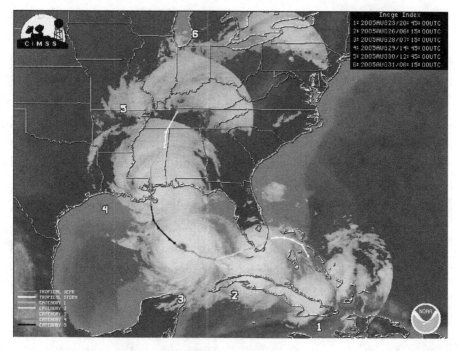

EXHIBIT 16.2   *Path of Hurricane Katrina*

Source: Axel Graumann et al., "Hurricane Katrina, A Climatological Perspective," Technical Report 2005-01 (Asheville, NC: U.S. Department of Commerce, U.S. National Oceanic and Atmospheric Administration, 2005).

By the time the storm reached the Gulf of Mexico, three-quarters of all manned oil platforms and drilling rigs in the area had been evacuated in anticipation of its arrival. Evacuations on land, however, were less thorough and slower to develop. Such was the case in New Orleans, where a mandatory order to evacuate was not issued until 24 hours before the storm struck the city. Despite this order, more than 100,000 people remained, being financially unable to flee, overconfident in their ability to weather the storm, or unwilling to leave their assets unguarded.

Late on August 28, Katrina began losing intensity, then turned northward, taking aim on the Louisiana and Mississippi coast. The storm came ashore in Plaquemines Parish, Louisiana, on the morning of August 29. By the time it made landfall, Katrina's wind speed had dropped to less than 130 miles per hour and had been downgraded to a Category 3 hurricane.

While the storm rapidly lost power as it moved inland, it was able to inflict considerable damage on the Gulf coast. Katrina knocked out power to 2.5 million customers and incapacitated the region's communication system. Thirty-eight 911 call centers were rendered inoperable, phone service to more than 3 million customers was interrupted, wireless phone infrastructure was damaged, and hundreds of television and radio stations were knocked off the air. Major ports in the region were closed, including Mobile, Alabama, as well as major shipping routes, including the Mississippi River and various Gulf-area waterways. Katrina's rain and storm surge flooded the coast, leaving some towns, such as Gulfport, Mississippi, under 10 feet of water. A number of communities, such as Waveland, Mississippi, were completely destroyed, and damage from the storm reached more than 150 miles inland. All told, 90,000 square miles, an area slightly larger than Great Britain, were affected by Katrina. In this area, nearly 2,000 people lost their lives and as many as three-quarters of a million people were displaced from their homes. The trail of destruction left behind by the Katrina made it the costliest and one of the most deadly storms ever to strike the United States.

New Orleans, with its intricate flood prevention system, was at the center of Katrina's devastation. When the hurricane made landfall, it created a storm surge approaching 20 feet in height. This wall of water eroded the outer layer of levees protecting the southeastern New Orleans region, crossed the swampland behind them, and easily over-topped the smaller, inner ring of levees protecting the city (see Exhibit 16.3). As the storm surge moved into Lake Borgne, the outer and secondary levees around the eastern part of New Orleans similarly failed. This surge also filled the Gulf Intracoastal Waterway and the Inner Harbor Navigation Channel beyond capacity, causing those flood-walls and levees to fail and allow water to flow toward downtown New Orleans.

Katrina then passed northward over Lake Pontchartrain, raising lake levels by 10 to 14 feet. New Orleans' lakeside levees were soon

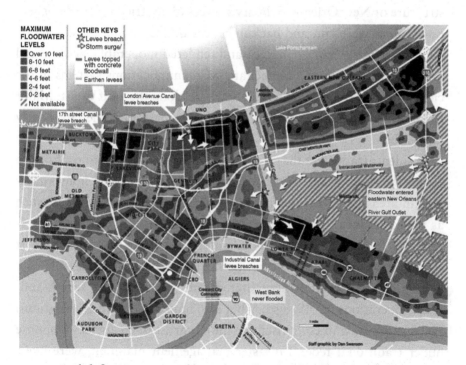

EXHIBIT **16.3**   *Location of levee breaches and levels of flooding*

Source: *Dan Swenson, "Multiple Failures,"* Times-Picayune, *December 8, 2005.*

overtopped, and the city's three drainage canals became filled with water flowing upstream from the lake. Two of these, the 17th Street and London Avenue canals, experienced breaches that allowed water to pour into the heart of New Orleans. Although the third canal did not fail, an unfinished section of floodwall allowed water to flow unimpeded into the city.

The failure of the canal flood protection system to hold back rising lake waters wreaked havoc. As water poured into the city, pumps that normally would help mitigate minor flooding were overwhelmed and stopped functioning. The waters continued to rise in New Orleans for four days until Lake Pontchartrain's levels began returning to normal. By this time, however, 80% of the city was under as much as 20 feet of water.

Hurricane Katrina and the resulting flood decimated the civil infrastructure of New Orleans. Primary sources of electricity were damaged, power lines were cut, and backup generators, including those used by many hospitals, were submerged and rendered inoperable. Sewage and drainage systems were incapacitated. Communications systems in the city suffered damage like that of elsewhere along the Gulf Coast. Major roads were impassible, making further evacuation of the city nearly impossible.

Residents trapped in the city climbed into attics and onto rooftops to escape the rising water. Those who were able to leave their homes gathered in areas that were not suitably equipped to serve as shelters, such as the Superdome, the Convention Center, and an overpass on Interstate 10. In these locations, food, water, and electricity were in short supply or nonexistent, and conditions quickly became intolerable.

Katrina's destruction necessitated one of the largest search-and-rescue operations in U.S. history but also impeded response operations. Local officials, who comprised the initial thrust of emergency response under traditional federal disaster management planning, were overwhelmed by the storm and flood. Throughout the region, police stations and fire departments were destroyed, many emergency responders were missing, and flooding forced the closure of emergency operations centers. A non-functioning 911 system, the lack of police radios, and downed telephone lines made coordination among local responders extremely difficult. Coordination was further obstructed by the inability of response crews to establish local operational command centers under flood conditions. The office of Mayor Ray Nagin, which was forced to operate out of a hotel, had no means of communication and could not oversee response coordination. With local agencies unable to mount a large-scale response, chaos soon gripped the city.

Anticipating some degree of flooding from Katrina, a small number of federal responders had been prepositioned in the area. When it became apparent that more federal assistance was needed, delivery of these resources was complicated by the flooding of major highways in the Gulf region. Even so, the U.S. Federal Emergency Management Agency (FEMA) was unprepared to provide all the necessary emergency supplies required by the disaster. When federal agents and supplies were delayed for days, Mayor Nagin issued what he described as a "desperate SOS" to the federal government. Louisiana representative Charles Boustany later described the early phases of emergency response by saying "The state resources were being overwhelmed, and we needed direct federal assistance, command and control, and security—all three of which were lacking."[2]

Even as federal officials and National Guard troops began arriving in the days following Katrina, much confusion plagued search-and-rescue efforts. In particular, incompatibility among responding agencies' communications systems made interagency coordination difficult. As a result, many victims were rescued from the floodwaters only to be delivered to locations where there was no food, water, or relief from the sun.

Threats to the personal safety of emergency responders further hampered search-and-rescue operations. If being exposed to extreme heat, downed power lines, bacteria, spilled oil, and toxic chemicals were not enough, they also had to face crime and lawlessness from looting and violence that had spread throughout the city. At one point, Mayor Nagin was forced to order 1,500 police officers—nearly the entire force—to turn their attention away from rescue operations in order to combat looting. Amid the anarchy, several emergency workers were attacked.

By September 1, state and federal officials had formulated an evacuation plan for flood victims and began relocating those inside the Superdome to shelters in other states. Eventually, tens of thousands of people were either bused or airlifted out of the city.

The U.S. Army Corps of Engineers (USACE) began repairing levees and pumping the floodwaters out of New Orleans soon after the hurricane had passed. As the floodwaters receded, the extent of the storm's impact on the city became more apparent. Eighty percent of the nearly 2,000 people who lost their lives as a result of the storm died in New Orleans. Damage in the greater New Orleans area, by itself, has been estimated in the hundreds of billions of dollars.

In the months following Katrina, FEMA struggled with ways to house the hundreds of thousands of people displaced by the storm. The agency arranged for more than $2 billion in temporary housing but had difficulty making it available to storm victims. More than 120,000 trailers and mobile homes were purchased by FEMA, yet one month after Katrina, only 109 families had been placed in them, leaving 48,000 people in shelters in Louisiana alone. Similarly, four cruise ships were leased as temporary shelters, but by the end of September 2005, they were less than half full.

The destruction and loss of life in New Orleans, while initiated by the storm itself, cannot be attributed entirely to Katrina. Numerous failures of the city's flood protection system, due to poor design and construction, deferred maintenance, and a lack of funding, left New Orleans susceptible to a hurricane of Katrina's magnitude. As the city filled with water, insufficient emergency planning and preparedness, and the inability of responders to communicate, compounded the hurricane's effects.

Katrina was a large and powerful storm. Although its strength waned just before landfall, the hurricane was still able to produce a massive storm surge that set in motion the failure of New Orleans' levees and floodwalls. The magnitude of the surge can be attributed to Katrina's size and shallow offshore waters that served to amplify its effects.

This surge could have been buffered by wetlands, which reduce such swells at a rate of one foot for every four miles of marsh. However, drilling for fossil fuels and engineering of the Mississippi River had destroyed wetlands in the Gulf beyond New Orleans at a rate of 25 miles per year. As a result, the city was left defenseless as Katrina and the storm surge continued unimpeded toward land.

The New Orleans flood protection system was designed in compartments, so that if one area of the city were to flood, other areas might be spared. Thus, widespread flooding of the city would be possible only if there were multiple failures in the system. However, when conceived, this system was intended to withstand only a "very strong Category 2" hurricane. On average, storms of this magnitude or stronger were expected to impact New Orleans once every 30 years. In comparison, structures such as oil rigs and flood protection for some cities that face the threat of strong storms are routinely designed to withstand natural disasters whose likelihood of occurrence is once every 10,000 years.

With such lenient design standards, the New Orleans flood protection system was considered far less dependable than other flood protection devices in the United States, such as major dams. Dam design in the United States is particularly strict, because failure of these structures is assumed to present a threat to major populations. Few dams in this country, however, present a risk to populations as large as that of greater New Orleans.

One inadequacy of the flood protection system was a lack of floodgates on canals and the navigation channel. Floodgates are dams that normally are left open to allow water to flow or vessels to pass. In the event of a storm, the gates are closed to prevent flooding of the channel. Had gates been included in the flood protection system for New

Orleans, water in the canals and navigation channel likely would not have reached levels high enough to cause levee and floodwall failures.

Once water reached elevations that overtopped the canal and channel floodwalls, it poured over the back side of the walls and scoured out a trench behind them. As the supporting soil was washed away, rising water pushed over the floodwalls. This situation occurred throughout the New Orleans system because most of the floodwalls were "I" type, designed with no protection against such erosion. This type of floodwall is less stable and more easily toppled than T-walls, partly because T-walls have a concrete splash pad built into their design that acts as a barrier against scouring erosion (see Exhibit 16.4). The design of the joints connecting adjacent floodwalls was also problematic; many failed under pressure from the rising water. Thus, the faulty joints allowed floodwalls that were not toppled to fail at the seams.

While poor design of flood system elements played a major role in flooding the city, in several instances the system failed without storm conditions reaching design levels. During construction, some floodwalls were not sunk deep enough; they were undercut by floodwaters. Other floodwalls were built on sediments that were prone to slipping, allowing the walls to be pushed over. Numerous sections of levees were constructed using sand and shell materials instead of clays, which are more

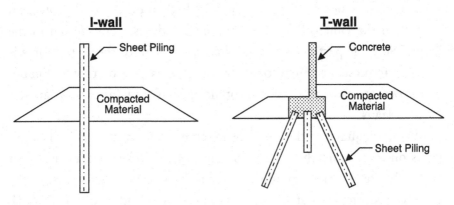

EXHIBIT 16.4 *Comparison of I-type versus T-type floodwalls.*

(Note: figure not to scale.)

resistant to erosion. Additionally, levee coverings used to mitigate erosion, such as stone, were not employed.

The construction of the flood protection system was incomplete in addition to being faulty. By the summer of 2005, system improvements initiated after Hurricane Betsy struck were still 12 years from completion. When Katrina arrived, an 11-mile section of levee along Lake Borgne was several feet lower than the already underdesigned construction standards. Similarly, an incomplete section of floodwall along the Orleans Canal in downtown New Orleans was six feet below specifications.

In some cases, proper maintenance and inspection before the storm would have served to strengthen weak points in the flood protection system. For example, USACE and local inspectors had given levees on the 17th Street Canal ratings of "acceptable" despite the presence of trees growing on them. These trees were neither reported nor removed. Such growth compromises structural integrity and is in violation of standards for levee protection. Moreover, some levees had settled by more than two feet since their construction but were not repaired, making them more likely to be overwhelmed by storm surges.

Some of the shortfalls in construction and maintenance can be attributed to difficulty in obtaining sufficient funding. Procuring federal money is often a complex and lengthy process. For example, USACE had long requested funds for completing levees along Lake Borgne, but they had not been granted when Katrina struck. Additionally, the amount of funding available for flood protection had grown progressively smaller at the same time that USACE was being asked to produce better results. Following the terrorist attacks of September 11, 2001, federal dollars were diverted from flood protection to support military operations in Afghanistan and Iraq. This political agenda caused funding for flood control to fall dramatically, prompting work on levees to be halted for the first time in 37 years. In 2005, USACE requested $27 million for flood protection around Lake Pontchartrain and $78 million for similar work in New Orleans; instead it received just $5.7 million and $36.5 million, respectively.

Even with shortfalls in funding, some of the money earmarked for flood control was never used for its intended purpose. According to a report by the U.S. Department of Defense, funds delivered to the city of New Orleans were diverted to more politically popular projects through mismanagement and corruption.

Insufficient funding also crippled emergency response planning. In 2004, an emergency exercise conducted by officials from the federal, Louisiana, and New Orleans governments exposed the significant risk that hurricanes posed to the city. Plans to prepare for an actual hurricane, however, were abandoned due to lack of funding. Among the plans to be developed were methods for providing shelter for storm victims and evacuating displaced people from the Superdome. One month before Katrina, federal, state, and local officials again convened to study emergency planning for hurricanes. The attendees determined that, in the absence of funding, evacuation planning was dangerously incomplete and that conditions were ripe for a mass-casualty event.

The funds for such planning, like those for levee construction and maintenance, had suffered as a result of the September 11, 2001, attacks. After the attacks, FEMA's focus was redirected away from mitigating natural disasters and toward antiterrorism. In 2003, the agency was placed under the Department of Homeland Security. Three-quarters of the grants that agency distributed for emergency preparedness were for combating terrorism rather than responding to natural disasters.

FEMA's shift in focus was but one issue that plagued it as the agency in charge of responding to Katrina. A number of critics have charged FEMA leadership with incompetence. Five of the agency's top eight officials, including then director Michael Brown, had no experience in crisis management prior to their appointment within FEMA. The disaster management background of Brown's superior, Homeland Security secretary Michael Chertoff, was nearly as meager. During the Katrina crisis, these officials showed little knowledge or understanding of the situation, claiming to be unaware of conditions within New Orleans (despite numerous media reports) and dismissing victims as people who simply chose not to evacuate.

The inexperience among federal officials compounded the difficulty in responding to a disaster that presented new challenges in emergency planning and response for all levels of government. Traditional methods for mitigating disasters were found to be highly ineffective in the face of such massive destruction. For example, federal response to disasters was based on the premise that local government would initiate the effort, or at least be able to direct federal assets. In the case of Katrina, however, local governments were incapacitated, which undermined the established response process. As the federal government began to mobilize, standard procedures, such as FEMA's methods for procuring and delivering supplies, proved inadequate. Local and state hurricane response plans were similarly ineffective. These governments had provisions for evacuation prior to the landfall of a major hurricane but were unprepared to evacuate the many thousands stranded by the flood that followed the storm.

In the days after Katrina, emergency responders were in short supply. Many were either missing or had abandoned their posts in the chaos that followed the storm. Moreover, 8,000 National Guard troops from the affected area—60% of the total force—had been deployed to Iraq and were unavailable for the response effort. Although troops were available in surrounding states, additional time and cost were required to transport them to the disaster area.

Available responders found their work hampered by numerous communication problems. The storm destroyed telephone and police radio systems, leaving responders in the field unable to communicate with those in charge of coordinating the response. FEMA had prepositioned two of its five mobile communications systems in the area before Katrina reached landfall, but this provision proved to be insufficient for such a large response effort. Additional communications infrastructure was not readily available and could not be put in place until three days after the storm, As the response effort progressed, communication among various agencies continued to be problematic, as systems used by the military were incompatible with those operated by local officials.

Less than a month after Hurricane Katrina, another hurricane, Rita, made landfall near the Louisiana–Texas border. Although Rita caused far less damage than Katrina, officials were better prepared the second time around. Over 3 million people were evacuated in the days prior to the storm, emptying the city of Houston and surrounding areas. Many officials attributed the low fatality count for the storm to this evacuation, which was more thorough than what transpired with Katrina.

The evacuation was still far from perfect, however, as officials were unprepared for the number of Gulf coast residents who attempted to evacuate. Millions of people fled the approaching storm, creating a traffic jam 100 miles long. After moving only 10 to 20 miles over nine hours, many cars overheated or ran out of gas. Ninety out of the 108 deaths indirectly attributed to Hurricane Rita were a result of the evacuation process. The majority of these fatalities occurred due to hyperthermia when the gridlock kept drivers from using air conditioning in the intense heat of late September.

Additional prestorm preparations included President Bush declaring an "incident of national significance" two days before Rita made landfall, setting in motion a federal response. A similar action had not been taken until two days after Katrina. As Rita approached land, 37,000 military troops were readied for response; by comparison, only 5,000 were available before Katrina. Federal officials stationed double the amount of search-and-rescue teams in the area and twice as many trailers of ice and water as they had with Katrina. Additionally, more than a dozen navy ships were stationed offshore with supplies and personnel. This increased preparation and attention to maintaining communication infrastructure were thought to have diminished adverse effects of storm.

Following the 2005 hurricane season, federal, state, and local officials began preparing for the next major hurricane. USACE worked around-the-clock to construct floodgates on New Orleans' three drainage canals. FEMA vastly increased the amount of supplies ready for a disaster, including preparing more than five times the amount of food for storm victims than was available during Katrina. FEMA also coordinated with the Louisiana National Guard to place satellite communication systems, handheld radios, and satellite cellular phones in each local government district to improve disaster communication. In addition, the agency helped to create a unified command post for coordinating response efforts. State and local officials have collaborated further with FEMA to create and rehearse more thorough evacuation plans for rescuing people prior to and following a hurricane. Plans for evacuating New Orleans still contain a number of oversights, however, such as an established list of shelters for evacuees and a plan for securing enough buses to transport the approximately 10,000 people who would require ground transportation under the new plan.

Residents of New Orleans have been slow to return to the city following Katrina. Nearly one year after the hurricane, New Orleans had less than half of its prestorm population. Cleanup and construction in the city continues, as does reconstruction and improvements to the city's flood defenses, a project that could take over a decade to complete.

Since the mid-1700s, New Orleans has experienced hurricane-induced flooding on an average of once every six and one-half years. This frequency, combined with the threat of rising sea levels and continued soil settling, suggests that improvements to the city's flood protection system may not be adequate to prevent another disaster.

Meanwhile, state and local governments beyond Louisiana have been slow to effect changes to emergency response plans and infrastructure in the wake of Katrina. This sluggishness is particularly disconcerting when viewed in the context of current meteorological trends indicating increases in both the number and the destructive potential of major Atlantic storms.

REFERENCES

Barbour, Haley. Speech to the Special Session of the Mississippi State Legislature, September 27, 2005. www.jacksonfreepress.com/comments.php?id=7332_0_7_0_C.

Blake, Eric S., et al. "The Deadliest, Costliest, and Most Intense United States Tropical Cyclones from 1851 to 2004 (and Other Frequently Requested Hurricane Facts)." NOAA Technical Memorandum NWS TPC-4. Miami, FL: Tropical Prediction Center, National Hurricane Center, U.S. National Oceanic and Atmospheric Administration, 2005.

Brown, Michael. Testimony before a Hearing on Hurricane Katrina, The Role of the Federal Emergency Management Agency. U.S. House Select Bipartisan Committee to Investigate the Preparation for and Response to Hurricane Katrina, 109th Congress, 1st session, September 27, 2005.

Burkett, Virginia R., David B. Zilkoski, and David A. Hart. "Sea-Level Rise and Subsidence: Implications for Flooding in New Orleans, Louisiana." In U.S. Geological Survey Open File Report 03-308, ed. Keith R. Prince and Devin L. Galloway. U.S. Geological Survey Subsidence Interest Group Conference, Proceedings of the Technical Meeting. Galveston, Texas, November 27–29, 2001.

Chertoff, Michael. Testimony before a Hearing on Hurricane Katrina: The Homeland Security Department's Preparation and Response. U.S. Senate Homeland Security and Governmental Affairs Committee, 109th Congress, 2nd session, February 15, 2006.

CNN. "A Disturbing View from Inside FEMA," November 4, 2005. www.cnn.com/2005/US/09/17/katrina.response/index.html.

CNN. "FEMA Chief Touts High-Tech Hurricane Response," June 1, 2006. http://cnn.com/2006/WEATHER/06/01/hurricane.forecast/index.html.

CNN. "FEMA Chief: Victims Bear Some Responsibility," September 1, 2005. www.cnn.com/2005/WEATHER/09/01/katrina.fema.brown/index.html.

CNN. "Katrina Kills 50 in One Mississippi County," August 30, 2005. www.cnn.com/2005/WEATHER/08/29/hurricane.katrina.

CNN. "Official: July until New Orleans Floodgates Ready," May 18, 2006. http://cnn.com/2006/US/05/18/nola.levees/index.html.

CNN. "Report: New Orleans Levee Planners Ignored Danger Signs," March 22, 2007. www.cnn.com/2007/US/03/22/new.orleans.levees.ap/index.html.

Connolly, Ceci. "'I Don't Think I've Ever Had a More Surreal Experience'; Veteran Rescue Workers Surprised by Challenges in Louisiana," *Washington Post*, September 12, 2005.

Emanuel, Kerry. Increasing Destructiveness of Tropical Cyclones over the Past 30 Years, *Nature* 436 (2005): 686–688.

Graumann, Axel, et al. "Hurricane Katrina, A Climatological Perspective," Technical Report 2005-01. Asheville, NC: U.S. Department of Commerce, U.S. National Oceanic and Atmospheric Administration, 2005.

Griffis, F. H. "Engineering Failures Exposed by Hurricane Katrina," *Technology in Society* 29 (2007): 189–195.

Holland, Greg J., and Peter J. Webster. "Heightened Tropical Cyclone Activity in the North Atlantic: Natural Variability or Climate Trend?" *Philosophical Transactions of the Royal Society A.* (doi: 10.1098/rsta.2007.2083) 2007.

Hsu, Spencer, and Steve Hendrix. "Hurricanes Katrina and Rita Were Like Night and Day," *Washington Post*, September 25, 2005.

Independent Levee Investigation Team. "Investigation of the Performance of the New Orleans Flood Protection Systems in Hurricane Katrina on August 29, 2005." Berkeley: University of California 2006.

Interagency Performance Evaluation Taskforce. "Performance Evaluation of the New Orleans and Southeast Louisiana Hurricane Protection System." Vicksburg, MS: U.S. Army Corps of Engineers, 2006.

International Association of Firefighters. "Reports from the Hurricane Frontlines: Katrina (August 29–September 6)," August 30, 2005. http://daily.iaff.org/Katrina/Katrina.htm?c=report1.

International Association of Firefighters. "Reports from the Hurricane Frontlines: Katrina (September 7–September 13)," September 10, 2005. http://daily.iaff.org/Katrina/Katrina.htm?c=report2.

Kates, R. W., et al. "Reconstruction of New Orleans After Hurricane Katrina: A Research Perspective," *Proceedings of the National Academy of Sciences* 103 (2006): 14,653–14,606.

Knabb, Richard D., Daniel P. Brown, and Jamie R. Rhome. "Tropical Cyclone Report: Hurricane Rita, 1826 September 2005." Miami, FL: National Hurricane Center, U.S. National Oceanic and Atmospheric Administration, 2006.

Knabb, Richard D., Jamie R. Rhome, and Daniel P. Brown. "Tropical Cyclone Report: Hurricane Katrina, 23–30 August 2005." Miami, FL: National Hurricane Center, U.S. National Oceanic and Atmospheric Administration, 2006.

LaCaze, Keith. "Activity Report on Hurricane Katrina." Baton Rouge, LA: Louisiana Department of Wildlife and Fisheries, Enforcement Division, 2005.

LaCaze, Keith. Testimony given at Congressional hearing on Managing the Crisis Evacuating New Orleans, U.S. Senate Homeland Security and Governmental Affairs Committee, 109th Congress, 2nd session, January 30, 2006.

Lean, Geoffrey. "Warnings Went Ignored as Bush Slashed Flood Defense Budget to Pay for Wars," *The Independent,* September 4, 2005.

Lipton, Eric. "Key Documents Regarding the Government Response to Katrina," *New York Times.* February 10, 2006, www.nytimes.com/ref/national/nationalspecial/10katrina-docs.html.

Lipton, Eric, and Leslie Eaton. "Housing for Storm's Evacuees Lagging Far Behind US Goals," *New York Times,* September 30, 2005.

Lipton, Eric, and Scott Shane. "Leader of Federal Effort Feels the Heat," *New York Times,* September 3, 2005.

Litman, Todd. "Lessons from Katrina and Rita: What Major Disasters Can Teach Transportation Planners,"*Journal of Transportation Engineering* (2006): Vol 132, 11–18.

Louisiana Office of the Governor. Response to U.S. Senate Committee on Homeland Security and Governmental Affairs Document and Information Request Dated October 7, 2005, and to the U.S. House of Representatives Select Committee to Investigate the Preparation for and Response to Hurricane Katrina, December 2, 2005.

Meeting transcript. New Orleans emergency response officials, 2005. www.nytimes.com/packages/pdf/national/20060210KATRINA/document4.pdf.

Mittal, Anu K. Testimony before a Hearing on Hurricane Protection Given to the U.S. Senate Committee on Homeland Security and Governmental Affairs, 109th Congress, 1st session, December 15, 2005.

Moran, Kenneth. Testimony before a Hearing on Ensuring Operability During Catastrophic Events Given to the U.S. House Committee on Homeland Security, Subcommittee on Emergency Preparedness, Science, and Technology, 109th Congress, 1st session, October 26, 2005.

Moran, Kenneth. Written Statement for a Hearing on Hurricane Katrina and Communications Interoperability, submitted to the U.S. Senate Committee on Commerce, Science, and Transportation, 109th Congress, 1st session. September 29, 2005.

Nagin, Ray. Testimony before a Hearing on Hurricane Katrina: Preparedness and Response by the State of Louisiana Given to the U.S. House Select Committee to Investigate the Preparation for and Response to Hurricane Katrina, 109th Congress, 1st session, December 14, 2005.

Nagin, Ray. Written Statement for a Hearing on Managing the Crisis: Evacuating New Orleans, submitted to the U.S. Senate Homeland Security and Governmental Affairs Committee, 109th Congress, 2nd session, February 1, 2006.

Pearce, Vincent. Written Statement Submitted for a Hearing on Hurricane Katrina: Managing the Crisis and Evacuating New Orleans Given to the U.S. Senate Homeland Security and Governmental Affairs Committee, 109th Congress, 2nd session, February 1, 2006.

Rhoads, Christopher. "Cut Off: At Center of Crisis, City Officials Faced Struggle to Keep in Touch," *Wall Street Journal*, September 9, 2005.

Riley, Warren J. Written Statement for a Hearing on Hurricane Katrina: Managing Law Enforcement and Communications in a Catastrophe, submitted to the U.S. Senate Committee on Homeland Security and Governmental Affairs, 109th Congress, 2nd session, February 6, 2006.

Roesgen, Susan. "New Orleans Evacuation Plan Has Holes," CNN, May 12, 2006. http://cnn.com/2006/US/05/11/new.orleans.evacuation/index.html.

Roig-Franzia, Manuel, and Spencer Hsu. "Many Evacuated, but Thousands Still Waiting," *Washington Post*, September 4, 2005.

Schneider, Saundra K. "Administrative Breakdowns in the Governmental Response to Hurricane Katrina," *Public Administration Review* 65 (2005): 515–516.

Select Bipartisan Committee to Investigate the Preparation for and Response to Hurricane Katrina. *A Failure of Initiative*. Washington, DC: U.S. Government Printing Office, 2006.

Sengupta, Kim. "Iraq War Delayed Katrina Relief Effort, Inquiry Finds," *The Independent*, October 3, 2005.

Thomas, Evan. "The Lost City," *Newsweek,* September 10, 2005.

Townsend, Francis Fragos. "The Federal Response to Hurricane Katrina: Lessons Learned." Washington, DC: The White House, 2006.

Watson, Rebecca. Written Statement for a Hearing on Global Oil Demand/Gasoline Prices, submitted to the U.S. Senate Committee on Energy and Natural Resources, 109th Congress, 1st session, September 6, 2005.

U.S. Department of Defense. "Army Corps of Engineers Fixes Levees, Drains New Orleans," September 15, 2005. www.defenselink.mil/news/newsarticle.aspx?id=17286.

U.S. Department of Defense, National Guard Bureau. "After Action Review: Hurricane Response September 2005," NGB J7. Arlington, VA: U.S. Department of Defense, National Guard Bureau, 2005.

U.S. Department of Energy. "Department of Energy's Hurricane Response Chronology, as Referred to by Secretary Bodman at Today's Senate Energy and Natural Resources Committee Hearing," October 27, 2005. http://energy.gov/news/2404.htm.

U.S. Department of Homeland Security. "United States Government Response to the Aftermath of Hurricane Katrina," September 1, 2005. www.dhs.gov/xnews/releases/press_release_0727.shtm.

U.S. Department of Transportation. "Largest Airlift in U.S. History to Get over 10,000 People Out of New Orleans by End of Today," September 3, 2005. www.dot.gov/affairs/dot12005.htm.

U.S. Environmental Protection Agency. "Environmental Assessment Summary for Areas of Jefferson, Orleans, St. Bernard, and Plaquemines Parishes Flooded as a Result of Hurricane Katrina," 2005. www.epa.gov/katrina/testresults/katrina_env_assessment_summary.htm.

U.S. Federal Emergency Management Agency. "Urban Search and Rescue Operations Completed," September 30, 2005. www.fema .gov/news/newsrelease.fema?id=19320.

Zachria, Anthony and Bela Patel. Deaths Related to Hurricane Rita and Mass Evacuation, *Chest.* 130 (4): p.124S.

NOTES

1. Independent Levee Investigation Team. "Investigation of the Performance of the New Orleans Flood Protection Systems in Hurricane Katrina on August 29, 2005." Berkeley: University of California, 2006.
2. Josh White and Peter Whoriskeyl, "Planning Response Are Faulted," *Washington Post*, September 2, 2005.

PART FOUR

SUCCESS STORIES

There have been times in the past when individuals and organizations have worked diligently ahead of time to address significant risks that they believed might occur in the future. They adhered to a responsible and proactive approach, where intense preparation and attention to detail would prove to be the difference between a catastrophic outcome and less severe consequences.

Two success stories are presented here. One involves a man-made accident in which, although some human lives were lost, by all rights there should have been no survivors. The other case focuses on a natural disaster that had the potential to inflict major damage to one of the most pristine spots in the world. Ironically, this success story involves some of the same players who were part of a man-made catastrophe described earlier in this book.

These cases are exemplary in demonstrating how a well-designed and carefully orchestrated risk management approach can alter an outcome in terms of life versus death or ecological destruction versus environmental protection. While certain individuals might appear to have performed heroic tasks, in reality they were just doing their jobs.

CHAPTER 17

UNITED AIRLINES FLIGHT 232

On July 19, 1989, while en route from Denver to Chicago, flying debris severed all three hydraulic systems on United Airlines Flight 232, leaving the pilot without any control of the DC-10 aircraft. Through the courageous effort of the cockpit crew and a highly coordinated emergency response, the plane was able to make a crash landing at the Sioux City, Iowa, airport. Due to these exemplary risk management practices, both in the air and on the ground, of the 296 passengers and crew onboard, 184 people survived the crash (see Exhibit 17.1).

In the early afternoon of July 19, 1989, passengers began boarding a United Airlines DC-10 aircraft at Denver's Stapleton Airport. One of the passengers, Denny Fitch, introduced himself to the flight crew as he entered the plane and made his way to the first-class section. Fitch, an off-duty DC-10 instructor pilot, settled into his seat, looking forward to an uneventful flight. He was entirely unaware that an unthinkable disaster was about to occur, one that he would help turn into an equally improbable success.

United Airlines Flight 232 departed Denver for Chicago at 2:09 PM. In the cockpit was Captain Al Haynes, a 33-year veteran with nearly 30,000 hours of flying time. Beside him sat First Officer William Records and Flight Engineer Dudley Dvorak, with 20,000 and 15,000 hours of flight time, respectively, on their resumes.

EXHIBIT 17.1   *Crash site of United Flight 232*

Source: www.airdisaster.com/special/special-ua232.shtml.

About an hour into the flight, the 8 attendants onboard began serving lunch to 285 passengers. The plane had climbed to 37,000 feet and had just crossed the Iowa border when the crew began executing a gentle right turn toward Chicago. Suddenly a deafening explosion shook the entire aircraft. The sound was so loud that the captain initially feared that the passenger compartment had decompressed. A quick scan of the flight controls, however, revealed that one of the engines had failed. Haynes gave the order to begin shutting it down.

The DC-10 is a three-jet engine aircraft with one engine under each wing and one in the tail. The failed engine on Flight 232 was the tail, also referred to as the number two engine. The plane still had its right and left engines available, however, which normally would be sufficient to carry the aircraft to a safe landing.

Haynes left Records to fly the plane while he and Dvorak carried out the shutdown procedure for the damaged engine. Dvorak read the first item on the procedure list: "Close the throttle." Haynes pulled the throttle lever, but it would not move, a problem he had not encountered before. When Dvorak continued to the second item, "Turn off the fuel supply," Haynes could not move the fuel supply lever, either. Haynes and Dvorak had just devised an alternate way to shut off the fuel to the number two engine when Records spoke up: "Al, I can't control the airplane."

The explosion of the engine had shot more than 70 pieces of shrapnel into the horizontal section of the plane's tail. These projectiles severed all three of the independent, redundant hydraulic flight control systems onboard. With hydraulic fluid completely drained from the aircraft, the crew seemingly had no means of controlling the plane.

Upon realizing the severity of the situation, Dvorak began contacting maintenance and air traffic control (ATC) centers to notify them of his circumstances and to seek advice. The maintenance experts had never encountered a similar problem. In fact, the probability of all three hydraulic systems failing at once was considered so low that the aircraft manufacturer, the Federal Aviation Administration, and United Airlines had no established a procedure for addressing such a scenario. According to the manufacturer's specifications, steering a DC-10 under these conditions would not be possible. Maintenance could offer no suggestions and, unknown to the flight crew, decided that Flight 232 was doomed.

Meanwhile, the plane continued its slow right turn and began descending. Haynes took over the controls as the plane began to roll over onto its back. As the tilt of the plane increased and the crew ran out of options, Haynes desperately throttled the left engine and reduced the thrust in the right. The plane then began to level out.

ATC directed Flight 232 to Sioux City Gateway Airport to attempt an emergency landing. Haynes then notified the passengers that the number two engine had been lost and instructed the flight attendants to prepare for the landing.

After about 15 minutes of manipulating the throttles in an attempt to steer the plane toward Sioux City, a flight attendant brought Finch to the cockpit. Although Finch was unable to provide any new information, he offered to assist in whatever way he could. Finch first went to the rear of the aircraft to confirm the damage. He then took over control of the throttles, affording the crew more freedom to work on the problem. For the next 30 minutes, Finch steered the plane with a throttle control in each hand, responding to commands from the crew.

As Flight 232 approached Sioux City Gateway, Fitch was unable to keep the airplane from completing a number of wide right circles as it continued descending (see Exhibit 17.2). Meanwhile, Haynes communicated with the Gateway airport air traffic controller to make preparations for landing. The crew then dumped the plane's excess fuel and worked in concert with the controller to steer the aircraft away from populated areas around Sioux City.

Rescue and firefighting vehicles gathered as Fitch attempted to line up the plane with the longest of Gateway's three runways. As the plane completed its final circle, however, Fitch was only able to align the air-

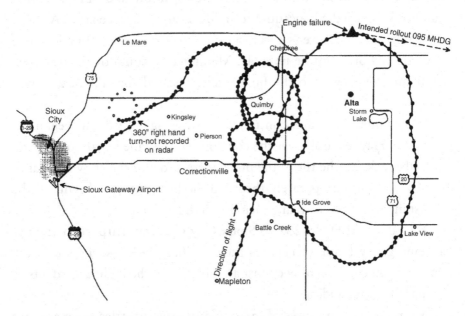

EXHIBIT 17.2   *Flight path of United 232 over Iowa*

Source: National Transportation Safety Board, Aircraft Accident Report—United Airlines Flight 232, McDonnell Douglas DC-10, Sioux Gateway Airport, Sioux City, Iowa, July 19, 1989. *Report No. NTSB/AAR-90/06, November 1990.*

craft with a shorter, 7,000-foot runway that was no longer in use. The controller cleared Flight 232 to use the shorter runway and scrambled rescue equipment that had been positioned there out of the way.

Fitch and the crew were able to straighten the plane out for landing, but they could not control the speed and descent rate. Whereas a speed of 160 miles per hour at a descent rate of 300 feet per second is the normal condition for landing a DC-10, United 232 was traveling at almost 250 miles per hour and dropping at more than 1,850 feet per second.

The plane touched down 45 minutes after the explosion, at approximately 4:00 PM. Although the aircraft landed just off of the runway center line, the left wing dipped at the last moment, striking the ground and spinning the plane to the side. The right landing gear ripped a large hole in the concrete runway as the plane broke apart and then burst into flames.

The center section of the aircraft, where most of the passengers were located, ended upside down in a cornfield 3,700 feet from the site of initial touchdown. Firefighters approached the wreckage cautiously in order not to injure the victims who had begun walking across the runway. The tall corn in the field, just one of the many obstacles responders faced, made it difficult for firefighters to see the wreckage and locate survivors. The limited number of available radio frequencies for the size of the recovery effort also hindered communication among responders. Additionally, a critical water delivery system malfunctioned as firefighters fought the flames. Despite these challenges, the firefighters were able to reach the plane, cut through seat belts to remove survivors trapped inside, and extinguish the blaze.

Crash victims were moved from the wreckage site to a well-organized triage area for transport to local hospitals. When the scale of the disaster became apparent, rescue workers requested additional vehicles. Thirty-four ambulances, some from as far as 60 miles away, responded to the call, along with 9 helicopters. All critical patients were evacuated from the scene within an hour of touchdown, with the remaining victims removed within another 45 minutes.

At the time of the crash, the two local hospitals activated their mass-casualty plans, assembling resources and personnel. By the time the first patients arrived, they encountered an orderly and efficient medical disaster response system.

Of the 296 people on board United Flight 232, 185 survived the crash and fire. Following an accident investigation and simulator testing of the event, a federal review board declared that a safe landing under such circumstances was essentially impossible, making the survival of any of Flight 232's passengers all the more extraordinary.

The failure of the number two engine was caused by a material defect and wear in an engine fan. The six-foot fan developed a crack and disintegrated during the flight, spraying fan blades and pieces of metal that severed all three independent hydraulic lines. The crack, which had occurred very early in the life of the engine part, had never been detected, despite six detailed inspections of the fan over its 18-year life.

That the Flight 232 crew was able to save the lives of 185 people is considered remarkable. This positive outcome can be attributed in part to the crew's experience; the four airmen had been flying for a total of 103 years. It can also be attributed to at least one crew member having trained on the use of unconventional aircraft control methods after the hydraulics-related crash of a Japan Airlines jumbo jet in 1985. Another critical factor was the crew's preparedness for handling in-flight emergencies. This preparation, referred to as Crew Resource Management (CRM) training, enabled the crew to communicate effectively, cooperate with one another, and carry out necessary tasks in the face of almost unimaginable adversity.

CRM training, which was adopted by the airline industry following a series of potentially avoidable mishaps in the 1970s and 1980s, aimed to increase the effectiveness of communication among cockpit teams in emergency situations. Poor communication had been a major factor in more than 70% of all airline accidents, and teamwork often suffered when stress levels were high. Thus, CRM sought to foster a group approach to problem solving and communication, in stark contrast to the previously accepted paradigm in which the captain was the unchallenged leader of the flight. According to CRM, in emergency situations, this kind of inclusive, efficient communication is even more important than skill in flying the aircraft.

On Flight 232, the superb team interaction and coordination demonstrated by the crew was a product of CRM training. A case in point was the discussion that took place among crew members on how to lower the landing gear in the absence of hydraulic power. Each airman offered suggestions, which were then discussed by the group, eventually leading to an agreed-on approach. In another instance, as Dvorak took Fitch's place at the controls to land the aircraft, he realized that Fitch was more proficient at using the throttles. He then suggested that Fitch perform the landing and returned to his supporting role. According to Haynes, without this kind of team-oriented approach and open communication, Flight 232 would likely have been a complete loss.

Effective communication also extended beyond the cockpit door. The captain reported that communication with the flight attendants was as good as could be expected while the officers attempted to fly the damaged aircraft. Flight attendants, in turn, were able to explain the situation to passengers and provide instructions in preparation for landing. Interaction between the flight crew and Gateway air traffic control was similarly solid. The radar worker speaking with Flight 232 remained calm throughout the ordeal, lowering the tension level in the cockpit and helping the crew maintain its composure.

Preparedness for the disaster was not limited to air personnel, however. Local officials in Sioux City had formed a disaster planning committee that met each month and held two simulated disasters exercises every year. In one such exercise, response personnel practiced for the emergency landing of a DC-10 aircraft at Gateway Airport, although a DC-10, like United Flight 232, had never landed at the airport before. Ironically, the exercise was held on the same runway used by the crippled plane.

The airport itself was also well equipped to handle the disaster. Sioux City Gateway was categorized as a "Category 6" airport according to National Fire Protection Association standards. This classification, based on the largest plane scheduled for landings at the airport, required one less rescue vehicle and half the amount of extinguishing agent than Gateway kept on hand.

Before Flight 232 had even touched down, local responders issued a "Level 3 Alert," which indicates that a plane has already crashed. This allowed early activation of Sioux City's crash response plan in anticipation of the emergency landing. As Flight 232 approached, airport resources were prepositioned along the runways, while Sioux City responders had mobilized to the south, in case the plane fell short of its target. This preparation allowed firefighters to respond quickly and effectively, saving many passengers' lives.

While credit belongs to preparation and training by the crew and responders, according to Captain Haynes, disaster mitigation also depended on a confluence of events almost as unlikely as the circumstances that set the episode in motion. For example, the engine failure took place on the only day of the month in which the 185th Iowa Air National Guard was on duty, making available 285 additional responders. The timing of the accident was similarly beneficial in that it coincided with shift changes at local hospitals. As a result, these hospitals had enough personnel on hand to allow for a doctor and assisting staff to be assigned to each ambulance as it arrived. Good afternoon weather, which can be unusual over the Midwest region of the United States in July, was critical in controlling the aircraft. Finally, the presence of an off-duty instructor pilot as a passenger on the plane presented the crew of Flight 232 with an invaluable additional resource for managing the crisis.

Haynes, Fitch, Records, and Dvorak all suffered varying degrees of injury in the crash, but each returned to work within 11 months of the accident. Haynes went on to speak publicly about the accident and the virtues of CRM training.

In 2003, a large cargo jet departing Baghdad International Airport was hit by a surface-to-air missile, destroying the plane's hydraulic systems. Fortunately, the captain of the aircraft had recently attended one of Haynes's lectures and was able to employ Flight 232's method of throttle control to land the jet safely.

The crash of Flight 232 also had a direct effect on the future design of DC-10 hydraulic systems. Following the accident, several fuses were installed in the tail section of the number three hydraulic line to prevent a complete loss of hydraulic fluid in the event of an accident. The close proximity of the three hydraulic lines within the plane's tail still makes their simultaneous failure a possibility, however. This was nearly the case in 2002, when a tire exploded on a DC-10 taking off from San Salvador, rupturing the first two hydraulic lines and nearly severing the third.

Researchers at NASA have recently developed Intelligent Flight Control (IFC), a software system that allows pilots to control aircraft when conventional controls are partially or completely damaged. The system registers the pilot's commands and compares how the plane responds to the way it should react if all flight controls were normal. By adjusting the plane's engines to make its actual response increasingly closer to the theoretical response, the plane becomes progressively easier for pilots to maneuver. In simulations, pilots aided by IFC were able to land damaged aircraft every time, while only 50% of pilots without the software achieved a similar outcome. The system was successfully tested aboard a military jet in February 2006 but is not yet available for commercial use.

REFERENCES

Bramesfeld, Götz, Mark D. Maughmer, and Steven M. Willits. "Piloting Strategies for Controlling a Transport Aircraft after Vertical-Tail Loss," *Journal of Aircraft* 43 (2006): 216–225. CNN. "DHL Halts Iraq Service after 'Hit,'" November 22, 2003. http://edition.cnn.com/2003/WORLD/meast/11/22/sprj.irq.dhl.ap.

Conroy, Mark T. "Aircraft Accidents that Caused Major Changes to Emergency Response Equipment and Procedures." Presentation to the International Forum on Emergency and Risk Management Singapore Aviation Academy, January 10–12, 2005.

Corder, Mike. "Crippled, but Not Crashed," *Scientific American* (August 2004.)

Driskell, James E., Eduardo Salas, and Joan Johnston. "Does Stress Lead to a Loss of Team Perspective?" *Group Dynamics: Theory, Research, and Practice* 3 (1999): 291–302.

Engleman, Ellen G. "Safety Recommendation," Recommendation Letter from the U.S. National Transportation Safety Board to the U.S. Federal Aviation Administration (No. A-03-40), August 21, 2003.

Haynes, Alfred C. "The Crash of United Flight 232." Presentation at Dryden Flight Research Facility, Edwards, California, May 24, 1991.

Haynes, Alfred C. "United 232: Coping with the 'One-in-a-Billion' Loss of All Flight Controls," *Accident Prevention* 48 (1991): 1–10. 1991.

Kilroy, Chris. "Special Report: United Airlines Flight 232." www.air disaster.com/special/special-ua232.shtml.

McKinney, Earl H. Jr. "How Swift Starting Action Teams Get Off the Ground: What United Flight 232 and Airline Flight Crews Can Tell Us about Team Communication," *Management Communication Quarterly* 19 (2005): 198–237.

National Fire Protection Association. "NFPA 403—Standard for Aircraft Rescue and Fire Fighting Services at Airports." Quincy, MA: Author, 2003.

Petersen, Rick, and La Vone Sopher. "Plane Crash," *American Journal of Nursing* 89 (1989): 1288–1289.

Roberts, Karlene H., and Robert Bea. "Must Accidents Happen? Lessons from High-Reliability Organizations," *Academy of Management Executive* 15 (2001): 70–78.

U.S. National Aeronautics and Space Administration. "Intelligent Flight Control System Tests" (March 2006). http://ase.arc.nasa.gov/news/story.php?id=332.

U.S. National Transportation Safety Board. "Aircraft Incident Report: United Airlines Flight 232, McDonnell Douglas DC-1040, Sioux Gateway Airport, Sioux City, Iowa, July 19, 1989." Washington, DC: Author 1990.

CHAPTER 18

ALASKA PIPELINE AND DENALI QUAKE

A major earthquake struck the Alaska mainland on November 3, 2002 along the Denali fault, which passes directly under the Trans-Alaska Pipeline (see Exhibit 18.1). Had the pipeline ruptured, it would have resulted in spillage of up to a million barrels of crude oil a day in an environmentally sensitive area. Yet not a drop of oil was released. This potential catastrophe was averted due to successful risk management in both the design of the pipeline system and the quality of maintenance, surveillance, and emergency preparedness.

Along the southern coast of Alaska, the Pacific plate of Earth's crust is slipping beneath the North American plate at a rate of two to three inches per year. This movement has caused and continues to cause frequent earthquakes, making Alaska the site of nearly 60% of those that occur in the United States. Moreover, of the 10 most severe earthquakes in recorded history, 3 have occurred on Alaskan soil.

In 1968, oil was discovered along the northern coast of Alaska. In the years that followed, major oil-producing countries of the world began decreasing the supply of crude oil to the United States. The resulting shortage made extracting Alaskan oil increasingly attractive to the industry as well as the federal government. Ice along Alaska's northern coast made shipment of oil by sea impossible unless it could be delivered by a means other than marine transport to the more southerly located port of Valdez (see Exhibit 18.2). The solution to this problem

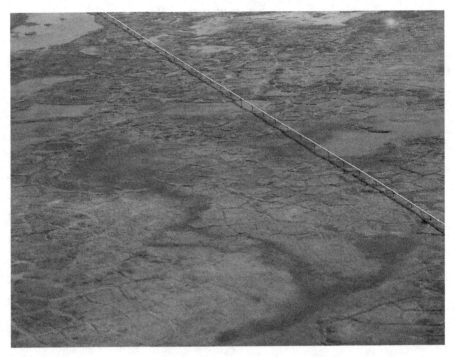

EXHIBIT **18.1**   *A Section of the Trans-Alaska Pipeline Crossing the Coastal Plain of Northern Alaska*

Source: Dave Houseknecht. USGS. Online: http://energy.usgs .gov/alaska/ak_cns_ images.html.

was to construct a pipeline from the northern coast to Valdez, where the oil could be loaded onto tankers for distribution to refineries on the U.S. mainland. The *Exxon Valdez* was one of these vessels.

Recognizing that construction of this pipeline would be a large infra-structure project, it was immediately opposed by several activist groups, due to concern for potential damage to Alaska's wildlife and pristine environment. The four-foot-diameter pipeline would run over more than 800 miles of remote wilderness, including 350 rivers, making any spill a potential environmental disaster. The prospect of an adverse event was compounded by Alaska's frequent and intense earthquakes, particularly since the pipeline would have to cross three active fault zones. The federal government acknowledged this concern by attaching

EXHIBIT 18.2   *Location of the Trans-Alaska Pipeline*

Source: U.S. Bureau of Land Management. 2002. Online:
http://tapseis.anl.gov/guide/photo/State-of-Alaska-Map.html.

a number of stipulations to the land grant for the pipeline, including a
design that would minimize environmental damage in the event of an
earthquake.

The project was awarded to the Alyeska Pipeline Company, a consortium of oil companies. On June 20, 1977, after three years of construction and an investment of $8 billion, oil began flowing through the
pipeline. Over the next 25 years, 14 billion barrels of crude oil would be
carried across the state.

The economic benefits from pipeline operation have been enormous. By 2002, $25 million worth of oil reached Valdez each day. Oil taxes and royalties generate enough revenue that Alaskans do not have to pay any income or sales taxes. These revenues have also enabled the state to fund numerous transportation, communication, and public works projects. Alaska has additionally used oil revenues to establish a multibillion-dollar fund to replace lost income should oil production diminish in the future.

Despite these economic benefits, many environmentalists remained wary of pipeline operation. Disasters like the grounding of the *Exxon Valdez* served as a reminder of the threat posed by oil production in Alaska. Then, in late October 2002, a 6.7-magnitude tremor was felt along the Denali Fault, which intersects the pipeline. Fortunately, it did not damage the pipeline, which lay far to the west of the epicenter. This quake proved to be a harbinger of things to come, however; 10 days later, a much larger earthquake would rock Alaska's interior and take direct aim on the Trans-Alaska Pipeline.

Just after noon, on November 3, 2002, a 7.9-magnitude earthquake struck approximately 90 miles south of Fairbanks. The quake started on the previously unknown Susitna Glacier fault, propagated along the Denali fault, and continued on to a third fault, the Totschunda. More than 200 miles of these faults ruptured over the course of approximately two minutes, with some sections of the Denali fault slipping by more than 22 feet. Thousands of landslides triggered by the tremors buried valleys under thick deposits of rock and ice, in some instances at locations more than 10 miles away from the fault lines. The earthquake touched off a series of small tremors in such far-off places as Yellowstone National Park, while nearly 3,500 miles away, outside of New Orleans, vibrations sloshed the waters of Lake Pontchartrain for several minutes.

This quake, which came to be known as the Denali fault earthquake, was similar in nature and magnitude to the devastating San Francisco earthquake of 1906. Fortunately, due to its remote location, the Denali quake caused far less destruction. The few homes located near the epicenter were damaged or destroyed, but no lives were lost and only one person was injured. The regional highway system, which comprised the majority of the area's infrastructure, suffered the most damage. Large holes and offsets opened on many roads, and the Northway Airport, located southeast of Fairbanks, was rendered unusable.

As the Denali quake began, the Trans-Alaska Pipeline's earthquake monitoring system (EMS) sensed the tremor and immediately began shutting off the flow of oil while compiling a list of locations for inspection and possible repair. Within a couple of hours, Alyeska response crews began inspecting sections of the line above- and belowground. The crews discovered that, while the fault rupture ran directly beneath the pipeline, miraculously the pipeline remained intact. The little damage the pipeline sustained primarily involved the displacement of a handful of supporting structures.

The pipeline remained shut down for a 66-hour period to accommodate damage inspection and initial repairs, at a cost of $1 million per hour. By early morning on November 6, less than three days after the area had received the major jolt, oil was flowing through the pipeline again. A major ecological and economic disaster had been averted.

The ability of the pipeline to survive the Denali quake when other structures failed can be attributed to thorough earthquake planning and cutting-edge design. During the pipeline design phase, an extensive field study was undertaken of the land that the pipeline would traverse. A joint team of U.S. Geological Survey personnel and contractors conducted a detailed examination of the proposed corridor and the faults located within it. This investigation generated the information required to make precise estimates of the potential for movement on the Denali fault.

Using this information, the pipeline design team determined that the fault could experience up to an 8.0-magnitude quake, which could cause as much as a 20-foot horizontal slip and a 5-foot vertical movement. It is notable that the November 3, 2002, earthquake registered a magnitude of 7.9 along the fault, causing 14 feet of horizontal slippage and 2.5 feet of vertical movement. Clearly, the design team's attention to detail resulted in the construction of a pipeline system that could survive this degree of trauma.

Pipeline design considerations were also influenced by the passage of the 1969 National Environmental Policy Act and a destructive quake that hit Southern California in 1971. In response, the federal government, which owned the land on which the Trans-Alaska Pipeline would be built, imposed design standards intended to protect the system from earthquakes over a 300-year period. While many viewed these standards as being overly conservative at the time, in hindsight they were entirely appropriate given the characteristics of the Denali quake.

Meeting these standards required a revolutionary earthquake design, more comprehensive than that used for any other structure in the United States with the exception of nuclear power plants. One prominent design feature was the zigzag pattern of the pipe, which accommodated fault movement as well as expansion and compression due to shifts in temperature (see Exhibit 18.3). Another innovation was with the pipeline supports, consisting of Teflon-coated "shoes" resting on beams coated with low-friction paint. These supports allowed the pipe to slide freely with tremors rather than buckling or breaking. Additionally, the pipe was constructed close to the ground, minimizing the distance it would fall if shaken completely off of its supports.

During the Denali fault earthquake, these design innovations performed exactly as intended, the pipeline remained intact, and no oil was spilled. Thus, $3 million in geological studies and corresponding design considerations helped to prevent an environmental disaster that could easily have topped $100 million.

Even with thorough planning and cutting-edge design, the pipeline may have failed during the Denali quake if not for outstanding maintenance. Over the 25 years from the time of construction to the November 2002 tremor, Alyeska conducted aerial surveillance of the system at least once every other week. The company carried out more meticulous inspections on a quarterly basis by surveying the entire pipeline

EXHIBIT **18.3**　*Examples of innovative earthquake design in the Trans-Alaska Pipeline*

Source: U.S. Geological Survey, "Rupture in South-Central Alaska—The Denali Fault Earthquake of 2002," USGS Fact Sheet 014-03 (Reston, VA: Author, 2003).

from the ground. Further assessments, focused specifically on the pipe support structures, were performed periodically. All surveillance and maintenance information was tracked using a database, and necessary repairs were carried out each summer.

When the Denali quake hit, the intricate EMS alerted Alyeska and set response measures in motion. The EMS consists of 11 computer-based earthquake seismograph stations located along the length of the pipeline.

During the Denali quake, six of these stations registered the event and automatically activated the procedure for shutting off the flow of oil. At the same time, the monitoring system alerted Alyeska pipeline control, calculated the severity of the tremor, assessed the potential for pipeline damage, and determined where the pipeline should be inspected. The EMS incorporated these assessments into checklists for use by response crews. The lists were sorted by technical discipline and distributed to field workers. Thus, the EMS provided for an immediate, highly focused response to the event, diminishing the effect of any potential pipe failures.

Response to the incident was further facilitated by a well-organized incident command system (ICS). The Alyeska ICS is a framework for emergency management that organizes the overall response into five categories: command, plans, operations, logistics, and finance. Each of these sections has a prescribed set of functions and responsibilities during emergency events. This prearranged structure provided the organization with the means necessary to carry out a large-scale response in a complex man-made and natural environment.

Aleyska's preparation for earthquakes extended beyond the ICS to include an earthquake preparedness plan (EPP) and an oil spill contingency plan (OSCP). The EPP includes a plan for rapid response, repair, and, if needed, shutdown of the pipeline following an earthquake. Alyeska employees were well trained in the plan's prescribed procedures. Also, necessary tools, such as damage assessment forms and placards, were kept on hand to speed postaccident analysis. In addition to response provisions, the EPP contains guidelines for modification of the pipeline system to ensure that all components continue to meet seismic design specifications.

The OSCP, while not specifically geared toward earthquakes, complements the EPP by providing information critical to responders in the event that a quake should cause an oil leak. Included is information on repair methods and equipment, oil migration paths, and tactics for minimizing environmental damage.

Another factor that allowed response workers to minimize pipeline downtime was unseasonably warm, dry weather. November in Alaska is typically characterized by cold temperatures and snow cover, which would have limited response crews to access the pipeline via snowmobiles and tracked vehicles. In the absence of snow cover, however, travel was accomplished with wheeled vehicles and helicopters, leading to reduced response times. Decreased travel time was especially important given the limited number of daylight hours in late-autumn Alaska.

In the wake of the Denali quake, Alyeska received praise from the government, industry, and the media for its ability to avert disaster and return the pipeline quickly and safely to operational status. The positive outcome of the event and increased confidence in Alyeska helped to pave the way for renewal of the pipeline's federal land grant in January 2003.

Examination of the earthquake and the pipeline's resilience has improved scientific and engineering knowledge of major quakes and how to reduce structural vulnerability to such events. It is hoped that lessons learned from the Denali tremor will one day serve to reduce potential damages in other earthquake-prone areas, such as Southern California.

In the meantime, the Trans-Alaska Pipeline System will continue to face the risks posed by the intense earthquakes that frequently occur in and around Alaska. Earthquakes are not the only threat, however. Pipeline vandalism has resulted in the release of tens of thousands of barrels of crude oil. Pipeline age and the onset of corrosion is another growing concern, recognized initially by the occurrence of numerous small spills following a routine shutdown of the pipeline in 2001. More recently, in March and August 2006, other corrosion-induced leaks were discovered in portions of the pipeline system located in northern Alaska.

REFERENCES

Baker, Allen. "Alyeska Begins Restarting Pipeline," *Anchorage Daily News*, November 6, 2002.

Birkland, Thomas A. "In the Wake of the *Exxon Valdez*," *Environment* 40 (1998): 4–9, 27–32.

Carlton, Jim. "Oil-Pipe Vandalism Highlights Concern about Line Security," *Wall Street Journal*, October 8, 2001.

Cluff, Lloyd S., et al. "Seismic Hazard Exposure for the Trans-Alaska Pipeline," *Proceedings of the Sixth U.S. Conference on Lifeline Earthquake Engineering*, Long Beach, California. 2003.

CNN. "Alaska Oil Shutdown Hikes Prices," August 7, 2006. www.cnn.com/2006/US/08/07/oilfield.shutdown.

Eberhart-Phillips, Donna, et al. "The 2002 Denali Fault Earthquake, Alaska: A Large Magnitude, Slip-Partitioned Event," *Science* 300 (2003): 1113–1118.

Haeussler, Peter J., and George Plafker. "Earthquakes in Alaska." USGS Open-File Report 95-624. Reston, VA: U.S. Geological Survey, 2003.

Hall, William J., et al. "Performance of the Trans-Alaska Pipeline in the November 3, 2002 Denali Fault Earthquake," *Proceedings of the Sixth U.S. Conference on Lifeline Earthquake Engineering*, Long Beach, California, 2003.

Johnson, Elden R., Michael C. Metz, and David A. Hackney. "Assessment of the Below-Ground Trans-Alaska Pipeline Following the Magnitude 7.9 Denali Fault Earthquake," *Proceedings of the Sixth U.S. Conference on Lifeline Earthquake Engineering*, Long Beach, California, 2003.

Kayen, Robert, et al. "Geotechnical Observations of the November 3, 2002 M7.9 Denali Fault Earthquake," *Proceedings of the Fifth International Conference on Case Histories in Geotechnical Engineering*, New York, 2004.

Loy, Wesley. "Pipeline Passes Earthquake Test," *Anchorage Daily News*, November 5, 2002.

Nyman, Douglas J., Elden R. Johnson, and Christopher H. Roach. "Trans-Alaska Pipeline Emergency Response and Recovery Following the November 3, 2002 Denali Fault Earthquake," *Proceedings of the Sixth U.S. Conference on Lifeline Earthquake Engineering*, Long Beach, California, 2003.

Pesznecker, Katie, and Doug O'Harra. "After the Quake: 'We Need Help,'" *Anchorage Daily News*, November 5, 2002.

Ratchkovski, N., and R. Hansen. "Earthquakes in Alaska—October 2002." Alaska Earthquake Information Center, Fairbanks, Alaska, 2003.

Sorensen, Steve P., and Keith J. Meyer. "Effect of the Denali Fault Rupture on the Trans-Alaska Pipeline," *Proceedings of the Sixth U.S. Conference on Lifeline Earthquake Engineering*, Long Beach, California, 2003.

Sorensen, Steve P., et al. "Response of the Above-Ground Trans-Alaska Pipeline to the Magnitude 7.9 Denali Fault Earthquake," *Proceedings of the Sixth U.S. Conference on Lifeline Earthquake Engineering*, Long Beach, California, 2003.

U.S. Bureau of Land Management. "Final Environmental Impact Statement: Renewal of the Federal Grant for the Trans-Alaska Pipeline System Right-of-Way." Washington, DC: Author, 2002.

U.S. Geological Survey. "Earthquake 'Top 10' Lists & Maps." 2007. http://earthquake.usgs.gov/eqcenter/top10.php.

U.S. Geological Survey. "Massive Alaskan Earthquake Rocks the Mainland," *Volcano Watch*, November 14, 2002.

U.S. Geological Survey. "Rupture in South-Central Alaska—The Denali Fault Earthquake of 2002," USGS Fact Sheet 014-03. Reston, VA: Author, 2003.

U.S. National Science and Technology Council, Committee on the Environment and Natural Resources, Subcommittee on Disaster Reduction. "Reducing Disaster Vulnerability through Science and Technology," 2003. www.sdr.gov/SDR_Report_ReducingDisaster Vulnerability2003.pdf.

CHAPTER 19

LESSONS LEARNED

The theme of this book is that much can be learned from past disasters that allow us to become better prepared for the future. It is not necessary for history to repeat itself.

Fifteen case studies of previous catastrophes have been presented, equally divided among man-made accidents, intentional acts, and natural disasters. Two "success" stories were also included to demonstrate how different the outcome can be when threatening situations are handled well. Collectively, these cases provide a wealth of information about how disasters evolve, what can go wrong, the aftermath of these events, and whether we remain vulnerable to the recurrence of a similar event. In this chapter, this information is transformed into important lessons we can learn and apply toward making our future world a safer place.

Exhibit 19.1 contains a list of the 10 risk factors introduced in Chapter 1, matched against each case that has been presented. An "x" is placed in the box where a specific risk factor had an important effect on the outcome of a particular case. For example, the exhibit shows that the cause and impact of the collapse of the Hyatt Regency walkways can be attributed to the risk factors of *design and construction flaws, economic pressures, schedule constraints, not following procedures,* and *communication failure.* The one exception to the use of an "x" in the exhibit is with regard to the success cases, where the symbol "**" is used to signify the presence of a specific risk factor in which proactive management contributed to a positive rather than an adverse outcome.

EXHIBIT 19.1 *Risk factor scorecard*

	Design and Construction Flaws	Deferred Maintenance	Economic Pressures	Schedule Constraints	Inadequate Training	Not Following Procedures	Lack of Planning and Preparedness	Communication Failure	Arrogance	Political Agendas
Hyatt Regency	x		x	x		x		x	x	
Bhopal	x	x	x		x	x	x	x	x	x
Chernobyl	x			x		x		x	x	x
Exxon Valdez	x		x			x	x	x	x	x
Challenger/Columbia	x	x	x	x		x		x	x	x
Oklahoma City	x						x	x		x
Aum Shinrikyo					x		x	x		x
USS Cole	x		x			x	x	x	x	x
World Trade Center	x		x				x	x		x
London	x		x				x	x		x
Edmund Fitzgerald	x	x	x	x		x	x	x	x	
Mount St. Helens			x			x	x	x		
South Canyon				x	x	x	x	x	x	
Sumatra–Andaman			x		x		x	x		
Hurricane Katrina	x	x	x			x	x	x		x
United Airlines 232	x				**	**	**	**		
Denali Quake	**	**				**	**	**		

It is important to recognize that the information presented in the exhibit is not intended to represent a formal statistical analysis. Rather, it is meant to illustrate trends that are indicative of significant risk-related considerations.

In reviewing Exhibit 19.1 and reflecting back on details of each case, 12 key lessons emerge.

Lesson 1: Risk factors work together to generate an event with disastrous consequences. As mentioned earlier, most of our systems and processes are designed with a built-in margin of safety. This buffer is created so that we can feel comfortable in what we are doing even if something goes wrong. Typically, if a single risk factor goes awry, such as not following a certain procedure, there is a system or process in place that will protect us from an adverse outcome. Depending on the circumstances, these safety measures could include equipment that warns us of a developing problem while it can still be fixed, a redundant capability to perform the same function that has failed, or the existence of a contingency plan to limit the damage if the problem cannot be contained.

Therefore, when a disaster occurs, typically more than a single risk factor is at work. As a result of multiple things having gone wrong, our margin of safety gets "consumed," and the situation is able to spiral out of control. The case studies strongly support this conclusion. As shown in Exhibit 19.1, every disaster can be attributed to the presence of multiple risk factors. Moreover, there are many instances in which a majority of risk factors were present. These include Bhopal, Chernobyl, *Exxon Valdez*, *Challenger/Columbia*, USS *Cole*, *Edmund Fitzgerald*, South Canyon, and Hurricane Katrina.

Lesson 2: Communication failure is a risk factor in every disaster, irrespective of whether the event is caused by accident, intentional act, or nature. The inability to share important information that is timely and accurate is a common denominator of every case we have reviewed. In each instance, this risk factor either caused the event to occur or contributed to the severity of the outcome.

Communication failure is a complex problem, because it involves man and machine. Failure can be attributed solely to an equipment problem, such as system overload (jammed phone lines in the port of Valdez), poor reception (within the World Trade Center towers), interoperability of different communication devices (between civilian and military responders during Hurricane Katrina), or lack of technology (no way to inform coastal residents of the approaching Sumatra tsunami).

In other situations, failure can occur because certain individuals neglect to pass along vital information or do not think it is important to do so. This failure can occur within an organization (among firefighters in South Canyon), between organizations (different levels of threat to the USS *Cole* as interpreted by the U.S. Department of Defense and the State Department), or between authorities and the general public (radiation exposure to the population in Chernobyl and the surrounding area).

Lesson 3: Take planning and preparedness seriously; it should never be short-changed. Along with communication failure, by far the most common risk factor is a lack of planning and preparedness. While managing this risk factor is vital to preventing man-made accidents and intentional acts from occurring, it is perhaps even more important in controlling the consequences of events, including those due to natural causes.

Effective planning and preparedness is based on the consideration of what might go wrong, the likelihood of its occurrence, and the potential consequences. Risk mitigation strategies then can be devised to address these scenarios. This is the process that was adopted by United Airlines through its Crew Resource Management training and by design engineers involved in building the Trans-Alaska Pipeline.

By contrast, the natural disaster cases were devoid of appropriate emergency response planning, as were most of the terrorism cases and roughly half of the man-made accidents. The terrorism cases also revealed another element of deficient planning and preparedness: the inability to perform and coordinate intelligence gathering so as to prevent the attack from taking place.

Lesson 4: Economic pressure is a chronic problem that appears as a risk factor in most man-made accidents and natural disasters and in some intentional acts. One of the most important repercussions of economic pressure is a decision to forgo investment in planning and preparedness due to lack of available resources. Several examples of this risk factor appearing with dramatic implications were presented, including the *Exxon Valdez* (response equipment not available for deployment), Mount St. Helens (lack of volcano monitoring capability), Hurricane Katrina (overwhelmed by the response needs of a Category 3 hurricane), and the London transit bombings (limited intelligence resources). While resource limitations can be a common management challenge, assigning available resources to the right priorities is an entirely different matter.

Often economic pressure and schedule constraints go hand in hand. A lack of resources can stimulate the need to hasten a project, while time-sensitive deadlines can result in limiting the level of quality control. Use of the fast-track construction method to build the Hyatt Regency, coupled with denial of a request to position an engineer on site, illustrates this point. Other examples include NASA's aggressive launch schedule using parts shared among several shuttles and the decision to squeeze in one more voyage of the *Edmund Fitzgerald* at minimum freeboard with winter weather approaching.

Lesson 5: Not following procedures is a significant problem in man-made accidents, and is also present in some natural disasters and intentional acts. The source of this risk factor can come from either ignoring known procedures or by lack of proper training. Development and implementation of standard operating procedures is the foundation on which successful organizations are built. Imposing a structure and discipline to the performance of repetitive tasks ensures that they are done properly every time. When these procedures are not followed or errors in judgment are made, the consequences can be serious. Such was the case when Gillum & Associates failed to follow the formal design review process and when plant workers at Bhopal allowed water to seep into a tank as part of a routine cleaning operation. Similar disregard for standard operating procedures aboard the USS *Cole* left the vessel and its occupants highly vulnerable to attack.

While in these instances not following procedures was the catalyst that led to the occurrence of a tragic event, the same risk factor can plague those attempting to respond to an incident in progress. Such was the case at South Canyon, where firefighters brought excessive risk on themselves by not following Standard Fire Fighting Orders and Watch Out Situations. In contrast, the crew of United 232 followed established guidelines, a decision that paid huge dividends.

In our haste to get people on the job or to fill in where help is needed, formal training often is deferred or not offered at all. In other circumstances, retraining is not provided at a time when personnel need to be exposed to new methods and practices. Evidence of this problem appears at Bhopal and in Tokyo (Aum Shinrikyo) as well as at South Canyon and in southern Asia (Sumatra-Andaman). These failures, while part of a general problem of not following procedures, can be attributed to not knowing what procedures to follow rather than not applying procedures that had been taught. The outcome, however, remains the same.

Lesson 6: Design and construction flaws are the bane of man-made accidents. Every man-made case we reviewed suffered from a problem that was related to either design or construction. Some of these flaws were readily apparent and widely known, such as the safety and containment system at Bhopal and the design of the Chernobyl reactor cooling system. In other situations, as with the *Exxon Valdez*, the protection system in place (single hull) was thought to be sufficient, until it was demonstrated that it could not be relied on.

However, the most important lesson associated with design and construction flaws is that small items in a complex facility or operation can prove lethal if attention to detail is absent. The hanger rod configuration of the Hyatt Regency walkways and the O-ring design used in the space shuttles are classic examples of how disaster can ensue if people in charge of design and construction are not vigilant about every aspect of system operation.

Lesson 7: Do not underestimate the significance of political agendas in creating high-risk situations. Without question, this is the key message associated with intentional acts. In every case, there was a strong political motivation for creating events of mass destruction. Al Qaeda, the international terrorist organization allegedly behind the attacks on the World Trade Center, USS *Cole*, and London transit system, had openly declared its contempt for U.S. and U.K. foreign policy. The assailants in the cases of Aum Shinrikyo and Oklahoma City were similarly politically motivated, albeit for different reasons. Of particular concern regarding the attacks on the London transit system, the Toyko subway system, and the Murrah Building is the fact that they were carried out by nationals rather than foreigners.

Somewhat surprising, perhaps, is the extent to which political agendas also appear as risk factors in man-made accidents. The Indian government's disregard for safety conditions at Bhopal, Russian policy to maintain a Cold War posture in the face of a nuclear crisis, the U.S. government's ambiguous response to the *Exxon Valdez* spill, and NASA's political motivation to protect a threatened program further illustrate the influence of political agendas in creating high-risk conditions.

Lesson 8: Arrogance among individuals and organizations is perhaps a far more significant risk factor than previously imagined. Individuals in a position of authority and organizations with a mandate to perform a certain operation are particularly susceptible to becoming arrogant over time. While a certain amount of arrogance can be healthy when it is channeled into strong team leadership, it can be just as easily abused.

The cases discussed herein present several instances of individual and organizational arrogance that likely contributed to adverse outcomes. Did Captain McSorley take unnecessary risks by navigating the

Edmund Fitzgerald as he did, because he had conquered everything that the Great Lakes had previously thrown at him? Were firefighters at South Canyon convinced they could overcome any peril that adverse weather might create? Did Duncan and Gillum believe that attention to detail was a waste of their precious time? Was the U.S. Navy's view of its maritime supremacy what caused it to discount certain threats? Did the Russian government and NASA diminish the value of human lives to preserve their status?

Lesson 9: The lack of uniform safety standards across different nations creates an uneven risk management playing field, conditions ripe for exploitation. While attempts are being made to promote uniform human health and environmental quality standards throughout the world, there remains a wide disparity in how countries value public safety. As a result, in places where safety is treated as a second-class citizen, there are likely to be more frequent incidents and with more severe consequences.

This problem is due to a strong desire on the part of developing countries to promote economic activity, creating incentives to attract foreign investment that often lack safety considerations. It is exemplified by what took place in Bhopal, where Union Carbide, without any objection from the Indian government, applied different safety standards than it used in its West Virginia plant.

In other instances, the problem may be due to a more casual regard for what constitutes a reasonable level of safety. Chernobyl illustrates this point, where the Russian standard of nuclear reactor safety was inferior to that applied in the United States and Western Europe.

Finally, the ignorance or lack of resources of a country or region can render safety to be a less prominent concern. The many countries that suffered from exposure to the Sumatra-Andaman tsunami had neither the knowledge nor the means to institute an effective warning system.

Lesson 10: Regardless of how well risks are being addressed, "luck" can change your fortunes one way or another. Circumstances beyond human control, often called luck, always influence the extent to which a potentially catastrophic situation becomes a reality. Sometimes, due to poor risk management, bad luck allows a vulnerable situation to unravel. Such was the case at South Canyon when the winds shifted unexpectedly, causing a blowup to occur in a location where firefighters had no means of escape.

In other instances, good luck enables a well-managed situation to prevail against seemingly long odds. This was experienced by United Flight 232, as despite everything that the air and ground crews did right, survival was aided by the lack of thunderstorm activity during a time when it is typically frequent, occurrence of the incident on the one day of the month that the Iowa Air National Guard was on duty, and the presence of an off-duty instructor pilot as a passenger on the aircraft.

Some people believe that you make your luck through effective planning and preparedness. If you consider a variety of disaster scenarios and devise strategies to limit their likelihood and severity, if faced with bad luck, there is a better chance that a contingency plan has been developed that can offset an unfortunate roll of the dice.

Lesson 11: It usually takes a disastrous event to convince people that something needs to be done. We are so engrossed in our daily lives that an important problem often is ignored until an event of disastrous proportions wakes us up and makes us take notice. Only then are public officials, industry leaders, and community activists tuned in to the need for reform and prepared to take appropriate action.

This is a consistent theme across all of the cases presented. Consider the creation of the Department of Homeland Security in the aftermath of the September 11 attacks, enactment of the Oil Pollution Act in response to the *Exxon Valdez* spill, restrictions on federal building access due to the Oklahoma City bombing, and the adoption of Responsible Care guidelines in the face of Bhopal gas leak. It is an unfortunate truth that we must suffer to a certain degree before help is on the way.

What is remarkable about the lessons learned from these cases is that they are easy to understand and make practical sense. Moreover, they can be put into daily use by individuals, communities, businesses, and governments. Simply put, the foundation of successful risk management is planning, preparedness, and communication. That forms the basis for establishing sound daily practices and creating opportunities for learning and knowledge building. In managing your daily activities, do not impose unreasonable economic and schedule pressures on what you are trying to accomplish. Pay attention to detail of how things are designed, built, and maintained. Recognize that certain individuals and organizations may be politically motivated or arrogant in ways that could be detrimental to your safety. And recognize that risk factors often work together to create a crisis situation, so be on the lookout for circumstances where these factors can become intertwined.

This prescription, if followed, will take you a long way toward a safer tomorrow, whether "luck" is on your side or not. However, adopting this approach is not a guarantee that one will be safe everywhere, all of the time. This leads us to the final lesson.

Lesson 12: Risk cannot be entirely avoided; nothing can be designed or built to perfection, nor last forever. Life is an inherent choice among alternative risks. Every minute of every day, somewhere in the world, people are hurt, property is damaged, and the ecology is harmed. Sometimes the impact is felt by a few people at a specific location, while in other circumstances, the impact can involve mass casualties over a large expanse.

No matter how hard we try to create a safe environment, it is not humanly possible to make life entirely risk free. Even if we had unlimited resources to invest in safety, we could not guarantee that nothing bad would happen. Consequently, we must recognize that life is an inherent choice among alternative risks. The key to managing these risks successfully is being able to identify them and establish priorities among them. Then we can direct our attention at *reducing*, but not *eliminating*, those risks of greatest concern.

For these reasons, it is incumbent on each of us to adjust our outlook and expectations about the level of protection we can realistically expect. Simply put, we need to become more tolerant of certain risks and recognize that sometimes bad things will happen even when we put our best foot forward . . . and that is just a fact of life.

EPILOGUE: WHERE DO WE GO FROM HERE?

We live in a changing, complex, and stressful world. Information abounds, technology advances, and people expect instant gratification. It is an age of terrorism, our climate is changing, and there is a constant struggle between man and machine. How can we make everything fit together so that we can feel safe?

In reviewing painful experiences of the past, we have learned that protecting our future cannot be left to chance. Strong messages have been delivered that can form the basis for individuals, communities, businesses, and governments to recognize and address risks that they each face by focusing on the risk factors that threaten their respective livelihood. Not every risk factor will be present in each situation that is confronted, nor will they be valued the same, but as long as there is an awareness of their presence and an understanding of their importance, effective measures can be taken.

In the world in which we live today, the risks that we face are compartmentalized, with concern for man-made accidents, intentional acts, and natural disasters the responsibility of different entities. Each group has its own priorities, separate resources are being used to address each problem, and limited coordination exists. Yet, as we have seen in the cases presented, man-made accidents, intentional acts, and natural disasters share many of the same risk factors and outcomes. This fact begs for a single "all-hazards" approach to risk management, a process that is holistic and systematic in nature.

Let's think about the ramifications of adopting a new approach based on this principle. For illustration purposes, consider a community that has a history of tornado activity, is home to several chemical and energy production facilities, and is the site of a major public transportation system. From the community's perspective, the health and well-being of its residents, businesses, and environment may be threatened by risks associated with these characteristics, ones that could prove disastrous under certain conditions. By considering these risks within an all-hazards context, each concern can be identified, evaluated, and prioritized. Out of this process can come a prudent decision regarding where and how to invest available resources to reduce those risks of greatest concern. Moreover, by managing all hazards under a single umbrella, there can be opportunities to reduce a specific risk while simultaneously decreasing other risks. For example, a call-out system to notify the affected population of a tornado alert could also be used to communicate a bomb threat or a chemical release.

While a community was used in this illustration, the identical process can be performed by governments, businesses, and even individuals, based on their respective concerns and the risk management decisions that they can control. Moreover, if the process is implemented in a way that is inclusive with other parties that influence or are affected by these risks, several benefits emerge. Better ideas and solutions are generated, there is a greater understanding of what is being done to improve safety, and there is increased confidence that a credible effort is being made.

We can ill afford not to recognize the need for change, nor should we wait any longer. As the cases have taught us, we remain vulnerable to the recurrence of many of the disasters that have taken place in our recent past. Moreover, changing conditions in our world are posing new challenges that will require making tough risk-related choices. For example, with the onset of global warming, we can expect more erratic weather conditions, such as more damaging hurricanes in the Gulf of Mexico and increased wildfire potential due to drought conditions elsewhere. There will be greater reliance on nuclear power production, with implications for facility safety. Concern is growing over possible contamination of our food and water supply as well as the changing political agendas of many nations over time. And then there are the more traditional risks that remain, such as those associated with transportation, chemical manufacturing, and earthquakes. Without an all-hazards approach to risk management, how can we make intelligent decisions about which risks to try to control?

Moreover, the risk factors come into sharper focus within the all-hazards approach. These factors should be prominent in the formulation of methods and practices that control the likelihood of an unfortunate event and limit the consequences should one occur.

So, what does this mean? Will we suffer another tragedy? Of course we will. Lower-priority risks that we have chosen not to address still can spawn a destructive event. However, the prospect of that happening is less likely than our vulnerability to what we judged to be more important risks. Even among the risks that we have opted to focus our attention on, a disastrous outcome could occur. However, it should be less likely to happen once investments in prevention and mitigation have been made.

The bottom line is that we can and should do much better at being a master rather than a victim of risk. We no longer need to be driven by fear for our safety. All it takes is a more organized approach to managing the risks that affect our daily lives coupled with a greater tolerance for unfortunate events that sometimes will occur no matter how hard we try. Peace of mind is well worth this commitment.

INDEX

273